This important collection of articles brings together distinguished experts from both the Classical and New Testament traditions of linguistic analysis to re-examine the thorny issue of definiteness and the use of definite expressions in post-classical Greek. The spotlight is firmly on the language of the NT (how Koine Greek usage differs from the classical language and how far it points the way towards medieval and modern practice), but anyone with a general interest in definiteness (e.g. what exactly it is, why and how definite expressions develop, or under what conditions they are used) will find rich food for thought in this very welcome addition to the field.

Geoffrey Horrocks, *Emeritus Professor of Comparative Philology, University of Cambridge*

One might think that the article in New Testament Greek has been thoroughly understood, especially since it is so ubiquitous. Yet with all the work that has been done on ὁ ἡ τό, this bequest of Hellas has many facets yet to be explored. The present anthology fills much of the vacuum, offering case studies, stimulating theories, and competing viewpoints. I enthusiastically commend this volume for gathering in one place up-to-date and thought-provoking treatments of the Greek article.

Daniel B. Wallace, *Senior Research Professor of New Testament Studies, Dallas Theological Seminary*

The Article in Post-Classical Greek

SIL International®
Publications in Translation and Textlinguistics
10

Publications in Translation and Textlinguistics is a peer-reviewed series published by SIL International®. The series is a venue for works concerned with all aspects of translation and textlinguistics, including translation theory, exegesis, pragmatics, and discourse analysis. While most volumes are authored by members of SIL, suitable works by others also form part of the series.

Series Editor
Susan McQuay

Content Staff
Lynn Frank, Content Editor
Gene Burnham, Proofreader

Production Staff
Lois Gourley, Composition Director
Judy Benjamin, Compositor
Barbara Alber, Cover Design

Cover Photograph
"Greek New Testament" by B. Vasiliy (www.flickr.com/photos/29811338@ N05/4949956227) is licensed under CC BY 4.0. (creativecommons.org/licenses/ by/4.0). Image modified by Barbara Alber.

The Article in Post-Classical Greek

Edited by

Daniel King

SIL International®
Dallas, Texas

Copies of this and other publications of SIL International® may be obtained through distributors such as Amazon, Barnes & Noble, other worldwide distributors and, for select volumes, publications.sil.org:

SIL International® Publications
7500 W. Camp Wisdom Road
Dallas, Texas 75236-5629 USA

General inquiry: publications_intl@sil.org
Pending order inquiry: sales@sil.org

Contents

Contributors

Mark Dubis is professor of biblical studies and languages and director of the Discipline-Specific Honors Program in the School of Theology and Missions at Union University in Jackson, Tennessee, USA. His special research interests are Petrine studies and Greek grammar and linguistics. He is author of *1 Peter: A Handbook on the Greek Text* in the Baylor Handbook on the Greek New Testament series (Baylor, 2010), as well as *Messianic Woes in First Peter: Suffering and Eschatology in 1 Peter 4:12–19* (Peter Lang, 2002).

Cristina Guardiano is associate professor of linguistics at the Università di Modena e Reggio Emilia (Italy). She specialised in historical syntax at the Università di Pisa, completing a doctoral thesis on the internal structure of determiner phrases in Ancient Greek. She is active in researching the parametric analysis of nominal phrases, the study of diachronic and dialectal syntactic variation, cross-linguistic comparison and phylogenetic reconstruction. She is a member of the SSWL research team and has been a research associate in the ERC Advanced Grant 'LanGeLin.' Recent articles include, "Adjective-noun combination in Romance and Greek of Southern Italy. Polydefiniteness revisited," *Journal of Greek Linguistics* (forthcoming); "Parameter theory and parametric comparison," in I. Roberts, *The Oxford Handbook of Universal Grammar* (Oxford: OUP, 2017); and "Definite articles in Ancient Greek," in Stephanie W. Jamison et al., *Proceedings of the 26th Annual UCLA Indo-European Conference* (Bremen: Hempen, 2016).

Daniel King is research fellow in Syriac studies and Semitic languages, Cardiff University, UK, and a translation consultant with SIL International. His research is principally concerned with methods and techniques of translation in antiquity especially between Greek and Syriac in the fields of philosophy and theology. He has published an edition of *The Earliest Syriac Translation of Aristotle's Categories* (Brill, 2010) as well as many articles in the field. Dr. King has a special interest in all aspects of the history of translation and currently lives and works in Tanzania on translation projects in the vernaculars of East Africa.

Stephen H. Levinsohn is a senior linguistics consultant with SIL International and a member of Wycliffe Bible Translators, having served in Colombia as a linguist and Bible translator with the Inga (Quechuan) people. He is particularly interested in discourse typology and how different discourse features are manifested in languages of different types. He first became interested in discourse features of New Testament Greek during a discourse-and-translation workshop in Panama in 1974, when it became apparent that more was known about the discourse features of Panamanian languages than of Greek. This led him to undertake doctoral studies at the University of Reading, UK, which were eventually published as *Textual Connections in Acts* (SBL Monograph Series 31, Atlanta: Scholars Press, 1987). Subsequent publications in English and Spanish, including *Discourse Features of New Testament Greek: A Coursebook on its Information Structure and Other Devices* (Dallas, TX: SIL International, 2002), are listed at https://www.sil.org/resources/search/contributor/levinsohn-stephen-h.

Maria Napoli is associate professor at the University of Eastern Piedmont, Vercelli, Italy. Her main research interests include: language change, typology, aspect and actionality, argument structure, (in)definiteness, and multilingualism in the ancient world. Her recent publications include: "Ditransitive verbs in Latin: a typological approach," *Journal of Latin Linguistics* 17/1 (2018); "Which type of bilingualism? A corpus-based approach to the use of Greek in Late Latin," *Lingue e Linguaggio* XVII/1 (2018); and a monograph, *Aspect and Actionality in Homeric Greek. A Contrastive Analysis* (FrancoAngeli: Milano, 2006).

Ronald D. Peters is professor of New Testament, Great Lakes Christian College, Lansing, Michigan, USA. His research interests include Greek language and linguistics, Luke-Acts, and Johannine writings. He is the author of *The Greek Article: A Functional Grammar of ὁ-items in the Greek New Testament with Special Emphasis on the Greek Article* (Brill, 2014).

Jenny Read-Heimerdinger. After graduating in Modern Languages in 1973 from the University of London, UK, she discovered the joys of Biblical Greek. Some five years later she studied New Testament manuscripts at the Catholic University of Lyons, France. By 1985 her fascination with biblical studies had materialised in an MA in Biblical Exegesis at the London School of Theology, followed in 1994 by a PhD from the University of Wales. Since that time, she has combined linguistic studies with textual investigations and has taught in universities around the world, most recently at the University of Wales. She is a research fellow of several institutions in the UK and has published a wide range of scholarly works, notably on the manuscript of Codex Bezae with particular reference to Luke's writings. Dr. Read-Heimerdinger is currently adapting her research for a popular readership.

Steven E. Runge is currently scholar-in-residence at Faithlife Corporation and research associate at the Department of Ancient Studies at Stellenbosch University, South Africa. His principal research interests are cognitive-functional descriptions of biblical languages, particularly the linguistic mismatches between English and Koine Greek. He authored *Discourse Grammar of the Greek New Testament: A Practical Introduction for Teaching and Exegesis* (Hendrickson, 2010), and is co-editor of *The Lexham Discourse Bible* (Logos, 2008–2014) and of *The Greek Verb Revisited: A Fresh Approach for Biblical Exegesis* (Lexham Press, 2016).

Figures

Tables

Abbreviations

CE	common era
D	determiner
DP	determiner phrase
E-language	external or externalized
N-ADJ	noun-adjective
NP	noun phrase
NT	New Testament
TH-items	definite article and demonstratives, 'that', 'the', 'this'
VO	verb object
WH-items	relative pronouns, 'who', 'which'
§	section
ø	nominal or adjectival that appears without the article
↑	indicates an absence
.....	shows lexical or grammatical variation
(*italics*)	words that vary in order (ch. 7)

Latin

pc.	*pauci*	'a few MSS'
lac.	*lacuna*	'a gap in the transmitted text'
LXX	*septuaginta*	'Septuagint'
	nomen regens	'substantive that governs the genitive; can also be represented by the article or a pronoun'
om.	*omittit or omisit*	'omits' or 'omitted'

Codices

ℵ01	Sinaiticus
B03	Vaticanus
C04	Ephraemi Rescriptus
D05	Bezae
𝔓46	Chester Beatty P. II
𝔓105	P Oxy 4406

1

Introduction

Daniel King

1.1 Previous studies on the article

In 1828 Middleton published his monograph *The Doctrine of the Greek Article*, which was focused in particular on the usage of the article in the language of the New Testament. The editor of the second (1833) edition was rather shocked to discover "how many men to whom I am accustomed to look with the highest respect have not even read the volume and how little its real doctrines and real value are known" (1833:v). Middleton had the good sense to perceive and to describe certain rules, or at least tendencies, such as frequent omission of the article following prepositions or in enumerations. He thus belongs to those who attempt to explain all the data on the basis of a relatively small number of underlying principles. To this extent his aim was more ambitious than that of many of his followers who, as we shall see, left a great deal of space to "authorial style." Middleton concedes the notion of authorial style, but not that it extends to the use of the article, which is more a matter of grammatical correctness (1833:117–120), a correctness that may be discerned in both the classical and the "sacred" authors. One of his key findings was that the Granville-Sharp rule was indeed valid not just in the New Testament but throughout Greek literature.[1]

In many ways, Middleton was well ahead of his time—he hints, without laying himself open to excessive criticism, at the opinion that New Testament Greek is a normal dialect rather than a sacred tongue, and he doubts that the authors of Scripture would have deliberately violated the rules of grammar for the sake of expressing sacred truths upon a higher plane. He often anticipated, by common sense, certain modern linguistic analyses; for instance he observed the use of the article with nouns whose existence in the setting was already obvious, referring to what more modern interpreters have called the "encyclopedic knowledge" of the reader or the "cognitively identifiable status" of a noun (Middleton 1833:32).

Nonetheless, consideration of the linguistic characteristics of the Greek article, the morpheme ὁ, in the post-Classical dialect(s) only makes a genuine beginning in the era of the papyri. From this point comparative evidence becomes readily available and a more measured appreciation of the place of the New Testament within the Koine begins to make itself felt in the research literature. Frank Eakin's (1916) essay in the American Journal of Philology, in which he considered the usage of the article in the papyri of the first two centuries CE, may be taken as an example of just such an approach. Eakin, for instance, takes especial note of the fact that both NT authors and the papyri had a tendency towards anarthrousness of proper noun phrases that constituted a marked difference from Attic usage. Deissmann had, of course, marked out the path for research of this type, focused on treating the language of the NT within its broader cultural environment. Eakin picked up on some key observations of Deissmann's and elaborated upon them. One of these is the important suggestion that the unmarked or default pattern of article usage is anarthrousness upon the first mention of a proper noun, while subsequent mentions have the article. This important point, as it relates to discourse analysis, has more recently been subjected to further study by Levinsohn and others, and will crop up a number of times in the current volume.

One other point Eakin makes that is worthy of note is that correcting scribes sometimes inserted the article where it had initially been omitted, not because they perceived any grammatical error, but merely because the corrector felt at that point that it would be more natural if it were present. In Matthew's gospel, chapter 27, Pilate is a major participant in the narrative, who is thus referred to anaphorically (i.e. arthrously) throughout the passage save for his introduction at verse 2, except only that in the text

---

[1] I.e. that two common nouns joined by 'and', in which the first is articular, the second anarthrous, have a single referent. It has been defended *in extenso* in more recent times by Wallace (2009). Classically, exceptions may be found, such as ὁ δ’ ἐκκλησιαστὴς καὶ δικαστὴς ἤδη περὶ παρόντων καὶ ἀφωρισμένων κρίνουσιν (Arist., *Rhet.*, 1,1,7), but they are rare.

carried by the major majuscules there is an unexpected omission of the article at verse 62, whereas in the text of the approximately contemporary P Oxy 4406 (𝔓105) the expected article is present. This is not a case of one scribe following "rules" and another making an error, but rather of varying conceptions of that slippery phenomenon we call discourse patterns. Such data as we see in this example of Matt 27:62 are obviously crying out for a discourse analytic approach rather than one that attempts to deduce a list of grammatical rules on a purely syntactic or semantic basis. Such "rules" cannot, for example, explain a pattern such as τὴν ἀδελφὴν ἀσπάζου καὶ τὴν Κύριλλαν, Ῥοδόπη ὑμᾶς καὶ Ἀρσίνοος ἀσπάζονται (P Oxy 117:16–18). Only a nuanced analysis of discourse function can really explain why the first-mentioned sister is articular while her colleagues go without. In the current volume, Read-Heimerdinger has focused especially on variants in order to elicit discourse-analytic patterns of usage.[2]

In that same era of early papyrus-research, Robertson published his substantial *Grammar of the New Testament in the Light of Historical Research* (1914). On the whole, Robertson contents himself with a list (albeit a long one) of the usages of the article as observable in the NT text, without attempting any "general" explanation of its meaning or function that would account for the manifold data presented. In contrast to most other treatments, Robertson insisted that the so-called "demonstrative use" of the article was a misnomer and that ὁ,ἡ,τό when used as a demonstrative was in truth a different lexeme. Robertson defines the article essentially as a "pointer." It is not needed for the indication of definiteness (an observation ratified by most recent scholarship, which identifies definiteness as a feature that may be present even when the article is absent). This basic "pointing" function is very common and helps to distinguish between a general idea and a definite token, such that μετὰ γυναικὸς ἐλάλει (John 4:27) may be easily differentiated from, say, βάλλει ὕδωρ εἰς τὸν νιπτῆρα (John 13:5). In this latter, the bowl is a definite token insofar as the reader may well expect the bowl to be present as a "prop" in the environment. Such a take on the notion of the "encyclopedic knowledge" of the reader has been again affirmed more recently in understandings of language based on relevance theory, and is applicable to a nuanced understanding of anaphora.

Robertson, however, remained wedded to the notion that, where free variation in the use or non-use of the article is observable, free authorial style ought to be deployed as the key explanation. He notes patterns of usage that differ between, say, Plato and the author of Acts, but this is a matter of personal difference only, not one of diachronic variation of any rules that could be deduced from the data (e.g. Robertson 1914:761). The upshot is that, for Robertson, post-Classical usage is one with the pure Attic—Mark's gospel will as naturally write καλὸν τὸ ἅλας (Mark 9:50) as Lysias would say θάνατος ἡ ζημία ἐστί (Lys. 13,69). Thus Robertson's conclusion more or

---

[2] Note also the comment on this point at Middleton (1833:xii).

less confirms the earlier, rather brief, treatment of Moulton's Prolegomena, that "in all essentials [the article's] use is in agreement with Attic" (Moulton 1906:81). Guardiano's paper in the current volume makes a significant suggestion as to just how the grammatical analysis of the article does differ between the Attic and the Koine dialects.

In terms of a linguistic theory of the article, little further was added in Blass and Debrunner's much-used grammar. It has, however, many useful observations, even some of a diachronic nature. Thus the papyri sometimes retain a classical usage that is not paralleled in the NT, such as expressions of the type πρὸ τοῦ δὲ περιτρέχων ὅπη τύχοιμι (Plato, *Symposium* 173a), without any infinitive following. New Testament scribes in general partake of a Koine-era shift towards the use of the relative pronoun where the article was to be expected, such that they are even on occasion guilty of "updating" good classical usage: ὃς μὲν οὕτως, ὃς δὲ οὕτως (1 Cor 7:7) is to be found in 𝔓46, but ὁ μὲν οὕτως, ὁ δὲ οὕτως in most of the majuscules. An alternative interpretation would be that the majuscules have Atticized Paul's Koine usage, but in either case the gradual shift towards the relative in such constructions seems clear enough.

Blass and Debrunner are also slightly more prone to resorting to the "Semitism" explanation than were Moulton or Robertson, for example in noun phrases consisting of an anarthrous *nomen regens* and a dependent genitive (Rom 1:16, δύναμις γὰρ θεοῦ ἐστιν εἰς σωτηρίαν). An important extension of this point, which is not totally to be dismissed in view of the special religious status of Septuagintal diction for NT authors, is the case of θεός, κύριος, and Χριστός. On the apparent free-variation of the article with proper nouns, however, Blass and Debrunner note only very general patterns of anaphora and again resort to arguments from authorial "style."

The "compilation" approach taken by many of these fundamental grammars, by which listings of usages with numerous examples was preferred to the quest for finding unifying themes, may be found also in some more recent treatments. Cignelli and Bottini's (1991) essay continues to use this method of organizing the data. But the observation, for instance, that one may describe the second τό in καθὼς κἀγὼ πάντα πᾶσιν ἀρέσκω μὴ ζητῶν τὸ ἐμαυτοῦ σύμφορον ἀλλὰ τὸ τῶν πολλῶν (1 Cor 10:33) as the "pronominal function" of the article is mere name-calling and does not in itself shed light on the grammatical substructures. In this treatment, "pronominal use" is followed by "individuating use" (which includes the article with unique objects, as well as anaphora, cognitively identifiable objects etc.), "generic use" (interpreted as a Hebraism), "substantive use," and so forth. One useful feature that is included is a discussion of indefiniteness and the developing use of τις and εἰς to fulfil this function. Some interpretations are offered which by themselves look too general or vague to be meaningful but which are crying out for further, and more sophisticated, consideration—such as the idea (Cignelli and Bottini 1991:172) that the postposed adjective with article repeated gives the adjective greater emphasis than an articular adjective preposing the head noun, as in ἐγώ εἰμι ὁ ποιμὴν ὁ καλός (John 10:11), which incidentally is treated as a Semitism on the basis of the parallel οἱ θεμέλιοι αὐτοῦ ἐν τοῖς ὄρεσιν τοῖς ἁγίοις (Ps 86:1).

In recent years, a number of studies have appeared which aim at that more unified linguistic explanation of the article that was lacking in the grammars mentioned. For classical Greek, Bakker's (2009) monograph on the Herodotean dialect is probably the most significant. Important also is the previous work of Guardiano and Napoli (Guardiano 2006; 2011; 2013; Napoli 2009), whose most recent research is contained in the present volume. Manolessou and Horrocks (2007) is an important starting point, however rather superficial on those questions that we most want answers to. These authors focus on two issues in particular, namely the original evolution of the article from a demonstrative, and the progressive extension of its usage to new contexts over time. They do not really ask the question about why in a given place the article is used or not, rather contenting themselves with observations of a general tendency towards increasingly "unmarked" usages over time. This analysis is based on cross-linguistic observations regarding developments from demonstratives to articles. Following work by Löbner (1985) on definites, they helpfully distinguish semantic from pragmatic definites (the former "represent functional concepts independently of the particular situation referred to," the latter "depend crucially on that situation for unambiguous reference") and then use this typology to note the spread of the article within the realm of semantic definites, where it generally is optional (Manolessou and Horrocks 2007:226). In this case, "its presence will normally point to a pragmatic function, e.g. to ensure discourse continuity, to convey contrast or emphasis" (2007:227). This discourse-focused analysis is taken up by Napoli's article in chapter 2 of the present volume, and may also be taken as symptomatic of the approach to the question taken by all the essays found here.

1.2 Brief summary of studies in this volume

I will turn now to a consideration of the findings of the authors of this volume. Napoli's paper is an exercise in uncovering not just the "function(s) of the article" but the ways in which definiteness might be encoded in Greek, and how strategies of encoding may have varied diachronically. Definiteness itself, she contends, is not simply a grammatical category, but rather one that can be understood at a discourse-pragmatic level, indicated by other than dedicated markers. In taking this route, she is moving the discussion away from the descriptive approaches to "usage." A marked feature of these former approaches was that they attempted merely to account for the data by categorizing it in a variety of ways. Napoli is also concerned with explaining the apparent optionality of the article in many environments, especially with generic noun phrases. Again, this search after general explanations is laudable and an important step beyond the merely descriptive.[3]

In section 2.3, Napoli offers us a "map" of logical and pragmatic definiteness and their sub-varieties. Logical definites she takes to mean proper nouns, together with nouns that have "uniqueness of reference." For these, logical definiteness is an inherent property. Then there are those nouns which are still logically definite but are so in a derived way, which are assumed to be so because of their semantic content. This category includes groups usually called "generics" and "abstracts." Pragmatic definites are those that may arise from the linguistic or extra-linguistic context, and hence includes, for example, what is more traditionally referred to as "anaphora."

The basic diachronic framework within which the analysis is carried out is that the article starts life as a pure demonstrative, moves towards taking a role in marking pragmatically definite noun phrases, and then at a later stage to marking logically definite noun phrases. Fundamentally, however, and despite differences that are perceptible, the Classical and post-Classical forms of the Greek language both belong to the same diachronic stage. These dialects use the article to mark pragmatic definites, with the reservation of certain bounded exceptions, such as prepositional phrases; whereas the article is not required to mark logical definiteness. This does not necessarily imply unmotivated usage, or that the presence or absence of the article before logically definite noun phrases is simply a matter of "style."

It becomes clear, then, in what way precisely the usage has shifted between the Classical and the post-Classical dialects. There has been a creep towards near-obligatoriness in the optional use of the article with generics and with unique entities, a process that was only completed in the medieval dialect. Only in specified syntactic contexts may the article be omitted before unique entities, for example; and similarly we find that in the case of proper nouns, anarthrousness is a marked discourse feature (an important factor also in the analyses of Read-Heimerdinger and of Levinsohn and Dubis in this volume). Even generic nouns (as Napoli shows in §2.5.1.2) are overwhelmingly + article in the Koine period, albeit that the trend is less clear (statistically) for abstracts.

In this field, therefore, we witness an extension in the use of the article across semantic categories of noun phrases. At the same time, there are hints of restrictions in other areas. In particular, Napoli takes note of the New Testament's tendency to restrict the pronominal use of the article, once such a staple of the classical dialect. This (hypothetical) tendency in particular would benefit from a comparative analysis on the basis of the grammar of the papyri from the same era.

---

[3] For a predecessor in this quest, see Bakker (2009:146).

Finally, Napoli makes the important point that syntactic and semantic definiteness and the use of the article should not be treated in isolation from indefiniteness and the development of an indefinite article τις/εἰς, the first beginnings of which are already discernible in the New Testament.

In chapter 3, Guardiano sets herself the task of describing the changes that have come about in the syntactical patterns of the article on the basis of universal comparanda. She argues that Greek may be analyzed in the same way as any living natural language and may be assigned typologically on the basis of its syntactic constraints upon the article. Using this method she can assign different stages of the Greek language to different general language types and hence identify the nature of the changes that occurred.

Her syntactical analysis depends in turn upon a parametric approach, a theory developed within generative grammar in order to describe fine distinctions between syntactical systems. Thus any natural language may be described in terms of its "settings" for a series of binary "switches." For example, the first mentioned is the switch ±grammaticalised article, followed by ±grammaticalised text anaphora. In this way a description of the syntactic patterns of any stage of the Greek language may be built up.

In section 3.3.1 we come to the first key claim regarding how the ancient forms of the Greek language may be described within this parametric approach. Guardiano finds that both Classical and Koine Greek do have a full definite article, and that it fulfils the conditions given, one of which is that "bare nominals" (i.e. when neither ὁ, ἡ, τὸ nor any other definite item is visible) in argument position are never assigned a definite reading. In section 3.3.2, the small differences in the syntactic constraints operating upon the article in the different stages of the language are identified: Modern Greek has, as it were, flicked "on" the switch for "strong article" which had not been activated in the earlier forms of the language, whereas post-Classical (Koine) had already flicked "on" the switch for "N-raising over GenO" in contrast to its classical predecessor. In section 3.4 she even ventures into Homeric grammar to demonstrate its quite different patterns of syntactic constraints, where she proposes that the data be explained as a mixture of grammatical stages of the language.

Thus Guardiano generalizes that the apparent variation in article use over time may be identified in quite specific ways and may be reduced to simple terms:

> The DP syntax...revealed itself as particularly conservative: surface differences between ancient and modern varieties are in fact manifestations of one single historical change. If the creation of the indefinite article and the necessity of an expletive article with proper names are structurally related, namely if they actually follow from the (re)setting of just one parameter (+strong article), we might expect them to be also chronologically related, namely that the establishment

of the numeral "one" as an obligatory marker of non-definite
singular count argument nouns and the systematic presence
of a lexical expletive with argument proper names took
place in parallel. (§3.5)

Readers will notice how different approaches to the problem of the article thus give rise to different conclusions about language change. Findings that are based on seeking out differences in syntactic constraints, as seen in Guardiano's paper, look different from the findings of those focused on semantics or discourse patterns.

Peters's essay in chapter 4 also seeks overarching linguistic explanations, rather than the disconnected series of rules that characterize traditional grammars of New Testament Greek. Unlike Napoli, however, this author of a recent monograph on the subject offers a single unifying theory which he believes can account for the semantic function of the article. Whereas older treatments held the article to be "basically" a determiner, to be rendered as English *the*, save in cases that had then to be explained as "exceptions," he offers the following hypothesis: "The Greek article is most closely akin to the relative pronoun, ... it orients identification of a referent to the speaker or writer who provides the necessary information for identification, and ... items modified by the article are characterized as concrete" (§4.1a). Looked at from the perspective of functional grammar, in which we may distinguish TH-forms (demonstratives) from WH-forms (relatives) on the basis of recoverability of information, Peters suggests that the Greek article should be treated as belonging to the latter category rather than to the former, with which it has often been associated: "In Greek, the article and relative pronoun are used to indicate that the speaker or writer is providing the information necessary for identification. Neither is used to direct the recipient to the information necessary for identification, nor do they indicate that the information is proximate or recoverable from the immediate situation, as is the case with the English demonstrative pronoun and definite article, respectively" (§4.2.1).

A prototypical case (discussed in §4.1a) is the article + participle construction, in which we may identify nothing other than an alternative means of expressing a relative clause, which orients identification to the writer who is providing the information necessary for identification of the noun phrase, rather than leaving this to be recoverable from context by the receiver as would be the case for TH-items such as Greek demonstratives or the English definite article. Constructions with μὲν...δέ can be similarly analyzed (§4.1b), since instances with the relative pronoun are found alongside the more common use with the article. Section 4.3 tackles the discourse function of the article, which for other authors (Runge, Levinsohn-Dubis) is really the core concern of grammatical explanation. The opposition concrete/abstract, which is deployed in section 4.2 to explain the article's grammatical function, here becomes the parallel opposition foreground/background, to which again the opposition +/− article corresponds. The article may thus be expressed as having a concretizing and a foregrounding function depending on the level or type of analysis offered. This discourse description appears to be in contrast to that offered elsewhere in this volume, for example by Read-Heimerdinger, in whose theory of the article with proper names the article is the unmarked, or backgrounded, form.

The benefits, as indeed the correctness, of Peters's analysis will need to be judged in competition with other analyses offered both in the current volume and elsewhere. The analysis of the article as a WH-form will need also to contend with those usages of the article which are more overtly demonstrative in nature, especially in the older dialects. If the linguistic analysis of the article is to be completely different for classical and the post-classical dialects, this also would constitute a significant divergence from the otherwise accepted dogma that the differences are only small (as Napoli and most older grammarians contend).

In chapter 5, Levinsohn and Dubis have applied previous studies on the discourse function of the article (especially Levinsohn's own work) to the New Testament text of 1 Peter. They begin from the assumption that the function of the article is to indicate "that the entity concerned is cognitively identifiable rather than definite," even claiming this to be the modern "consensus" on the matter. Also vital for their presentation is the hypothesis (not new here, but tested through the analysis itself) that initial occurrences of entities are by default anarthrous, that subsequent occurrences are by default arthrous, and that it follows that any subsequent occurrences that are anarthrous may be read as marked for some particular discourse function, that is they are being foregrounded in some way.[4]

Their basic presentation of the article as a marker of identifiability is certainly shared by Runge and Read-Heimerdinger, whose essays in this volume share the same foundation, which is in turn grounded in an information structural analysis. This shared analytical framework differs in some important respects from that of Peters, whose theory of the article as a relative assumes an orientation towards the speaker rather than the hearer and who, while seeing in the article a means of expressing grounding, denies its cohesive function, which is a key component for Levinsohn and Dubis. Similarly they disagree with Peters, and with Porter before him, on the question of salience. For Levinsohn and Dubis, as for Runge, the article does not in and of itself imply a +salience feature, but only a +identifiability feature. This is a significant difference.

---

[4] This is different from the findings of Fee for John's gospel (Fee 1971). He notes no such pattern, only a series of grammatical conditions that seem to be functioning to determine whether or not a name has the article. A further, if unsystematic, survey of this text, however does suggest there may be leverage for the Levinsohn/Read-Heimerdinger thesis even here: the name Μάρθα follows the pattern predicted by their hypothesis, though the name Πιλᾶτος does not do so with equal clarity.

In section 5.2, the authors proceed to explain the reasons for anarthrousness especially in nouns that are clearly cognitively identifiable. In a variety of contexts they explain how the lack of an article may give thematic prominence (salience) to an identifiable entity. Again we see the importance of not assigning a particular function to the article without an awareness both of fundamental principles of discourse and also of information structure.

The bulk of the paper concerns an analysis of portions of 1 Peter, with the aim of assessing whether the given hypotheses make sense—looking not just at the presence of the article but also for its absence, also including adjectivals in their analysis. They then offer particular investigations of the use of the article with the nouns πνεῦμα and Χριστός, and also with infinitivals.

A brief comment: Gildersleeve offered a list of texts that aimed to give evidence for the general infrequency of arthrous forms, even in anaphora, among classical authors (Gildersleeve 1911:229–230). If, then, the NT situation is as Levinsohn and Dubis suggest, there has been a not insignificant change over time. For classical texts, it would be harder to maintain the basic principle that +article is the unmarked form subsequent to the first mention of a participant.

In chapter 6, Steven Runge's paper also explores functions rather than meanings, in a variety of noun phrase types, distinguishing prototypical from non-prototypical uses of the article, identifying those uses that were becoming commoner over time and how they served to offer a multitude of strategies for the elaboration of discourse. He too depends upon an information structure basis for understanding the article's discourse function as marking that which is "cognitively identifiable," preferring this to the binary notion of definiteness, which is not so closely and uniquely tied to the article. The marking of identifiability, thus defined, constitutes what Runge calls the "prototypical" use of the Greek article in the texts he has studied. He would add to this the "less prototypical" uses which include the nominalizing function of the article with infinitives, adverbials, and adjectivals, a function that more closely allies with Greenberg's third stage of grammaticalization in which the article's function becomes one of merely marking nominals. The use of the article in place of a pronoun, or as a subject-switcher, falls, for Runge, into the same general category, as also do articles placed "unnecessarily" in the midst of a noun phrase. In his search for a discourse-based explanation of this last type, Runge deploys the notion of the "packaging" of discourse elements in discrete bundles for easier processing. Noun phrases of the type τὴν δόξαν τὴν ἰδίαν may be thus explained in contrast to semantically parallel cases such as τὰ ἴδια πρόβατα. The use of the article in constructions of this sort does not, on the whole, serve to narrow down the referent of a noun phrase, but rather functions to offer thematically salient information.

In chapter 7, Read-Heimerdinger offers another essay in the application of discourse analytic principles to the problem of the Greek article. She affirms what for many is now considered dogma, that the feature "definiteness" is not to be tied to the presence/absence of the article itself. In the case of the NT, the analysis of the article's actual discourse function(s) is made considerably more challenging by the presence of such a large cohort of variants. Read-Heimerdinger, however, turns this into a virtue since it offers the opportunity to witness a multiplicity of scribes/authors expressing the same narrative but with differing patterns of discourse usage. In particular her comparison of the Vaticanus with the Bezan text of the book of Acts offers fertile soil for this type of study. The text of the Bezan codex, albeit that it differs in significant ways from the "standard" text of the printed editions, ought not to be treated either as deviant or merely as a repository of variant readings, but rather as an alternative presentation of the narrative itself, one that shows a deep understanding of Jewish contexts and a different perspective on a number of episodes.

The author begins from the fundamental observation (which we have noted at least as far back as Deissmann) that upon first occurrence proper names are anarthrous, with subsequent mentions being anaphoric and hence arthrous. The discourse implication is that anarthrous occurrences of a name (other than the first instance) are marked as foregrounded. This discourse-based observation applies not merely at the level of the book as a whole but also to embedded narratives as discourse units within the book, and this is where the value of the Bezan text makes itself felt in its greater sensitivity to indicating these "embedded narratives" by means of just such a discourse feature. Furthermore, participants in the wider narrative need from time-to-time to be "re-introduced" by an anarthrous usage (§7.2.2b), which thereby marks that a new narrative section has begun, at least so far as the scribe in question interprets the structure of his narrative. This accounts for much of the variation in the use of article with proper nouns among NT manuscripts. The author points out that her findings for the book of Acts are broadly similar to those of Sansone for Plato, that the article is "more at home with topic than with focus," that is, that focused elements tend towards anarthrousness. Thus a far more nuanced conclusion may be reached than simply observing that the article with proper nouns is anaphoric.

The author continues her study by investigating whether the same rules hold for the article with place names as for personal names. While the same rules do not hold absolutely, nonetheless the discourse patterns remain (broadly speaking the discourse salience of anarthrousness), and the differences in this regard between Vaticanus and Bezae may still be attended to. The latter's pattern of usage indicates a different focus of attention within the grander sweep of the narrative. She concedes that the names of cities do not seem to fall so clearly beneath this analysis.

In her conclusion, Read-Heimerdinger briefly compares her findings with the classical and the modern dialects. She suggests that the Koine usage is actually closer in this regard to the latter than it is to the former.

It is a suggestive notion, although dependent in its understanding of the classical discourse function of the article upon older analyses (such as that of Gildersleeve 1911), which were published before the modern analysis of discourse was developed. She adds the important rider that finding discourse principles is not a matter of statistical frequency. In a given text, highlighting may occur frequently, but it does not follow that it is "unmarked" just because of its frequency.

For the reader of the New Testament, these articles constitute a vital summary of contemporary, theoretically sound interpretations of the linguistic functions of the article in a way that will inform exegesis of the text especially in the field of larger discourse units. However, there is a significant payoff also for the as-yet significantly under-researched field of Koine linguistics. Whether or not a unified grammar of the Koine form(s) of Greek is an attainable object, each discrete building block that contributes towards such an edifice constitutes a key stage of the linguistic research. Comparative work, exploring in detail the data of the papyri and other post-classical authors, especially those preceding the Atticistic revival, is a major desideratum which would allow us to be in possession of a holistic view of the subject that is hardly attainable on the basis only of a restricted text corpus. Nonetheless, starting points have certainly been attained, and moreover ones that may to a certain extent be relied upon and further tested and refined.

References

Bakker, Stéphanie J. 2009. *The noun phrase in ancient Greek: A functional analysis of the order and articulation of NP constituents in Herodotus.* Amsterdam Studies in Classical Philology 15. Leiden: Brill.

Blass, Friedrich, and Albert Debrunner. 1961. *A Greek grammar of the New Testament and other early Christian literature.* Translated and edited by Robert W. Funk. Chicago: University of Chicago Press.

Cignelli, Lino, and G. Claudio Bottini. 1991. L'articolo nel greco biblico. *Review of Liber Annuus* 41:159–99.

Eakin, Frank. 1916. The Greek article in first and second century papyri. *Review of The American Journal of Philology* 37(3):333–40.

Fee, Gordon D. 1971. The use of the definite article with personal names in the gospel of John. *Review of New Testament Studies* 17(2):168–83.

Gildersleeve, Basil Lanneau. 1911. *Syntax of classical Greek from Homer to Demosthenes 2: The syntax of the simple sentence continued, embracing the doctrine of the article.* New York: American Book Company.

Guardiano, Cristina. 2006. The diachronic evolution of the Greek article: Parametric hypotheses. In Mark Janse, B. Joseph, and A. Ralli (eds.), *Proceedings of the 2nd International Conference of Modern Greek Dialects and Linguistic Theory*, Mytilene, Greece, 30 September–3 October 2004, 99–114. Mytilene, Greece: University of Patras.

Guardiano, Cristina. 2011. Parametric changes in the history of the Greek article. In Dianne Jonas, John Whitman, and Andrew Garrett (eds.), *Grammatical change: Origins, nature, outcomes*, 179–97. Oxford: University Press.

Guardiano, Cristina. 2013. The Greek definite article across time. *Review of Studies in Greek Linguistics* 33:76–91.

Manolessou, Io, and Geoffrey Horrocks. 2007. The development of the definite article in Greek. *Studies in Greek Linguistics* 27:224–236.

Middleton, Thomas Fanshaw, and Hugh J. Rose. 1833. *The doctrine of the Greek article applied to the criticism and illustration of the New Testament.* Second edition. Cambridge, UK: J. & J. J. Deighton.

Moulton, James Hope. 1906. *A Grammar of New Testament Greek 1: Prolegomena*. Edinburgh: T. & T. Clark.

Napoli, Maria. 2009. Aspects of definiteness in Greek. *Studies in Language* 33:569–611.

Robertson, A. T. 1914. *A Grammar of the Greek New Testament in the light of historical research*. New York: Hodder & Stoughton.

Wallace, Daniel B. 2009. *Granville Sharp's canon and its kin: Semantics and significance*. Studies in Biblical Greek 14. New York: Peter Lang.

2

Functions of the Definite Article from Classical Greek to New Testament Greek

Maria Napoli

2.1 Introduction

The present chapter provides an overview of the use of the Greek article from a diachronic perspective, by focusing on two different stages of the language:* Classical Greek and Koine Greek as represented, in particular, by New Testament Greek.[1] My aim is not to offer an exhaustive description and classification of all the types of occurrences of the definite article in both

---

* The insightful remarks of the editor, Daniel King, and of an anonymous reviewer are gratefully acknowledged.

[1] It is widely accepted that New Testament Greek "is neither a separate dialect of the Koine, nor a pure language inspired by the Holy Ghost, nor again 'une langue judéo-grecque chrétienne', but simply the language which, at the time of the composition of the various books of the OT, of the gospels and of the apocrypha, was in common use in all Greek speaking countries" (Costas 1997:53), i.e. Hellenistic Greek. At the same time, it has been recognized that New Testament Greek represents "conversational Koine," i.e. the spoken language of educated people, which should be distinguished from "literary Koine," i.e. the language of authors such as Polybius, Epictetus, Plutarch etc..., which represents "a more polished Koine" (Wallace 1996:21–22; 23–30). On the Koine, see also Horrocks (2010:75–90).

Classical Greek and in New Testament Greek, which have been extensively portrayed in many grammars and contributions.[2] I will rather concentrate on those functions attested in the New Testament which are more relevant to a comparison with the situation in Classical Greek.

The organization of this paper is as follows: section 2.2 contains a brief introduction to the category of (in)definiteness in Ancient Greek,[3] and to the development of the definite article in this language. In section 2.3, I will outline the theoretical groundwork for my study, by introducing the distinction between LOGICAL DEFINITENESS and PRAGMATIC DEFINITENESS, which is of crucial importance in the description of the Greek data. On the basis of this distinction, a map of definiteness will be presented illustrating the main uses of the definite article within the theoretical framework of functional typology. Section 2.4 deals with the distribution of the definite article in Classical Greek, by concentrating on its being optional or obligatory. Section 2.5 summarizes the main uses of the definite article in New Testament Greek. Section 2.6 concludes with some observations.

2.2 (In)definiteness in the history of the Greek language

Definiteness can be regarded as a universal semantic category. Notwithstanding, the definite/indefinite opposition is not obligatorily encoded by dedicated markers. In languages which express the notion of definiteness, it may be encoded by articles or by other morphological, syntactic or pragmatic strategies. In languages with definite and/or indefinite articles, they do not necessarily complete the paradigm of (in)definiteness, since articles may compete with other linguistic strategies at

---

[2] On Classical Greek, the reader is referred to the detailed description in Gildersleeve (1911:215–332), and more recently, in Cooper (1998:353–484); for more bibliographical references, see also Napoli (2009), and §§2.2 and 2.4 in this paper. On New Testament Greek, see §2.5. It should be noted that, unfortunately, a quantitative study of the various uses of the article in New Testament Greek is still lacking: this work is made particularly difficult since New Testament "suffers from high levels of variation across manuscripts with respect to the presence/absence of the article in specific contexts" (Manolessou and Horrocks 2007:231). This is true, in particular, for proper nouns: see Read-Heimerdinger (2002:117–118).

[3] In this chapter, the label "Ancient Greek" is used such as to include Mycenaean Greek, Homeric Greek, Classical Greek and post-Classical Greek (i.e. Koine Greek), in contrast to the labels "Medieval Greek" and "Modern Greek." Greek examples mentioned here are taken from a corpus of data based on my research on Classical Greek and on the texts of Gospels, or from previous literature (in this case, the source is cited below the example). Classical Greek texts and translations of the examples quoted are taken from the Loeb editions. The text of the New Testament is taken from Nestle-Aland XXVIII. Translations from the New Testament are based on the English text of the NRSV (New Revised Standard Version) with modification, in some cases, of the relevant portions.

a discourse-pragmatic level, especially pronominal forms and zero-articles. On the other hand, in languages without articles, noun phrases may be vague with regard to (in)definiteness (see §2.4). Only in languages which overtly encode noun phrases as definite by means of dedicated markers, can definiteness be interpreted as a grammatical category (see Lyons 1999:86–89; 274–275).

Ancient Greek is one of these languages, since it has developed a definite article, inflecting for number, gender and case. It lacks an indefinite article, although it uses the numeral 'one' (εἷς, μία, ἕν) and indefinite pronouns, the most frequent of which are τις 'anyone' and οὐδείς 'no one, none'.[4] In this respect, Ancient Greek differs from Modern Greek, which has both a definite article and an indefinite article, corresponding to the numeral 'one', inflecting for gender and case, but employed only in the singular number.

What makes the Greek language particularly interesting is the fact that it documents different stages of the development of (in)definiteness. Proto-Indo-European is traditionally described as a language with neither definite nor indefinite articles. In Greek, the demonstrative pronoun ὁ, ἡ, τό developed into a dedicated marker of definiteness, that is, into a definite article, as frequently happens from a cross-linguistic point of view. Whereas in Mycenaean Greek, there are no traces of the use of this demonstrative pronoun as a definite article (see Bartoněk 2003), it has been supposed that "à l'époque d'Homère, la langue courante connaissait déjà l'article" (Chantraine 1953:165). However, as recognized by Chantraine (1953) himself, and confirmed by more recent studies,[5] in Homer, ὁ, ἡ, τό basically still has the function of a demonstrative form, and is not systematically employed to mark definiteness. In other words, it can be said that only Classical Greek attests the accomplishment of the development of a definite article as an autonomous grammatical category, and that "what is found as an article in [Classical Greek] is not more than a demonstrative in Homeric Greek which is also used as a personal and a relative pronoun" (Hewson 2014:420).

At a syntactic level, this innovation had a fundamental role in the creation of the noun phrase as a distinct structure, operating "as a configurational rather than as a morphology-based entity" (Hewson

---

[4] There is no agreement on the function of these forms—mainly of τις—with respect to the PARAMETER OF SPECIFICITY (on this notion, see von Heusinger 2002). Some scholars claim that τις occurs only with a specific value, by denoting a referent whose identity is unknown to the hearer (cf. Faure 2014), whereas others argue that it may be employed as both specific and non-specific (cf. Biraud 1991:221, Bentein 2014:159–160). Cf. example (45.b) in §2.5.4.

[5] See, among others, Lombardi Vallauri (2002), Basset (2006), Manolessou and Horrocks (2007), Guardiano (2013), Hewson (2014).

2014:421).[6] However, from a semantic point of view, the picture seems to be more complex, due to the many diverse functions of the Greek definite article, and also to its optionality. In literature on this topic, it is often claimed that in Classical Greek the definite article may occur or not with the following categories of nouns, without any apparent constraint: proper nouns, nouns of unique entities, generics, abstract nouns, that is, the same kinds of nouns with which Modern Greek compulsorily uses the definite article. Gildersleeve (1911) pointed out that the presence of the definite article with these nouns entirely depends on the individual stylistic choices of Classical authors, who may decide to use or omit it without any relevant difference in the denotation of the noun phrase. I quote a case illustrating the so-called "optional" use of the definite article in Classical Greek:

(1) a. Ἀλλ' εἰ ἀπιστοίην, ὥσπερ οἱ σοφοί,
        οὐκ ἂν ἄτοπος εἴην
        'If I disbelieved, as the wise men do,
        I should not be extraordinary' (Plato, *Phaedrus* 229 c7)

    b. "Οὔτοι ἀπόβλητον ἔπος" εἶναι δεῖ,
        ὦ Φαῖδρε, ὃ ἂν εἴπωσι σοφοί […]
        'The word, Phaedrus, which the wise
        speak must not be rejected' (Plato, *Phaedrus* 260 a5–6)

In both (1.a) and (1.b), σοφός is a substantivized adjective inflected in the plural, used as a generic noun and, then, meaning 'wise men' (as a class). However, in (1.a), it is preceded by the definite article, whereas in (1.b) it appears without any determiner, apparently without any semantic difference.

In section 2.4, I will try to show how the idea of "optional choice" is an oversimplification, and that a different and more satisfying analysis of this phenomenon is possible if we examine it from a diachronic point of view. Before doing this, I will discuss some theoretical issues related to the category of definiteness, and mainly concerning the approach that will be taken here as the starting point for the analysis of the Greek data.

---

[6] It is worth quoting also from Faure (2014:443): "as for its syntax, the definite article occupies a special position in the Greek NP, as clearly shown by Biraud (1991). It does not commute with anything, but creates a domain within which noun modifiers can occur […], and outside which other terms bearing on the NP are found." From this point of view, the syntax of the article is the same in Classical Greek and in New Testament Greek. On the Greek noun phrase see also Bakker (2009) and Perdicoyianni-Paleologou (2014).

2.3 A map of definiteness: The main uses of definite articles across languages

Broadly speaking, what seems to be relevant to the use of definite articles is what we may call a PRESUPPOSITION OF IDENTIFICATION (see Comrie 1989:128, 135): the speaker marks an entity as definite since he or she presupposes that the hearer is able to recognize its reference or its existence and uniquely identify it, thanks to the information delivered by the context (linguistic or extra-linguistic) or to the semantic content of the noun phrase. In order to single out the underlying principle of definiteness, different theories have been proposed and developed, which are based on semantic and/or pragmatic notions such as UNIQUENESS (Russel 1905), FAMILIARITY (Christophersen 1939), INCLUSIVENESS (Hawkins 1978), IDENTIFIABILITY (among others, Comrie 1989), GRAMMATICALIZATION OF IDENTIFIABILITY (Lyons 1999), and, more recently, SALIENCE (von Heusinger 2013), which corresponds to a combination of the uniqueness theory and the familiarity theory (von Heusinger 2013:349, 362).

However, the variety and complexity of the cross-linguistic uses of definite articles can hardly be accounted for by invoking a single "descriptive" notion like those mentioned above, which are able to portray only some aspects of definiteness as a conceptual category.[7] For the same reason, although the assumption that "the general function of the article in Greek is to mark the referent as identifiable" (Bakker 2009:162) may be considered correct, such a principle does not give an exhaustive account of all its different uses.

In this paper, I follow Napoli (2009), who proposed to distinguish between LOGICAL DEFINITENESS and PRAGMATIC DEFINITENESS on the basis of Löbner's distinction between two separate uses of definites, belonging to semantic definiteness and pragmatic definiteness, respectively. Löbner explains:

> In those cases which I want to call "semantic definites" the referent of the definite is established independently of the immediate situation or context of utterance. [...] "Pragmatically definite" NPs, on the other hand, are essentially dependent on special situations and contexts for the non-ambiguity (and existence) of a referent. (1995:298)

By starting from the distinction between logical definiteness and pragmatic definiteness, the main cross-linguistic uses of definite articles with nouns may be summarized as in figure 2.1:[8]

---

[7] The reader is referred to Lyons (1999), Abbott (2010), and Elbourne (2013), among others, for a review of the debate on definiteness within different theoretical frameworks.

[8] As already pointed out in Napoli (2009:578n13), fn 13, the map of definiteness represented in figure 2.1 does not cover all uses of definite articles from a typological point of view, especially considering that some of these uses are language-specific (see, for instance, the "syntactic" uses of the definite article in §2.5.3 in this paper).

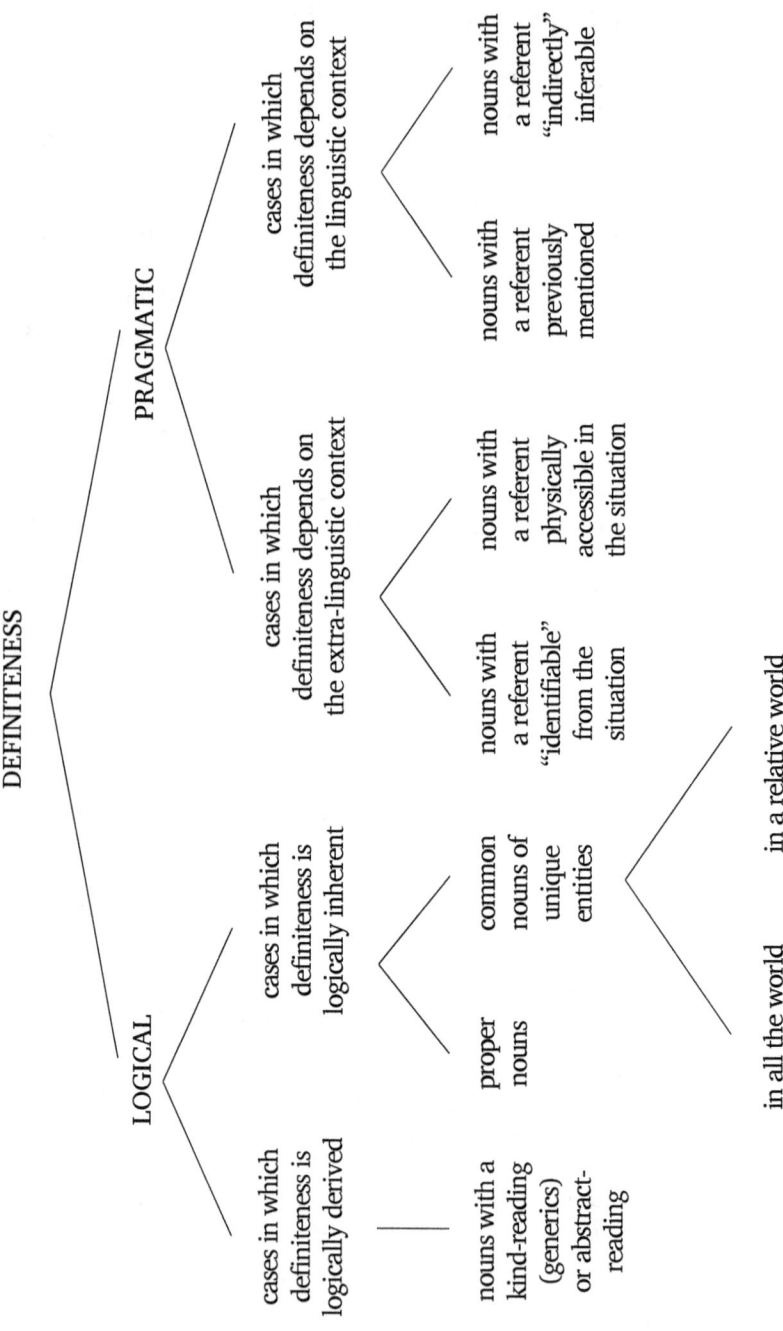

Figure 2.1. Map of definiteness as conveyed by articles. (Adapted from Napoli 2009:578. Used by permission. Contact the publisher, John Benjamins, for permission to re-use or reprint in any form.)

Having outlined a possible "map of definiteness," I now turn to a brief illustration of the domains of logical definiteness and pragmatic definiteness, and to their diachronic relationship.

2.3.1 Logical definiteness

Nouns may be logically definite due to their semantic content. This means that their definiteness does not depend on context but entirely on semantics, that is, on the fact that they represent an entity of which only one exists. Interestingly enough, languages with articles greatly differ in terms of logical definiteness; they do not necessarily mark the logical definiteness of proper nouns and common nouns by means of definite articles.

In figure 2.1, under the label "logical definiteness" two different subtypes have been included: (i) nouns whose definiteness is LOGICALLY DERIVED; (ii) nouns whose definiteness is LOGICALLY INHERENT. This type includes prototypically definite nouns, that is, common nouns denoting unique entities and proper nouns. Nouns of unique entities have been subdivided into two subtypes, generally having the same behaviour in terms of definiteness, but differing in terms of number: (i) nouns denoting something which is unique in all the world, without regard to variation in space or time, like *the moon, the sun, the atmosphere,* etc.; they are normally incompatible with plural markers and with the indefinite article, like proper nouns; (ii) nouns denoting something which is unique in a relative world, that is with respect to a specific space or time, shared only by a restricted group of people, like *the Queen of England, the Prime Minister of Italy,* etc.; in principle, these common nouns are compatible with plural markers and with the indefinite article.[9]

Interestingly enough, whereas languages with a definite article tend to employ it with nouns of unique entities, there is much more variation as regards its use with proper nouns. Some languages, like English, do not admit the definite article with proper nouns; on the contrary, in other languages, proper nouns are compulsory or optionally accompanied by the definite article, as in Modern Greek and Italian, respectively. Finally,

---

[9] In simple terms, many *queens* exist across the world and across time, but there is only one *Queen of England* at the moment, and this makes her *the Queen* (cf. Hawkins 1978). Obviously, the fact that proper nouns and nouns of unique entities like *the sun* are typically incompatible with plural and indefinite markers, since they presuppose uniqueness of reference, does not mean that they can never be used as plural or indefinite. On the contrary, this is possible under particular readings. For example, proper nouns may be converted into common nouns by means of a plural marker or an indefinite article, in order to represent prototypical instances of a given category. Similarly, "there are situations in which we might speak of our sun as one of many or entertain the possibility of there existing another universe" (Lyons 1999:8).

there are languages with a dedicated article for proper nouns, like some Austronesian languages (see Lyons 1999:121–124).

As mentioned above, the definiteness of nouns may be logically "derived" – this refers to generics and abstracts, which are not semantically definite, but may presuppose uniqueness of reference as a result of a semantic interpretation. GENERICS may be defined as common nouns referring not to a specific individual or entity, but to a class as a whole, distinguished by some particular properties which make it "unique," and which are shared by all its members, differentiating them from members of other classes. For example, in the sentence *dogs bark*, the noun *dogs* necessarily has a generic reading, referring to dogs as a class rather than to specific dogs (see Lyons 1999:189). To use Givón's (1978:293–294) words, "if a nominal is 'non-referential' or 'generic', the speaker does not have a commitment to its existence within the relevant universe of discourse. Rather, in the latter case, the speaker is engaged in discussing the genus or its properties, but does not commit him/ herself to the existence of any specific individual member of that genus."

From a typological point of view, generics may correspond to definite, indefinite or bare noun phrases: in English, bare plurals, definite singulars, indefinite singulars – and, more rarely, definite plurals – may be used as generics; in Italian, genericity is conveyed by definite singulars, definite plurals or indefinite singulars. However, the commonest strategy of expressing genericity – especially in European languages with a definite article – corresponds to the use of definite nouns (Lyons 1999:192; Behrens 2005:278). As regards Greek, Classical texts document different types of generics: they may be definite singulars, definite plurals, bare plurals or bare singulars; on the contrary, in Modern Greek, a generic reading of a noun phrase is possible only if it corresponds to a definite plural or, less frequently, to a definite singular, whereas a noun phrase marked by an indefinite article cannot express genericity (Alexiadou, Haegeman and Stavrou 2007:176).

To sum up, languages typically make use of more than one single type of noun phrase with a generic interpretation. Interestingly enough, the different types of generics in an individual language tend to be synonymous, but this does not mean that these types are necessarily interchangeable: factors such as the semantics of the verb, its aspectual content and its modal function may influence the choice of the more appropriate generic noun phrase. However, other contextual factors together with the status of the definite article in that language may play a role.[10] I quote the following well-known case, discussed by Lyons (1999:182–183):

(2) a.   **The dodo** is extinct.
    b.   **Dodos** are extinct.
    c.   *__A dodo__ is extinct.

---

[10] See Hawkins (1978:214 f.), Lyons (1999:179 f.), Napoli (2009:583–587), and also §2.4 and §2.5.1.2. in this chapter.

As shown in (2.a) and (2.b), a definite singular generic and a bare plural generic are admitted with a predicate like 'to be extinct', denoting an accidental property rather than an inherent feature. The impossibility of using an indefinite singular generic as in example (2.c) depends on the fact that it corresponds to a property-generic (Lyons 1999:183): indefinite singular generics designate neither a class as a whole nor an individual member of it, but the crucial property characterizing that class. For this reason, indefinite singular generics cannot be used to the same extent as definite generics or bare generics.

ABSTRACT NOUNS like 'hope', 'truth', 'virtue', denoting something which is typically "nonobservable" and "nonmeasurable" (Quirk et al. 1985:247), have been regarded as resembling proper nouns, with which they share "unique identifiability" (Anderson 2007:234). At the same time, like generics, "what they identify is not discretely identifiable as an individual unit" (Anderson 2007:235). Across languages, abstracts may be typically bare, as in English, or typically definite, as in Italian and French, where they are generally preceded by the definite article. This is illustrated below by means of an English sentence (from Quirk et al. 1985:286) and its Italian translation:

(3) a. **Happiness** is often the product of **honesty**.
   b. **La felicità** spesso è il risultato **dell' onestà**
      the happiness often is the result of.the honesty

An abstract noun can also be interpreted as having a concrete, discrete, reading: beauty is the quality of being beautiful, but it may also denote a person who is beautiful. In this case, the abstract noun takes the indefinite article:

(4) She has always been a **beauty**.

Abstracts may also take the indefinite article both in English and Italian, for instance, when they are premodified or postmodified, especially by an adjective or a relative sentence[11] (exceptionally also with those abstract nouns which are typically noncount). Two English examples are quoted below (from Quirk et al. 1985:287), to be compared with the case in (5c):

(5) a. She played the oboe with **(a) charming sensitivity**
   b. She played the oboe with **a sensitivity that** delighted the critics
   c. *She played the oboe with **a sensitivity**

It should be hypothesized that the function of the indefinite article in similar contexts is to focus on a single instance of the quality represented.

---

[11] I would like to thank Davide Ricca for drawing my attention to this point.

This function is in contrast with the "uniqueness-requirement," which is characteristic of the definite article. This may explain why in Italian, where abstracts are normally marked by the definite article, the same nouns are necessarily bare or indefinite in contexts like those mentioned above. In light of the foregoing, it cannot be denied that the indefinite article represents a marked choice for this category of nouns, as well as for generics (although for different reasons; see above).

To conclude, what justifies the presence of generics and abstracts in the map of definiteness in figure 2.1 is the fact that both these types are not typically indefinite; on the contrary, genericity and abstractness are often denoted by definite noun phrases in languages with articles, and/ or by bare noun phrases. Their indefinite use generally corresponds to a marked or more restricted use. However, differing from proper nouns and nouns of unique entities, which are inherently definite, the definiteness of generics and abstracts is a matter of logical inference, since it depends on a semantic interpretation: in the case of a generic noun, it depends on the fact that this noun represents the typical instance of the unique category to which it belongs; in the case of an abstract noun, it depends on the fact that it denotes an entity perceived of as unique in its non-discrete (i.e. mass) reading.

2.3.2 Pragmatic definiteness

Under the label "pragmatic definiteness" all cases may be included in which a given noun is marked by the definite article because the speaker presupposes that the hearer can identify its referent thanks to the linguistic context or the extra-linguistic context. On the basis of this, in figure 2.1, two subtypes of pragmatic definiteness have been distinguished.

2.3.2.1 Dependant on linguistic context

This first case, "pragmatic definiteness that is dependent on the linguistic context," results in anaphoric uses of the definite article. ANAPHORA deserves special attention since it tends to be systematically, although not exclusively, associated with definite articles.[12] In anaphoric processes, the reference of a given element is not established by interpretation of its descriptive content, but is acquired thanks to its having been previously introduced, in general by means of an indefinite description: the two elements are then co-referential (direct anaphora).[13]

---

[12] To give an example, in Ancient Greek there are three main types of nominal anaphora, represented by: (1) the definite article; (2) pronouns; (3) null anaphora (Haug 2014).

[13] To quote from Hawkins (1978:108), "The act of referring anaphorically involves a form of instruction to the hearer to match the linguistic referent of the definite description with a particular object in his mind, an object which has been entered

A slightly different anaphoric process is represented by indirect anaphora, including those cases in which the referent of a definite description can be inferred from the referent of another linguistic element:

> Indirect anaphora is based on the inferences that the hearer can make because a specific referent has been previously mentioned; the mention of this referent indirectly introduces a range of other referents which are related to it (because they are physically part of it or because they are associated with it on a more abstract, intellectual level). This inferred relationship allows the speaker to use the definite article when speaking of one of these referents, even though it has not been explicitly mentioned before. (Napoli 2009:572)

This means that in indirect anaphora the reference of a definite description is still determined by the previous mention of a linguistic element, but the two elements are not co-referential; they are rather connected on the basis of an associative process. Hawkins, who used the label ASSOCIATIVE ANAPHORA (1978:123–124), observed that if a speaker mentions a book, he can immediately talk about the author, the title, the content, etc.

Under the label "nouns with a referent 'indirectly' inferable" we could include also those cases in which the definiteness of the noun phrase depends upon the linguistic structure of the noun phrase itself: it has been noted that such "linguistic uses" of the definite article are highly language-specific. In English, for instance, the definite article is employed in the following cases, that Hawkins (1978) grouped under the label 'unfamiliar use': (i) establishing relative clauses, such as *What's wrong with Bill? Oh, **the** woman who dated him last night was nasty to him.* (Hawkins 1978:132); (ii) associative clauses like **the** bottom of **the** sea, **the** marine life of **the** sea, etc. (Hawkins 1978:138)[14]; (iii) NP complements (e.g. **the** fact that..., **the** rumor that...); (iv) nominal modifiers (*I don't like **the** colour red*, Hawkins 1978:146–147).

---

into his memory store in the course of some previous conversation with the speaker." As pointed out by Hawkins himself (1978), also the case in which the referent of the anaphoric definite noun phrase is not identical to its first indefinite mention should be considered as an instance of direct anaphora. In the following sentence, for example, the definite noun phrase *the oath* is not co-referential with a noun phrase, but with a verb (from Hawkins 1978:107):

(i) Bill *swore. The oath* embarrassed his mother.

[14] If an associative relationship exists between two objects, definite genitive expressions are normally found in English; associative clauses "incorporate both the trigger and the associate of a pragmatically permissible associative anaphoric sequence" (Hawkins 1978:139).

2.3.2.2 *Dependant on extra-linguistic context*

As displayed in figure 2.1, a different instance of pragmatic definiteness is represented by cases in which the noun is definite because of the extra-linguistic context. In this respect, two subtypes should be distinguished: (i) the definite noun is an entity physically accessible in the extra-linguistic context, shared by speaker and hearer; (ii) the definite noun is an entity not directly accessible.

In the first subtype, the fact that an object is visible and unique at the moment of speaking allows the use of the definite article (see Hawkins 1978:110).[15] This means that the article is employed with a deictic force. The second subtype includes those cases in which the definite noun corresponds to an entity which is neither visible nor physically accessible in the situation of utterance. Nonetheless, it is identifiable on the basis of the extra-linguistic context: its reference is inferred by means of shared knowledge (both speaker and hearer are aware of a situation in which that specific referent exists, for example because it is widely known) or of evidence taken from the context itself (the situation provides the framework for the identification of the referent). As with indirect anaphora, shared knowledge may play a role, with the difference that the framework is provided by the textual information previously given (i.e. by the utterance, discourse, sentence, etc.), rather than by the situation itself.

2.3.3 A diachronic approach to definite articles

As mentioned above, from a cross-linguistic point of view, articles can mark all subtypes of definiteness displayed in figure 2.1, or only some of them. However, given the distinction between logical definiteness and pragmatic definiteness, there are some interesting tendencies across languages concerning the development of definite articles which confirm the validity of this distinction also at a diachronic level.

Definite articles generally develop from demonstrative pronouns (see §2.2),[16] by assuming, at first, both deictic and anaphoric functions, to the extent that it is generally difficult to draw a clear-cut distinction between deixis and anaphora (Schroeder 2006:545). Later, definite articles tend to lose their original pronominal deictic force and are mainly used

---

[15] In Hawkins' (1978) terminology, this is labelled as VISIBLE SITUATION USE. He distinguished this case from the IMMEDIATE SITUATION USE (1978:114), in which the referent is not concretely visible, as in the notice *Beware of the dog*. The hearer/reader is informed of the existence of a given entity and is instructed to use the extra-linguistic context in order to identify which entity is referred to, even though he cannot see it.

[16] Apart from the seminal work by Greenberg (1978), a vast literature exists on this topic. Among others, the reader is referred to Harris (1980), Lyons (1999), Schroeder (2006), and Abraham (2007).

anaphorically: "From there, the use of the article may spread to non-ana-phoric uses" (Schroeder 2006:601).

In other words, the development of definite articles begins at the level of pragmatic definiteness (see Manolessou and Horrocks 2007:225, 227; Napoli 2009:580–583). In the beginning, languages systematically employ the definite article in those contexts in which it is functional, by gradually generalizing such pragmatic uses. Only later, the definite article may be extended to the domain of logical definiteness (i.e. to proper nouns, nouns having unique reference, generics and abstracts). If the use of the definite article becomes obligatory in this domain, it can be said that it has reached the final stage of its development as a marker of definiteness, as roughly illustrated in the schema in table 2.1:

Table 2.1. Stages in the development of definiteness

Stage 0	There is no systematic expression of definiteness by any dedicated means.
Stage 1	The definite article develops from a demonstrative pronoun, by showing both deictic and anaphoric function.
Stage 2	The definite article generalizes as a marker of pragmatic definiteness.
Stage 3	The definite article is optionally extended to the domain of logical definiteness (to all subtypes or only some of them).
Stage 4	The definite article generalizes as an obligatory marker of logical definiteness.

Languages may reach different stages in the diachronic development of definiteness.[17] Whereas Modern Greek has reached stage 4,[18] both Classical Greek and post-Classical Greek seem to belong to stage 3, due to the non-obligatory use of the definite article with logically definite nouns. In this respect, it is worth quoting from Manolessou and Horrocks (2007:227), who rightly noted that:

---

[17] Obviously, in examining definite articles from a diachronic point of view, the boundaries between the different stages may be not well-defined and easy to distinguish. It should also be mentioned that Greenberg (1978), who posited three stages in the diachrony of markers of definiteness, claimed that the definite article becomes merely a gender morpheme or a marker of nominality at the final stage of its development. On this see the discussion in Lyons (1999:337–339).

[18] As is well-known, there is a significant debate on the nature of the definite article in Modern Greek, and in particular on its "redundant" or "expletive" nature. For the sake of brevity, this topic cannot be discussed here: the reader is referred to Napoli (2009) and Alexiadou (2014:15–52), who have taken position against this interpretation.

> within the latter domain [of logical definiteness] (comprising proper names, generics and unique reference nouns, prepositional phrases of non-specific reference, etc.) we should not be surprised...to find significant cross-linguistic variation with respect to the use or absence of the article. Article use may eventually become obligatory with definites of all kinds, but if it remains optional with inherent functional concepts, its presence will normally point to a pragmatic function, e.g. to ensure discourse continuity, to convey contrast or emphasis, etc.

As we will see shortly, this is exactly what Classical Greek and post-Classical Greek attest.

2.4 Obligatoriness and optionality in Greek: Definite article versus zero article

In this section, I will discuss the notions of obligatoriness and optionality as related to the use of the Greek definite article in the domains of pragmatic definiteness and, mainly, of logical definiteness, by focusing on proper nouns, generics and abstracts, which may appear as definite or as bare (i.e. with a zero article). Finally, it will be considered how the existence of a zero article, which may be semantically definite or indefinite, may influence the development of (in)definiteness.

In the literature on definiteness in Classical Greek, two assumptions are frequently found concerning the use of the definite article: (i) it is regularly and primarily employed for anaphoric reference; (ii) it is "optional" with nouns whose definiteness is logically inherent or derived, that is mainly with proper nouns, nouns of unique entities, generics, and abstract nouns (see §2.2).

Although the assumption in (i) is certainly true,[19] what is relevant to our discussion is the fact that the definite article is obligatory not only when anaphora is involved, but, more generally, in all typical cases of pragmatic definiteness, that is when the speaker presupposes that the referent is identifiable also on account of the extra-linguistic context. This seems to happen in both Classical Greek[20] and post-Classical Greek, as represented by New Testament Greek (see §2.5).

---

[19] Interestingly enough, already "Apollonius Dyscolus noted that *anaphorá* was the core use of the Greek article" [c. 130 CE] (Haug 2014:107).

[20] See Lombardi Vallauri (2002), Manolessou and Horrocks (2007:22), Bakker (2009:162), Napoli (2009:582). There are, however, some contexts in which the definite article may be omitted although the noun refers to an identifiable entity (Bakker 2009:172–182). First of all, the article is often omitted in prepositional phrases, especially when forming fixed expressions and formulas: "prepositional

At the same time, although it cannot be denied that the definite article is not obligatory with the nominal categories mentioned in (ii), this does not mean that "its use is the consequence of a casual choice, nor that the alternatives (the presence or the absence of the article itself) are completely equivalent. On the contrary, the possibility of such an option turns out to be limited, at least in some contexts, by pragmatic forces" (Napoli 2009:574). Such pragmatic forces correspond mainly to the function of re-topicalising a constituent, of facilitating referent tracking, of pointing to the salience of the referent;[21] also anaphora plays a significant role, especially with proper nouns.

In Napoli (2009), I have shown how in Classical Greek a proper noun tends to be preceded by the definite article the second time it is mentioned, especially when the corresponding referent is a central topic in the discourse, whereas the same proper noun is often bare in all subsequent mentions. Moreover, in texts with a dialogical form, it may happen that the first occurrence of the definite article with a proper noun is found at a certain distance from the first mention of that proper noun without any article. In other words, what seems to be relevant to the presence of the definite article is the second "context" in which this name appears – and not necessarily its second "mention" when this mention is close to the first, especially if it is in the second context that the referent of the proper noun is established as the topic of the discourse. To illustrate this point, it is worth quoting the following case:

---

phrases and other formulae may dispense with the article as in the earlier language. [...] Anaphora or contrast may bring back the article at any time and there is no pedantical uniformity." (Gildersleeve 1911:259); on New Testament Greek see Turner (1963:174–175,179) and §2.5.4 in this paper. Second, when two or more substantives are connected by the conjunction καὶ, the article may be used only after the first noun, suggesting "unity" (Gildersleeve 1911:277, Bakker 2009:177, and fn. 51), or may be repeated with all coordinated nouns (on this so-called "Granville-Sharp rule" in New Testament Greek, see Wallace 1996:270–306). A rarer possibility is to use coordinated nouns without any article: this is found only with nouns denoting concepts like 'home and earth', or 'wife and children' (Bakker 2009:178). For interesting analyses of the alternation of definite article and zero see also Levinsohn and Dubis (this volume), and Read-Heimerdinger (this volume).
[21] See Sansone (1993); see also Manolessou and Horrocks (2007:230–231), who draw attention to the fact that in Classical Greek, apart from stylistic differences,

> it still remains the case that only the more *important* referents routinely have the article, and typically only when reintroduced in alternation with other participants, i.e. when there is a clear switch of topic/focus. Hence the article is routinely omitted even with key participants in the absence of such retopicalisation, as also in parentheticals (which are by definition outside the main discourse) and reported speech (which is taken from a different discourse context).

As regards the factors influencing the use and non-use of the article in New Testament Greek, see also the papers in this volume by Levinsohn and Dubis, by Read-Heimerdinger and by Runge.

(6) a. καὶ οἶμαι κάλλιστα ἀνθρώπων λέγειν περὶ Ὁμήρου [...],
        οὔτε ἄλλος οὐδεὶς τῶν πώποτε γενομένων ἔσχεν εἰπεῖν
        οὕτω πολλὰς καὶ καλὰς διανοίας περὶ Ὁμήρου ὅσας ἐγώ
        'And I think I speak about Homer better than anybody [...],
        nor did anyone who has ever lived have so many
        and such fine comments to offer on Homer as I have.'
        (Plato, *Ion* 530 c8–d3)

    b. καὶ μὴν ἄξιόν γε ἀκοῦσαι, ὦ Σώκρατες,
        ὡς εὖ κεκόσμηκα τὸν Ὅμηρον
        'And indeed it is worth hearing, Socrates,
        how well I have embellished Homer.' (Plato, *Ion* 530 d6–7)
        (cited from Napoli 2009:593–594)

In these examples, Ion, a rhapsode, utters the name "Homer" without any article at the beginning and at the end of his discourse in (6.a), which are also the first two occurrences of this name in the dialogue. After a brief intervention by Socrates, who invites Ion to tell him more about this subject, Ion himself mentions Homer's name with the definite article (6.b), declaring that, indeed, he will speak about the poet. From a statistical point of view, Homer's name occurs forty-seven times in the dialogue, but (6.b) corresponds to its sole occurrence with the definite article, representing also the second context in which the proper noun is mentioned by Ion.

As regards the issue of obligatoriness and optionality, it should be noted that a diachronic approach to definiteness raises many questions. The following is one of the most interesting and least explored: how do the categories of definiteness and indefiniteness affect each other in the rise and evolution of their respective markers? In order to answer this question, one should firstly examine whether and to what extent the development and distribution of definite articles are influenced by the existence or absence of dedicated markers for indefiniteness, and vice versa. Obviously, in languages with a definite and an indefinite article, both definiteness and indefiniteness are overtly marked, whereas in languages explicitly codifying only definiteness,[22] the definite article does not compete with any indefinite article. As a consequence, in these languages the opposition between definite/indefinite is not grammaticalized to its full extent: the absence of a definite article (i.e.

---

[22] The opposite phenomenon is possible, since there are languages with an indefinite marker but without a definite marker (see Dryer 2013a, 2013b). However, typological generalizations predict that "among languages with an article it is most common to have only a definite article. What is second most common is to have both a definite and an indefinite article, and it is by far least common to have only an indefinite article" (Plank and Moravcsik 1996:204). In Maˇvea, for instance, it is the lack of any article which marks definiteness, as opposed to the use of the article *aite*, expressing indefiniteness, and of the article *le*, expressing specificity, whereas *te...aite* introduces indefinite non-specific entities (Guérin 2007).

zero article) does not necessarily imply an indefinite referent (intended as an individual or entity whose referential identity is unknown to the hearer). In other words, a bare noun phrase may be, in principle, ambiguous, that is it may be interpreted not only as indefinite, but also as definite. It is the speaker/writer who decides to make the "(in)definite" nature of the referent explicit. This is the case in Kutenai (isolate; western North America), where the definite article is not obligatory on definite noun phrases, with the consequence that a noun lacking the definite article may have a definite or indefinite reading (Dryer 2013b). It may be supposed that a similar state-of-affairs strengthens the pragmatic force of the definite article: given that there is no explicit mark of indefiniteness, and that bare noun phrases may be interpreted both as definite or indefinite, the use of the definite article tends to generalize at first in all cases in which there is ambiguity.

Consider that Ancient Greek is a language without an indefinite article, and that since its first appearance in Classical Greek the definite article functions as a "fully developed article" (Manolessou and Horrocks 2007:229) used obligatorily with common nouns for all kinds of pragmatic definiteness, and extended to logically definite nouns in the same contexts, although only optionally. One may wonder then, to what extent the lack of an indefinite article favoured the evolution and distribution of the definite article, as well as its assuming "pragmatic force." As a matter of fact, in Classical Greek the number of bare nouns which may be ambiguous between a definite and an indefinite reading is quite limited. Obviously, this ambiguity does not concern proper nouns and nouns of typical unique entities, since they are inherently definite (see §2.3.1). Things are different as regards nouns used with a generic or abstract reading (and also nouns used in prepositional phrases; see §2.5.4). With these nouns, the fact the Greek definite article is "strongly pragmatical" is what may justify not only its presence, but also its absence. I will try to make this point clearer by commenting upon the examples below:

(7) a. Ἐννοεῖς οὖν, ἔφη, ὅτι, ἐπειδὰν ἀποθάνῃ **ὁ ἄνθρωπος**,
τὸ μὲν ὁρατὸν αὐτοῦ, τὸ σῶμα [...]
'Observe, he went on, that when a man dies,
the visible part of him, the body...' (Plato, *Phaedrus* 80 c2–3)

b. ἐμοὶ γὰρ δοκεῖ ὁμοίως λέγεσθαι ταῦτα ὥσπερ ἄν τις
περὶ **ἀνθρώπου ὑφάντου πρεσβύτου** ἀποθανόντος λέγοι
τοῦτον τὸν λόγον, ὅτι οὐκ ἀπόλωλεν **ὁ ἄνθρωπος**, ἀλλ᾽ ἔστι που σῶς
'It seems to me that it is much as if one should say about an old weaver
who had died, that the man had not perished but was safe.'
(Plato, *Phaedrus* 87 b4–7)

c.   καὶ οὐδέν τι μᾶλλον τούτου ἕνεκα **ἄνθρωπός** ἐστιν
     ἱματίου φαυλότερον οὐδ' ἀσθενέστερον
     'Yet a man is not feebler or weaker
     than a cloak on that account at all.' (Plato, *Phaedrus* 87 d1–3)

As already mentioned (§2.3.1), in Classical Greek generics may be marked by the definite article or may be bare, both in the singular and in the plural number: the different types are not necessarily interchangeable, since contextual factors may determine which type of noun phrase is more appropriate in order to convey genericity. It may be supposed that one of these factors is the status of the definite article, including the fact that in Greek the definite article is not opposed to an indefinite article. The passages quoted in example (7) are taken from the same dialogue by Plato. The noun ἄνθρωπος is used with a generic value in both (7a) and (7c). However, as opposed to the case in (7c), the subordinate clause in (7a) shows the occurrence of ἄνθρωπος with the definite article: interestingly enough, the verb (θνῄσκω 'to die') is punctual and inflected as an aorist, whereas in (7c) the verb is stative and inflected as a present. This is consistent with a tendency proper to Classical Greek, that is, the choice of a bare singular with a generic value if the focus is on a specific property of the class. On the other hand, in example (7b), ἄνθρωπος is not generic: it is accompanied by a definite article, which has an anaphoric value and, then, is "pragmatically" necessary, since it distinctively refers to the man ('an old weaver') mentioned before (although it sets up a hypothetical referent). Apart from contextual reasons which may have favoured the use of a bare singular in (7c), it should be noted that the use of the definite article would have created an ambiguity between a generic reading and a referential reading: ὁ ἄνθρωπος could have been interpreted as referring to the same man as in (7b). This ambiguity is avoided thanks to the use of a bare noun. In Modern Greek, after the development of the indefinite article, the syntactic contexts in which a bare noun is allowed become quite limited,[23] and the definite article occurs as an obligatory mark of (nominal) genericity.

As regards abstract nouns, it has already been observed that they may appear as definite or as bare in Classical Greek. Both ἡ ἀρετή and ἀρετή may correspond to 'virtue' as an abstract concept. Sansone (1993) analyzed the occurrence of ἀρετή in three Platonic dialogues, and concluded that the presence of the article is justified by different pragmatically based

---

[23] In general, in Modern Greek the article is absent only in the following contexts (Holton, Mackridge, and Philippaki-Warburton 1997:282–285): (i) with nouns having a partitive value; (ii) in predicative position; (iii) in more or less fixed collocations made up of a verb plus noun, a preposition plus noun (if the preposition is not employed in a concrete sense), or a noun phrase preceded by another noun phrase (if the noun is abstract and in the genitive case).

features. If we agree with this conclusion, which is consistent with what we observed in this section on the optional use of the definite article, we should assume that the occurrence of abstracts as bare is the "unmarked" choice for these nouns in Greek, as well as for proper nouns and nouns of unique entities. In other words, we may suppose that the most natural reading of ἀρετή is 'virtue', and not 'a virtue'. This may explain cases like those mentioned below:

(8) ἐγὼ οὖν, ὦ Πρωταγόρα, εἰς ταῦτα ἀποβλέπων
    οὐχ ἡγοῦμαι διδακτὸν εἶναι **ἀρετήν** · [...]
    εἰ οὖν ἔχεις ἐναργέστερον ἡμῖν ἐπιδεῖξαι
    ὡς διδακτόν ἐστιν **ἡ ἀρετή**, μὴ φθονήσῃς ἀλλ' ἐπίδειξον
    'I therefore, Protagoras, in view of these facts, believe that virtue is not teachable [...]. So if you can demonstrate to us more explicitly that virtue is teachable, do not grudge us your demonstration.' (Plato, *Protagoras* 320 b4–c1)

(9) Οἰκτρὸς δ' οὐχ ὁ πεινῶν ἤ τι τοιοῦτον πάσχων,
    ἀλλ' ὁ σωφρονῶν ἤ **τινα ἀρετὴν** ἤ μέρος ἔχων ταύτης,
    ἄν τινα ξυμφορὰν πρὸς τούτοις κεκτῆται
    'The man who suffers from hunger or the like is not the man who deserves pity, but he who, while possessing (a) temperance or (a) virtue of some sort, or a share thereof, gains in addition evil fortune.' (Plato, *Leges* 936 b3–b5)

In the passage quoted in (8), ἀρετή, denoting the abstract concept of 'virtue', occurs twice: in the first occurrence, it is bare, whereas in the second it is preceded by the definite article. This can be considered as anaphoric and at the same time has the function of re-topicalising the corresponding referent, which is the topic of the subsequent discourse by Socrates (note, moreover, that in its second mention ἀρετή is in the nominative case, corresponding to the subject of the embedded dependent clause). A different use of the same noun is found in (9), where the indefinite pronoun τινα precedes ἀρετήν, having a concrete meaning and identifying a particular good quality displayed by someone. Since the most basic reading of ἀρετή as a bare noun would have been 'virtue', the presence of an indefinite marker is necessary to denote an individual, "non-unique" virtue. This use resembles the exceptional occurrence of the indefinite article with abstract nouns in languages like English or Italian (see §2.3.1).

Having discussed these fundamental preliminary issues, I now turn to the presentation of the data from the New Testament.

2.5 The definite article in New Testament Greek

According to many scholars, Classical Greek and Koine Greek (including New Testament Greek) employ the definite article in the same way, with not much variation. The article is still optional with the same categories of nouns as was the case in Classical Greek, and the same pragmatic factors are at work.[24] In the following pages, I will illustrate the distribution of the definite article in the domains of logical definiteness and pragmatic definiteness in New Testament Greek, by focusing on the similarities and differences between this stage of language and Classical Greek.[25]

2.5.1 The domain of logical definiteness

In the domain of logical definiteness, nouns are not compulsorily marked by the definite article in New Testament Greek, as was also the case in Classical Greek. However, it seems that on the basis of previous literature (although a comprehensive quantitative study of this is lacking), a certain regularity may be noted in the use of the article, which is employed more often than not with some categories of nouns, particularly generics and nouns of unique entities. Interestingly enough, according to the provisional conclusion in Manolessou and Horrocks (2007:232), data from Medieval Greek (i.e. literary vernacular texts from the 12th–15th c.) show that the article is still optional with proper names and with "generic" prepositional phrases, but "had now become obligatory with other types of semantic definites (generics etc.)." Finally, there is evidence that the definite article began to be used compulsorily with proper names some time before the 15th century.[26]

---

[24] See, among others, Blass and Debrunner (1961:131–132), Turner (1963:165, 172), Manolessou and Horrocks (2007:231), and Guardiano (2013:89).

[25] Two syntactic phenomena common to both stages of the Greek language should be mentioned here, which will not be further treated for brevity's sake. First of all, in genitive phrases, the noun in the genitive case tends to have the same behaviour as its head noun in terms of (in)definiteness: this means that both nouns are definite or bare. However, this "rule" presents a lot of exceptions both in Classical Greek and New Testament Greek (cf. Turner 1963:179–180; Wallace 1996:239, 250–252). Second, when a noun is modified by an adjective with an attributive function, three different positions are admitted, correspondingly and respectively: (i) article-adjective-noun; (ii) article-noun-article-adjective; (iii) noun-article-adjective. The first position attributes major emphasis to the adjective (Robertson 1914:776), whereas in the second position "both substantive and adjective receive emphasis and the adjective is added as a sort of climax in apposition with a separate adjective" (Robertson 1914:777). The third position is quite rare (see Gildersleeve 1911:280–284, Wallace 1996:306–307).

[26] "Other than when used with adpositional modifiers, or in certain traditional formulae of legal texts, which continue to show optionality, see e.g. the acts of Manolis Varouchas 1597–1613" (Manolessou and Horrocks 2007:233).

2.5.1.1 The definite article with nouns of unique entities and proper nouns

In New Testament Greek, nouns referring to unique entities such as ἥλιος, σελήνη, οὐρανός, etc., tend to be marked by the definite article with the exception of prepositional phrases and fixed expressions or formulas,[27] which are typically bare also in Classical Greek, independently of the type of noun (see fn. 20). For example, κόσμος is always bare in the formula ἀπὸ καταβολῆς (or ἀρχῆς) κόσμου (Matt 24:21, 25:34, Mark 10:6). In other words, whereas in Classical Greek these nouns may appear with or without the definite article, the presence of which can often be explained by invoking pragmatic principles (see Gildersleeve 1911:255 and §2.4 in this paper), in the New Testament the rule seems to be represented by the presence of the definite article,[28] although it is still not obligatory with them.

To give an example, in the Gospels, there are twelve occurrences of ἥλιος, ten of which are arthrous, two anarthrous. Example (10) is an instance of the arthrous usage, while (11) and (12) represent the two "exceptions," where ἥλιος is found, respectively, in a genitive absolute construction and preceded by a preposition:

(10)   Τότε οἱ δίκαιοι ἐκλάμψουσιν ὡς **ὁ ἥλιος**
       ἐν τῇ βασιλείᾳ τοῦ πατρὸς αὐτῶν
       'Then the righteous will shine like the sun
       in the kingdom of their Father' (Matt 13:43)

(11)   **ἡλίου** δὲ ἀνατείλαντος ἐκαυματίσθη
       'But when the sun rose, they [the seeds] were scorched.' (Matt 13:6)

(12)   καὶ ἔσονται σημεῖα **ἐν ἡλίῳ** καὶ σελήνῃ καὶ ἄστροις
       'There will be signs in the sun, the moon, and the stars.' (Luke 21:25)

The issue of "definite" proper nouns (including proper names of individuals, geographical names of countries, towns, cities, rivers, etc.) is probably the most complex, because of the high degree of variation in the use of the article. It has been assumed that in New Testament Greek "the situation with proper names has apparently remained essentially unchanged" (Manolessou and Horrocks 2007:231) as compared to the situation in Classical Greek (see Gildersleeve 1911:229–255), and that the definite article is extensively

---

[27] See Stuart (1837:35), Blass and Debrunner (1961:132–133), and Wallace (1996:223–224, 248–249).

[28] Considering this tendency, it is not surprising that that the occurrence of θεός 'god' without the definite article has stirred up a significant debate on its correct theological interpretation and translation. However, its lack of an article is not surprising in light of the optionality of the definite article with nouns of unique entities: the reader is referred to Wallace (1996:266–269) and Levinsohn (2000:162–165).

used with them (see Müth 2011:16). In general terms, the first mention of a proper name lacks the definite article, but the subsequent instances may show it (Read-Heimerdinger 2002:120).

As a matter of fact, some scholars have tried to find principles governing the use of the article with this range of nouns, such as anaphora (Blass and Debrunner 1961:137), but also familiarity (Turner 1963:166), emphasis and designation of title or case, mainly for indeclinable names (Porter 1994:107). However, the major part of them have focused on the fact that proper nouns "employ or omit the article *ad libitum scriptoris*" (Stuart 1837:35; see also Blass and Debrunner 1961:136, Turner 1963:166). This state of affairs has led Wallace (1996:246), among others, to assume that "we are unable to articulate clear and consistent principles as to why the article is used in a given instance [i.e. with proper names]. (For example, although sometimes it is due to anaphora, there are too many exceptions to make this a major principle.)"

A very interesting contribution to this issue has been provided by Heimerdinger and Levinsohn (1992), who examined the occurrence of names of people in the texts of Acts (on the basis of the Codex Bezae).[29] The main rule governing the use of the article with these names can be summarized by quoting Read-Heimerdinger's (2002:119) words: "The unmarked way of mentioning a person by name is with the article. The omission of the article indicates that attention is being drawn to the person being named." This means that the presence of the article with proper nouns may be evaluated as "neutral," whereas its absence is "not neutral," and has the functional purpose of drawing special attention to the person referred to at the point of the narrative. As pointed out by the authors, this is consistent also with the fact that the first mention of a proper name tends to be bare. In other words, the absence of the article would be marked and mainly related to the function of expressing saliency, involving both prominent participants and prominent speeches (i.e. participants whose speeches are of central importance: see also Levinsohn 2000:156). This includes also the mechanisms of reactivation of participants (see Levinsohn 2000:152–155).

If Heimerdinger and Levinsohn's (1992) conclusions were confirmed by more data concerning both New Testament Greek and, more in general, Koine Greek, this would be a significant result in the diachronic study of definite proper nouns from Ancient Greek to Modern Greek. If it is true that in Classical Greek the use of the definite article with proper nouns spread from contexts in which pragmatic forces play a role, being marked (see §2.4), to Modern Greek, where its use with such nouns

---

[29] For a detailed description and examples see also Levinsohn (2000:148–167) and Read-Heimerdinger (2002:116–144). More recently, see Read-Heimerdinger (2011) (and ch. 7 of this volume), which examines names of places in the Book of Acts, confirming Heimerdinger and Levinsohn's (1992) conclusions.

becomes entirely a matter of logical definiteness, being obligatory, that is unmarked, Koine Greek would represent an intermediate stage: in this stage, the definite article is already unmarked and linked only to logical definiteness, although it is not still compulsory, its absence being admitted under special readings.

Obviously, much more research is needed in order to support this hypothesis. (In this respect, see the contribution by Read-Heimerdinger in this volume, and also §6.2.1.2 in Runge's paper, this volume).

2.5.1.2 The definite article with generics and abstracts

As mentioned in section 2.5.1, in the New Testament "the omission of the article with generics is much less common than previously" (Manolessou and Horrocks 2007:231; see also Robertson 1914:757), although its use has not yet become obligatory. An interesting example is the following, where the first generic noun is definite, whereas the second is bare:

(13)   ἡ γυνὴ δὲ δόξα ἀνδρός ἐστιν
         'The wife is the glory of (her) husband.' (1 Cor 11:7)
         (cited from Wallace 1996:254)

Although from some contexts, like that mentioned in (13), one could argue that definite and bare generics are interchangeable, it is more correct to claim that they are not completely synonymous.[30] This is consistent with the cross-linguistic tendency documented also in Classical Greek (see §2.3.1 and §2.4). As regards (13), it should be noted that ἡ γυνή functions as a subject, while ἀνδρός is part of a genitive phrase, and is bare following its head noun (see fn. 25).

Moreover, although a quantitative analysis would be desirable, it seems that in the New Testament, generic noun phrases correspond to plural definites more often than to singular definites. This is particularly interesting in the light of the fact that in Modern Greek genericity is typically expressed by definite plural nouns (see §2.3.1). If one looks at the occurrences of the noun ἄνθρωπος in the Gospels, there is evidence for this hypothesis. These occurrences are displayed in table 2.2 with regard to the nominative and dative cases in the singular and plural.

---

[30] See Wallace (1996:253). The author also draws attention to the fact that some nouns typically take the article and others do not (1996:227). However, he does not add more detailed material or statistical data in order to illustrate this point.

Table 2.2. Occurrences of the noun ἄνθρωπος 'man' in the Gospels

Types of occurrences	With a definite article			
	Singular		Plural	
	ὁ ἄνθρωπος	τῷ ἀνθρώπῳ	οἱ ἄνθρωποι	τοῖς ἀνθρώποις
Generic	6	–	9	10
Definite, non-generic	8	5	2	1
With a demonstrative pronoun	9	5	–	–
Total	23	10	11	11

	Without a definite article			
	Singular		Plural	
	ἄνθρωπος	ἀνθρώπῳ	ἄνθρωποι	ἀνθρώποις
Generic	8	1	–	7 (always with a preposition)
Predicative	6	–	–	–
Indefinite (bare)	34	8	–	1
Indefinite (with τις)	8	1	–	–
Other determiners (interrogative τίς, numeral)	4	–	1	
Total	60	10	1	8

As shown in table 2.2, the noun ἄνθρωπος occurs with a generic value twenty-five times with the definite article, and sixteen times with a generic value without any article. Plural definite generics are more frequent than singular definite generics (19 vs. 6 occurrences), and also than bare plural generics (19 vs. 7 occurrences). It is worth noting that bare plural generics are not attested in the nominative case, but only in the dative case, and are always part of a prepositional phrase. Finally, ἄνθρωπος frequently appears in the nominative with an indefinite value, especially to introduce a new referent or, in some cases, to set up a hypothetical referent. When the noun has a generic value, the choice of zero article often suggests a distributive reading in the singular ('man' corresponding to 'each man'). Three examples are mentioned below, by illustrating the use of ἄνθρωπος as a definite singular, a bare singular and a definite plural, respectively:

(14)   τὸ σάββατον διὰ **τὸν ἄνθρωπον** ἐγένετο καὶ
οὐχ **ὁ ἄνθρωπος** διὰ τὸ σάββατον
'The sabbath was made for humankind,
and not humankind for the sabbath.' (Mark 2:27)

(15)   Ἕνεκα τούτου καταλείψει **ἄνθρωπος** τὸν πατέρα καὶ τὴν μητέρα
καὶ κολληθήσεται τῇ γυναικὶ αὐτοῦ
'For this reason a man shall leave his father and mother
and be joined to his wife.' (Matt 19:5)

(16)   μακάριοί ἐστε ὅταν μισήσωσιν ὑμᾶς **οἱ ἄνθρωποι**
'Blessed are you when people hate you.' (Luke 6:22)

On the basis of previous literature, abstract nouns occur with the article more frequently than without it (Wallace 1996:226), "especially when it is desired to lay emphasis on the quality spoken about or to denote it as one previously mentioned" (Nunn 1913:57), that is, with an anaphoric function. Nonetheless, scholars have recognized that, as in Classical Greek, abstracts may appear as definite or bare without any "vital difference" (Robertson 1914:794; see also Turner 1963:176–178, Wallace 1996:249). An example of a definite abstract noun is quoted below:

(17)   ἀποχωρεῖτε ἀπ' ἐμοῦ οἱ ἐργαζόμενοι **τὴν ἀνομίαν**
'Go away from me, you evildoers.' (Matt 7:23)

However, the number of occurrences with or without the article depends also on the type of noun and on the context. For example, in the Gospels, ἀλήθεια is accompanied by the definite article eighteen times (4 times in a prepositional phrase), whereas it is bare fourteen times.

(18)   ἐκεῖνος ἀνθρωποκτόνος ἦν ἀπ' ἀρχῆς,
καὶ ἐν **τῇ ἀληθείᾳ** οὐκ ἔστηκεν,
ὅτι οὐκ ἔστιν **ἀλήθεια** ἐν αὐτῷ
'He was a murderer from the beginning
and does not stand in the truth,
because there is no truth in him.' (John 8:44)[31]

---

[31] This passage is preceded by two other passages in which ἀλήθεια occurs 3 times, and is always definite: see John 8:32, 8:40.

(19)   ἐγὼ δὲ ὅτι **τὴν ἀλήθειαν** λέγω, οὐ πιστεύετέ μοι.
        Τίς ἐξ ὑμῶν ἐλέγχει με περὶ ἁμαρτίας;
        Εἰ **ἀλήθειαν** λέγω, διὰ τί ὑμεῖς οὐ πιστεύετέ μοι;
        'But because I tell the truth, you do not believe me.
        Which of you convicts me of sin?
        If I tell the truth, why do you not believe me?' (John 8:45–46)

On the other hand, εἰρήνη is definite only four times (as a nominative or an accusative), and is bare twenty-one times. However, when it is bare, it mainly occurs in prepositional phrases and/or in given formulas:

(20)   καὶ λέγει αὐτοῖς **Εἰρήνη** ὑμῖν
        'And Jesus said to them: "Peace be with you."' (Luke 24.36)

To conclude, there is evidence from the data that the article has not become obligatory with abstracts in New Testament Greek, and that it is difficult to recognize a uniform principle governing its presence and also its absence with such nouns.

2.5.2 The domain of pragmatic definiteness

2.5.2.1 Definiteness as determined by the extra-linguistic context

As pointed out in section 2.3.2.2, the presence of the definite article may be influenced by the extra-linguistic context. The article may be used (i) with a noun denoting a referent which is concretely given in the physical space, or (ii) with a noun corresponding to a neither visible nor physically accessible entity, whose referential identity is established on the basis of shared knowledge or evidence taken from the situation itself.

According to Wallace (1996:221), the use sketched in (i) – labelled DEICTIC or POINTING ARTICLE by him – is not frequent in Koine Greek, where the article tends to be replaced or strengthened with the demonstrative pronoun. An instance of type (i) is exemplified by means of the passages in (21):

(21) a.   καὶ εἶδεν **πλοῖα δύο** ἑστῶτα παρὰ τὴν λίμνην·
           οἱ δὲ ἁλιεῖς ἀπ' αὐτῶν ἀποβάντες ἔπλυνον τὰ δίκτυα
           'Jesus saw two boats there at the shore of the lake;
           the fishermen had gone out of them and were washing their nets.'
           (Luke 5:2)

     b.   ὡς δὲ ἐπαύσατο λαλῶν, εἶπεν πρὸς τὸν Σίμωνα, Ἐπανάγαγε
           εἰς τὸ βάθος καὶ χαλάσατε **τὰ δίκτυα** ὑμῶν εἰς ἄγραν
           'When he had finished speaking, he said to Simon, "Put out into the
           deep water and let down your nets for a catch."' (Luke 5:4)

In Jesus' direct discourse cited in (21.b), the mention of τὰ δίκτυα as definite is determined by the fact that the nets are visible on the scene, as can be inferred from the preceding description (21.a). Note, moreover, that τὰ δίκτυα is definite also in (21.a) because of indirect anaphora: the mention of πλοῖα δύο sets up a series of referents which are identifiable since they are part of the first referent, that is, ὁι ... ἁλιεῖς and, indeed, τὰ δίκτυα.

As an illustration of type (ii), I quote the following passage:

(22)   εἶτα βάλλει ὕδωρ εἰς **τὸν νιπτῆρα** καὶ
         ἤρξατο νίπτειν τοὺς πόδας τῶν μαθητῶν
         'Then he poured water into the basin and
         began to wash the disciples' feet.' (John 13:5)
         (cited from from Stuart 1837:37)

The occurrence of the definite article before the noun νιπτῆρα – the referent of which neither was mentioned before nor can be inferred from the presence of another referent to which it belongs concretely or conceptually (i.e. because of direct or indirect anaphora) – may be explained only if we take into account that the writer presupposes that his readers know that a wash-basin is usually placed in a guest chamber. In the New Testament, one very frequently finds definite nouns referring to objects well-known to the writers and their contemporaries; that is, nouns whose definite status is a matter of shared knowledge.

2.5.2.2 Definiteness as determined by the linguistic context

Anaphora

Scholars who have dealt with the definite article in New Testament Greek have recognized that its occurrence with an anaphoric value corresponds to its most widespread and regular use. This is consistent with the behaviour of the article in Classical Greek. An example of direct anaphora is found in (23), where the noun γυνή 'woman' is bare in its first mention, but, later, it is preceded by the anaphoric definite article:

(23)   Καὶ ἰδοὺ γυνὴ αἱμορροοῦσα δώδεκα ἔτη προσελθοῦσα
         ὄπισθεν ἥψατο τοῦ κρασπέδου τοῦ ἱματίου αὐτοῦ [...].
         Καὶ ἐσώθη ἡ γυνὴ ἀπὸ τῆς ὥρας ἐκείνης
         'Then suddenly a woman who had been suffering from haemor-
         rhages for twelve years came up behind him and touched the
         fringe of his cloak [...]. And instantly the woman was made well.'
         (Matt 9:20, 22)

As mentioned before (fn. 13), one can speak of direct anaphora also when the anaphoric noun phrase and its first mention are not "identical." This case is also documented in New Testament Greek, as shown in (24). More precisely, in (24.b), βαπτίσματος is definite because of anaphora: however, its first mention is not represented by a noun, but by the corresponding verb (24.a).

(24) a. ἢ ἀγνοεῖτε ὅτι ὅσοι **ἐβαπτίσθημεν** εἰς Χριστὸν ᾿Ιησοῦν
εἰς τὸν θάνατον αὐτοῦ **ἐβαπτίσθημεν**;
'Do you not know that all of us who have been baptized into Christ Jesus were baptized into his death?' (Rom 6:3)

  b. συνετάφημεν οὖν αὐτῷ διὰ **τοῦ βαπτίσματος** εἰς τὸν θάνατον
'Therefore we have been buried with him by that baptism into death.' (Rom 6:4)
(cited from Wallace 1996:219)

The use of the definite article in indirect anaphora is also attested in the New Testament:

(25) Καὶ ἦλθεν εἰς Ναζαρά, οὗ ἦν τεθραμμένος, καὶ εἰσῆλθεν
κατὰ τὸ εἰωθὸς αὐτῷ ἐν τῇ ἡμέρᾳ τῶν σαββάτων
εἰς τὴν συναγωγήν, καὶ ἀνέστη ἀναγνῶναι.
Καὶ ἐπεδόθη αὐτῷ **βιβλίον** τοῦ προφήτου ᾿Ησαίου,
καὶ ἀνοίξας τὸ **βιβλίον** εὗρεν [τὸν] τόπον οὗ ἦν γεγραμμένον,
[...] καὶ πτύξας τὸ **βιβλίον** ἀποδοὺς τῷ ὑπηρέτῃ ἐκάθισεν
'When he came to Nazareth, where he had been brought up, he went to the synagogue on the sabbath day, as was his custom. He stood up to read, and the scroll of the prophet Isaiah was given to him. He unrolled the scroll and found the place where it was written [...]. And he rolled up the scroll, gave it back to the attendant, and sat down.' (Luke 4:16–17, 20)

The passage in (25) may illustrate both direct and indirect anaphora. βιβλίον is anarthrous in its first mention, corresponding to new, salient, information, whereas it is accompanied by the definite article in its two subsequent mentions, having an anaphoric value. In the same passage, the word 'attendant' is preceded by the definite article, although no previous mention of an attendant has been made: this is possible because of the mechanism of indirect anaphora. The noun phrase τῷ ὑπηρέτῃ attaches anaphorically to the words 'synagogue' and 'book', which establish a hypothetical set of referents related to them: one of this is, indeed, 'the attendant', who had some typical duties at the synagogue.[32]

---

[32] On the same passage see Nunn (1913:56) and Wallace (1996:217), who quotes it as an instance of "the ARTICLE OF SIMPLE IDENTIFICATION," which is regarded by him

The definite article co-occurring with other determiners

In the following pages, I will briefly look at the main contexts in which the definite article co-occurs with another determiner in the New Testament. This phenomenon is wide-spread also in Classical Greek, where the definite article "tends to co-occur with the other definite determiners and even with some quantifiers. Moreover, it defines a syntactic domain in which the other determiners can or cannot appear depending on their characteristics" (Faure 2014:442).

A well-known case is represented by the co-occurrence with demonstratives, which are "almost always accompanied by the definite article" (Bentein 2014:159) in Classical Greek, mainly if used attributively; they may occur before the article or may follow a definite noun phrase.[33] Demonstratives have exactly the same behaviour in New Testament Greek, where this use is systematic according to Wallace (1996:241). On the contrary, this phenomenon is quite rare from a typological perspective (see Lyons 1999:118–121). Two examples are given below, illustrating the two different types of word order:

(26)   Ἔλεγεν δὲ **ταύτην τὴν** παραβολήν
         'Then he told this parable.' (Luke 13:6)

(27)   Τίνι δὲ ὁμοιώσω **τὴν** γενεὰν **ταύτην**;
         'But to what will I compare this generation?' (Matt 11:16)

Another frequent use of the definite article at both stages of the Greek language is its co-occurrence with possessive pronouns,[34] as in (28):

(28)   οὗ γάρ εἰσιν δύο ἢ τρεῖς συνηγμένοι εἰς τὸ ἐμὸν ὄνομα […]
         'For where two or three are gathered in my name…' (Matt 18:20)

However, it seems that in Classical Greek the range of pronouns with which the definite article is attested is wider than in New Testament Greek. For instance, in Classical Greek, the article may occur with personal and

---

as one of the functions of the INDIVIDUALIZING ARTICLE (as opposed to the GENERIC ARTICLE).

[33] According to some scholars, the different word order corresponds to a different function: if the demonstrative precedes, there is special emphasis on it (see Biraud 1991:43–45, Bentein 2014:159). However, there are divergent opinions on this, as well as on how to interpret the presence of the definite article in this type of noun phrase (see Faure 2014:444, Hewson 2014:421, Bakker 2009:183–189).

[34] In this respect, Ancient Greek is significantly different from languages like English or Irish, where a possessive noun phrase is not marked by the definite article (Lyons 1999:22, 124–125, Bakker 2009:181). See also §2.5.3. for the so-called "possessive use" of the definite article.

reflexive pronouns, "in familiar language" (Gildersleeve 1911:268), for which see example (29). This is a usage that, to my knowledge, is not found in the New Testament.

(29)   ποῖ, ἔφην ἐγώ, λέγεις, καὶ παρὰ τίνας **τοὺς ὑμᾶς**;
        "'Where do you mean?" I asked; "and what is your company?'"
        (Plato, *Lysis* 203 b5)
        (from Gildersleeve 1911:268)

As regards the occurrence of the article with quantifiers like πᾶς, ὅλος, etc., in Classical Greek "the situation is even more puzzling, as some of them are in the domain of the article (οἱ ὀλίγοι), while others can be inside or outside, or even appear without any article" (Faure 2014:445). In New Testament Greek, a similar state of affairs is found, since quantifiers and, in general, pronominal adjectives may occur with the definite article or as bare.[35]

Finally, an interesting case to which very little attention has been paid is represented by the indefinite pronoun ὁ, ἡ, τό δεῖνα 'such a one, so-and-so': δεῖνα, frequently indeclinable, is preceded by the definite article, considered as "the only signal of gender" (Dressler and Katsouda 2014:155). The only occurrence in New Testament Greek is represented by the following example, where τὸν δεῖνα seems to have a specific indefinite reading:

(30)   ὁ δὲ εἶπεν, Ὑπάγετε εἰς τὴν πόλιν πρὸς **τὸν δεῖνα** καὶ εἴπατε αὐτῷ...
        'He said, "Go into the city to a certain man, and say to him..."'
        (Matt 26:18)

One could wonder whether the decreasing use of this pronominal form, which is not particularly frequent in Classical Greek anyway, is related to some change in the (in)definiteness system. However, in order to answer this question more research is obviously needed.

2.5.3 The "syntactic" role of the definite article

In studying definiteness in Classical Greek, many scholars have focused on the fact that "the definite article may in some cases play only a syntactic role" (Faure 2014:443). This primarily concerns two phenomena, that is, its occurrence with parts of speech different from the noun, and its occurrence with a pronominal value.[36]

---

[35] Blass and Debrunner (1961:143–144), Wallace (1996:253).

[36] These types of occurrences have not been included in the map of definiteness displayed in fig. 2.1, which is based only on the uses of the article with a noun. It would be interesting to explore how the syntactic role of the definite article, as labelled above, is related to its other uses, both from a synchronic and diachronic point of view. However, this investigation is beyond the scope of this paper.

In Greek, the definite article may be used with adjectives, infinitives, participles, adverbs, and prepositional phrases in order to turn them into noun phrases (see Gildersleeve 1911:263–268; also Hewson 2014:421–422). In New Testament Greek, the substantivizing function of the definite article is common especially with participles and adjectives, as well as in Classical Greek, where this use is regular in prose (Gildersleeve 1911:262); it is common also with adverbs and infinitives (which, however, may function as substantives also without the article), whereas it is less frequent with prepositional phrases, and rare with particles (Wallace 1996:231–237). Two examples are mentioned below displaying the substantivizing function of the article with an infinitive and a prepositional phrase (on the use with a genitive phrase see the end of this section):

(31)   τὸ δὲ **καθίσαι** ἐκ δεξιῶν μου ἢ ἐξ εὐωνύμων οὐκ ἔστιν ἐμὸν δοῦναι
        'But to sit at my right hand and at my left hand is not mine to grant.'
        (Mark 10:40)
        (cited from Wallace 1996:234)

(32)   **οἱ ἐκ** περιτομῆς
        'The circumcised...' (Acts 10:45)
        (cited from Wallace 1996:236)

As regards the pronominal use of the definite article in New Testament Greek, it seems much reduced as compared to Classical Greek (Turner 1963:36). First of all, a properly "demonstrative" use of the definite article is not frequently attested in the New Testament (Stuart 1837:54), as opposed to Classical and Homeric Greek, which obviously employs ὁ, ἡ, τό as a substantive demonstrative "with more freedom than the Attic" (Gildersleeve 1911:224). In Classical Greek the definite article often occurs in construction with μέν and δέ with a contrastive value (ὁ μὲν ... ὁ δέ 'the one...the other'), especially with reference to people or things already mentioned (Gildersleeve 1911:216). This use is found also in New Testament Greek; what changes is the extent to which it is documented, including its frequency, since it is "quite rare" (Wallace 1997:212; see also Blass and Debrunner 1961:131). Moreover, in the NT the article is found only as a nominative in this construction (Wallace 1997:211–212),[37] whereas in Classical Greek (and, also, in Homeric Greek) it may occur in other syntactic cases (many examples in Gildersleeve 1911:216–219).

Other contexts in which the definite article may occur as an independent pronoun both in Classical Greek and New Testament Greek are the following: the article functions as (i) a personal pronoun; (ii) a relative pronoun; (iii) a possessive pronoun.

---

[37] Eph 4:11 represents an exception to Wallace's statement (Daniel King, personal communication).

In the New Testament, when the article substitutes a third personal pronoun, it is inflected as a nominative and is generally preceded by δέ, indicating a change in the subject (i.e. it does not refer to the same subject as in the preceding sentence), as illustrated in (33). This is also very common in Classical Greek, although on occasion ὁ δέ can also be used to refer to the preceding subject (Gildersleeve 1911:220–221).

(33)   οἱ δὲ αὐτῷ λέγουσιν, Θέλεις οὖν ἀπελθόντες
         συλλέξωμεν αὐτά; ὁ δέ φησιν [...]
         'The slaves said to him, "Then do you want us to go
         and gather them?"' But he replied... (Matt 13:28–29)

As mentioned above, another use which is common to both stages of the Greek language concerns the occurrence of ὁ, ἡ, τό after a noun in the place of a relative pronoun (see Gildersleeve 1911:226; Wallace 1997:214).

Finally, the definite article may be found in contexts in which the notion of possession is involved, lacking any overt possessive marker. The possessive use of the definite article is mainly found with nouns denoting parts of the body, kinship terms or personal belongings (i.e. with inalienable possession). In Classical Greek this use is common in prose, but less frequent in poetry (Gildersleeve 1911:227, Bakker 2009:180). However, in New Testament Greek, a genitive of possession often appears after a definite noun phrase, especially with kinship terms. Compare (34), where no overt possessive form is found, with (35), which explicitly codifies possession by means of the genitive of the personal pronoun αὐτός.

(34)   μὴ ἔχοντος δὲ αὐτοῦ ἀποδοῦναι ἐκέλευσεν αὐτὸν ὁ κύριος πραθῆναι
         καὶ **τὴν γυναῖκα** καὶ τὰ τέκνα καὶ πάντα ὅσα ἔχει
         'As he could not pay, his lord ordered him to be sold,
         together with his wife and children and all his possessions.'
         (Matt 18:25)

(35)   Ἰωσὴφ ἀπὸ τοῦ ὕπνου ἐποίησεν ὡς προσέταξεν αὐτῷ
         ὁ ἄγγελος Κυρίου καὶ παρέλαβεν **τὴν γυναῖκα αὐτοῦ**
         'When Joseph awoke from sleep, he did as the angel of the Lord
         commanded him; he took her as his wife.' (Matt 1:24)

Note that a genitive of possession may be preceded by a definite article, normally implying a kinship term (see Nunn 1913:59) as in (36), or, more rarely, in the case of the neutral article, the noun 'things' (37):

(36)   καὶ προβὰς ὀλίγον εἶδεν Ἰάκωβον **τὸν** τοῦ Ζεβεδαίου
         'As he went a little farther, he saw James son of Zebedee.'
         (Mark 1:19)

(37)   ἄρα οὖν **τὰ** τῆς εἰρήνης διώκωμεν καὶ
        τὰ τῆς οἰκοδομῆς τῆς εἰς ἀλλήλους
        'Let us then pursue what makes for peace and for mutual upbuilding.'
        (Rom 14:19)
        (cited from Wallace 1996:235)

Sometimes, this use has been interpreted as an instance of the function
of the definite article as a relative pronoun (see Wallace 1996:235n51):
another possible interpretation is to consider the article as having a substan-
tivising function, as in examples (31) and (32). The same pattern is already
documented in Classical Greek (Gildersleeve 1911:266–267).

2.5.4 Bare nouns: Definite or indefinite?

As pointed out at the end of section 2.4, the fact that Ancient Greek lacks an
indefinite article possibly has a role in the distribution of the definite article, in particular as opposed to zero article. In principle, bare noun phrases
are not necessarily indefinite, but may be interpreted as definite. This has
been recognized by scholars dealing with New Testament Greek, who have
acknowledged the presence of definiteness in the absence of ὁ, ἡ, τό.[38]
   Apart from the case of generics and abstracts discussed in section 2.4, in
the Greek language there are other contexts in which a noun does not need
to be accompanied by the definite article in order for it to be definite: for
instance, with cardinal and ordinal numerals no article generally occurs.[39]
As already seen in the preceding pages, this is true also for nouns belonging
to prepositional phrases, which may lack the definite article even if they
are not indefinite. Obviously, this does not entail that all bare nouns in
prepositional phrases are definite. This is illustrated by means of the following example, where a new referent is introduced by a prepositional phrase
without any definite article, and must be read as indefinite:

(38)   καὶ ἀποστελεῖ τοὺς ἀγγέλους αὐτοῦ **μετὰ σάλπιγγος μεγάλης**
        'And he will send out his angels with a loud trumpet call.'
        (Matt 24:31)

Despite the tendency observed above, the definite article may be introduced
in prepositional phrases for pragmatic reasons (for instance, because of
anaphora) or because it has a syntactic function. As an illustration I quote
the following examples from my corpus:

---

[38] See Robertson (1914:790), Wallace (1996:243), Read-Heimerdinger (2002:116),
Levinsohn (2000:148).

[39] See Turner (1963:178), Blass and Debrunner (1961:133–134), Wallace (1996:247–
248).

(39) a. Ἄνθρωπος ἦν οἰκοδεσπότης ὅστις ἐφύτευσεν ἀμπελῶνα […],
   καὶ ἐξέδοτο αὐτὸν **γεωργοῖς**, καὶ ἀμπεδήμησεν
   'There was a landowner who planted a vineyard […].
   Then he leased it to tenants and went to another country.'
   (Matt 21:33)

b. ὅτε δὲ ἤγγισεν ὁ καιρὸς τῶν καρπῶν, ἀπέστειλεν τοὺς δούλους
   αὐτοῦ **πρὸς τοὺς γεωργοὺς** λαβεῖν τοὺς καρποὺς αὐτοῦ
   'When the harvest time had come, he sent his slaves
   to the tenants to collect his produce.' (Matt 21:34)

(40) a. ἐγὼ μὲν ὑμᾶς βαπτίζω **ἐν ὕδατι** εἰς μετάνοιαν
   'I baptize you with water for repentance.' (Matt 3:11)

b. καὶ ἐγένετο ἐν ἐκείναις ταῖς ἡμέραις ἦλθεν Ἰησοῦς ἀπὸ Ναζαρὲτ
   τῆς Γαλιλαίας καὶ **ἐβαπτίσθη** εἰς **τὸν Ἰορδάνην** ὑπὸ Ἰωάννου.
   Καὶ εὐθὺς ἀναβαίνων **ἐκ τοῦ ὕδατος** εἶδεν σχιζομένους τοὺς οὐρανοὺς
   'In those days Jesus came from Nazareth of Galilee and was baptized by John in the Jordan. And just as he was coming up out of
   the water, he saw the heavens torn apart.' (Mark 1:9–10)

In (39.b), anaphora determines the use of the definite article with γεωργούς,
co-referential with the indefinite description in (39.a), representing the first
mention of this referent. Similarly, the mass noun ὕδωρ 'water', which is
bare in the prepositional phrase in (40.a), is preceded by the definite article
in (40.b), which may be interpreted as a case of indirect anaphora: the
mention of the ceremony of "baptism" and of the river Jordan allows the
use of the article in the prepositional phrase with ἐκ (Jesus comes up from
the water of the Jordan after having been baptized). As opposed to the cases
in (39.b) and (40.b), in (41.b) the definite article does not occur, although,
apparently, the noun had been introduced before (41.a):

(41) a. Ἔρχεται γυνὴ ἐκ τῆς Σαμαρείας ἀντλῆσαι ὕδωρ
   'A woman of Samaria came to draw water.' (John 4:7)

b. Καὶ ἐπὶ τούτῳ ἦλθαν οἱ μαθηταὶ αὐτοῦ,
   καὶ ἐθαύμαζον ὅτι **μετὰ γυναικὸς** ἐλάλει
   'Just then his disciples came.
   They were astonished that he was speaking with a woman.'
   (John 4:27)

The presence of the definite article with γυναικός in (41.b) would have
pointed to a referent identifiable from the linguistic context, that is, the
woman introduced before (in 41.a). However, what is focused on in (41.b)

is the point of view of Jesus' disciples, to whom that specific woman is unknown (since they had not seen her before). The choice of zero article draws attention to this aspect, that is, to the fact that the disciples marvel that Jesus is speaking with somebody who is a woman (and not with that woman in particular). In other words, as already assumed at the end of section 2.4, the pragmatic force of the definite article is what may determine not only its presence, but also its absence.

Another case which is worth commenting on is the following: it is usually claimed that nouns with a predicative function in the nominative case tend to be bare, as opposed to subjects (Wallace 1996:43, 242–243). However, this is only a tendency. In general, Greek predicative bare nouns must be interpreted as non-referential, which determines the choice of zero article (see Faure 2014:442). However, in Classical Greek a predicative noun may be preceded by the article "in sentences of identification" (Gildersleeve 1911:325–327), that is, when the noun is referential (see also Bakker 2009:192). An example from Herodotus is quoted below:

(42)   Κατὰ ταῦτα τὰ ἔπεα συνεχέοντο αἱ γνῶμαι
       τῶν φαμένων **τὰς νέας τὸ ξύλινον** τεῖχος εἶναι
       'On the basis of these verses the opinion of those who said
       that the ships were the wooden wall became doubtful.' (Herodotus
       7.142.3)
       (cited from Bakker 2009:193)

As regards New Testament Greek, Colwell (1933) examined this issue in his doctoral dissertation, and published the results of his research in a paper in which he formulated what is known as Colwell's rule: "a definite predicate nominative has the article when it follows the verb, it does not have the article when it precedes the verb" (Colwell 1933:13). Compare (43.a) with (43.b):

(43)a.   Ἐγώ εἰμι **τὸ φῶς** τοῦ κόσμου
         'I am the light of the world.' (John 8:12)

     b. **φῶς** εἰμι τοῦ κόσμου
         'I am the light of the world.' (John 9:5)
         (cited from Colwell 1993:14)

On the basis of these data, Colwell (1933:20–21) concluded that

> a predicate nominative which precedes the verb cannot be
> translated as an indefinite or a "qualitative" noun solely
> because of the absence of the article; if the context suggests
> that the predicate is definite, it should be translated as a
> definite noun in spite of the absence of the article. In the

case of a predicate noun which follows the verb the reverse is true; the absence of the article in this position is a much more reliable indication that the noun is indefinite.

Firstly, it should be recognized that there are some exceptions to Colwell's rule, as he himself acknowledged. Second, as rightly remarked by Wallace, this rule does not imply that all nominatives with a predicative function preceding the verb must be read as definite, although "this is how the rule has been misunderstood by most scholars" (Wallace 1996:260).[40]

In conclusion, what is relevant to our discussion is the fact that in the New Testament nouns functioning predicatively in the nominative case may be bare even when they are definite, showing, at least in part, the same feature of "non-obligatoriness" that is attested in Classical Greek. Similarly, the assumption that in the New Testament "normally a subject will have the article (unless it is a pronoun or proper name)" inevitably encounters "exceptions," as Wallace himself admits (1996:242).[41] An example is quoted below, where there are two coordinated sentences; the subject of the first sentence is definite, but the subject of the second sentence is bare.

(44)   Τότε ἀφίησιν αὐτὸν **ὁ διάβολος**,
        καὶ ἰδοὺ **ἄγγελοι** προσῆλθον καὶ διηκόνουν αὐτῷ
        'Then the devil left him, and suddenly angels came and waited on him.' (Matt 4:11)

In other words, although it is true that a noun with the syntactic role of subject often corresponds to the topic of a sentence, and that "in all languages, an expression which refers to the topic of a sentence is typically definite or generic" (Gundel 1988:232), evidently this does not mean that all subjects are marked by a definite article. In a language like Greek, subjects are obviously bare if they correspond to a new element introduced in the discourse, such as ἄγγελοι in (44).

In concluding this section, it is worth discussing briefly the case of specific indefinite noun phrases. In order to do that, I quote three cases from John's Gospel:

---

[40] For a more detailed discussion and relevant examples cf. Wallace (1996:256–270). See also Blass and Debrunner (1961:142).

[41] See Wallace (1996:242n67): "Even with non-proper nouns, however, there are plenty of examples where the subject is anarthrous."

(45) a. Ἐγένετο **ἄνθρωπος** ἀπεσταλμένος παρὰ θεοῦ,
ὄνομα αὐτῷ Ἰωάνης
'There was a man, sent from God, whose name was John.'
(John 1:6)

   b. ἦν δὲ **τις ἄνθρωπος** ἐκεῖ τριάκοντα [καὶ] ὀκτὼ ἔτη
ἔχων ἐν τῇ ἀσθενείᾳ αὐτοῦ
'A certain man was there who had been ill for thirty-eight years.'
(John 5:5)

   c. οὐδὲ λογίζεσθε ὅτι συμφέρει ὑμῖν ἵνα **εἷς ἄνθρωπος** ἀποθάνῃ
ὑπὲρ τοῦ λαοῦ καὶ μὴ ὅλον τὸ ἔθνος ἀπόληται
'You do not understand that it is better for you to have one man die
for the people than to have the whole nation destroyed.'
(John 11:50)

In New Testament Greek, an indefinite specific entity may be introduced
by a bare noun (45.a) or by a noun accompanied by the indefinite pronoun
τις (45.b); εἷς, μία, ἕν is still generally used as a numeral, meaning 'one,
the only one' as in (45.c). It would be interesting to examine to what extent
these three different types of indefinite specific noun phrases are employed
in the New Testament and, more in general, in post-Classical Greek, in order
to shed light on the mechanism leading to the development of an indefinite
article in Modern Greek. This issue has not yet been extensively investigated
and certainly deserves more research.

2.6 Conclusions

The data discussed in section 2.5 show that in the New Testament the definite article has the same functions and distribution as in Classical Greek: it
covers all the typical uses associated with pragmatic definiteness, whereas
it is still not compulsorily employed with nouns belonging to the domain of
logical definiteness. It may also have the function of substantivizing various
parts of speech, and may assume the value of a pronoun, as in Classical
authors.

At the same time, there is trace of some changes in the definiteness
system, consistent with the evolution of the definite article into an obligatory marker of logical definiteness, a process fully realised in Modern Greek.
It seems that the use of the definite article as a pronoun (in particular,
as a demonstrative pronoun) is much reduced in the New Testament. On
the other hand, the definite article is more extensively employed in the
domain of logical definiteness, especially with nouns of unique entities and
generics (mainly plural generics). Recent findings on proper nouns suggest
that the article is the unmarked choice for these nouns as compared with

zero article, which appears to be related to the introduction or reactivation of prominent participants, by focusing on the notion of saliency.

A detailed quantitative investigation of this issue, as well as of the various uses of the definite article described here, could shed more light on how the article spread from contexts of pragmatic definiteness to logical definiteness in post-Classical Greek, especially if one takes into account its competing with zero article and with markers of indefiniteness. This future research, needless to say, may offer interesting contributions to the study of diachronic principles governing the development of definiteness.

References

Abbott, Barbara. 2010. *Reference.* Oxford Surveys in Semantics and Pragmatics. Oxford: University Press.

Abraham, Werner. 2007. The discourse-functional crystallization of the historically original demonstrative. In Elisabeth Stark, Elisabeth Leiss, and Werner Abraham (eds.), *Nominal determination: Typology, context, constraints, and historical emergence,* 241–256. Amsterdam: Benjamins.

Alexiadou, Artemis, Liliane Haegeman, and Melita Stavrou. 2007. *Noun phrase in the generative perspective.* Studies in Generative Grammar 71. Berlin: Mouton de Gruyter.

Alexiadou, Artemis. 2014. *Multiple determiners and the structure of DPs.* Linguistik Aktuell/Linguistics Today 211. Amsterdam: Benjamins.

Anderson, John M. 2007. *The grammar of names.* Oxford: University Press.

Bakker, Stéphanie J. 2009. *The noun phrase in Ancient Greek: A functional analysis of the order and articulation of NP constituents in Herodotus.* Amsterdam Studies in Classical Philology 15. Leiden: Brill.

Bartoněk, Antonin. 2003. *Handbuch des mykenischen Griechisch.* Heidelberg: Winter.

Basset, Louis. 2006. La préfiguration dans l'épopée homérique de l'article défini du grec classique. In Emilio Crespo, Jesús de la Villa, and A.R. Revuelta (eds.), *Word classes and related topics in Ancient Greek: Proceedings of the conference on 'Greek syntax and word classes' held in Madrid on 18–21 June 2003,* 105–120. Louvain-La-Neuve: Peeters.

Behrens, Leila. 2005. Genericity from a cross-linguistic perspective. *Linguistics* 43(2):275–344.

Bentein, Klaas. 2014. Pronouns (demonstrative, interrogative, indefinite, relative). In Giannakis, 158–161.

Biraud, Michèle. 1991. *La determination du nom en grec classique.* Publications de la Faculté des lettres et sciences humaines de Nice. Paris: Les Belles Lettres.

Blass, Friedrich, and Albert Debrunner. 1961. *A Greek grammar of the New Testament and other early Christian literature.* Translated and edited by Robert W. Funk. Chicago: University of Chicago Press.

Chantraine, Pierre. 1953. *Grammaire Homérique*. Paris': Collection de philologie classique 1. Paris: Klincksieck.

Christophersen, Paul. 1939. *The articles: A study of their theory and use in English*. Copenhagen: Munksgaard.

Colwell, Ernest C. 1933. A definite rule for the use of the article in the Greek New Testament. *Journal of Biblical Literature* 52:12–21.

Comrie, Bernard. [1981] 1989. *Language universals and linguistic typology: Syntax and morphology*. Oxford: Blackwell.

Cooper, Guy L. 1998. *Attic Greek Prose Syntax*, 2 vols. After K. W. Krüger. Ann Arbor: University of Michigan Press.

Costas, Procope S. 1997 [1937]. *An outline of the history of the Greek language: With particular emphasis on the Koine and the subsequent periods*. Chicago: Ares.

Dressler, Wolfgang, and Georgia Katsouda. 2014. Pronominal system. In Giannakis, 150–158.

Dryer, Matthew S. 2013a. Definite articles. In Matthew S. Dryer and Martin Haspelmath (eds.), *The world atlas of language structures online*. Leipzig: Max Planck Institute for Evolutionary Anthropology. Accessed May 16, 2018. http://wals.info/chapter/37.

Dryer, Matthew S. 2013b. Indefinite articles. In Matthew S. Dryer and Martin Haspelmath (eds.), *The world atlas of language structures online*. Leipzig: Max Planck Institute for Evolutionary Anthropology. Accessed May 16, 2018. http://wals.info/chapter/37.

Elbourne, Paul. 2013. *Definite descriptions*. Oxford Studies in Semantics and Pragmatics 1. Oxford: University Press.

Faure, Richard. 2014. *Determiners*. In Giannakis, 422–426.

Giannakis, Georgios K., ed. 2014. *Encyclopedia of ancient Greek language and linguistics*. Leiden: Brill.

Gildersleeve, Basil L. 1911. *Syntax of Classical Greek from Homer to Demosthenes 2: The syntax of the simple sentence continued, embracing the doctrine of the article*. New York: American Book Company.

Givón, Talmy. 1978. Definiteness and referentiality. In Joseph H. Greenberg (ed.), *Universals of human language*, 293–330. Stanford: Stanford University Press.

Greenberg, Joseph H. 1978. How does a language acquire gender markers? In Joseph H. Greenberg (ed.), *Universals of human language*, 49–82. Stanford: Stanford University Press.

Guardiano, Cristina. 2013. The Greek definite article across time. *Studies in Greek Linguistics*, 33:76–91.

Guérin, Valérie. 2007. Definiteness and specificity in Mavea. *Oceanic Linguistics* 46:538–553.

Gundel, Jeanette K. 1988. Universals of topic-comment structure. In Michael Hammond, Edith Moravczik, and Jessica Wirth (eds.), *Studies in syntactic typology,* 209–239. Amsterdam: Benjamins.

Harris, Martin B. 1980. The marking of definiteness: A diachronic perspective. In Elizabeth C. Traugott, Rebecca Labrum, and Susan Shepherd (eds.), *Papers from the 4th international conference on historical linguistics, Stanford, March 26–30, 1979*, 75–86. Current Issues in Linguistic Theory 14. Amsterdam: Benjamins.

Haug, Dag. 2014. Anaphoric processes. In Giannakis, 107–113.

Hawkins, John A. 1978. *Definiteness and indefiniteness: A study in reference and grammaticality prediction.* London: Croom Helm.

[Read-]Heimerdinger, Jenny, and Stephen H. Levinsohn. 1992. The use of the definite article before names of people in the Greek text of Acts with particular reference to Codex Bezae. *Filología Neotestamentaria* 5(9):15–44.

von Heusinger, Klaus. 2002. Specificity and definiteness in sentence and discourse structure. *Journal of Semantics* 19:245–274.

von Heusinger, Klaus. 2013. The salience theory of definiteness. In Allesandro Capone, Franco Lo Piparo, and Marco Carapezza (eds.), *Perspectives on linguistic pragmatics*, 349–374. Berlin: Springer.

Hewson, John. 2014. Definiteness/Definite article. In Giannakis, 419–422.

Holton, David, Peter Mackridge, and Irene Philippaki-Warburton. 1997. *Greek: A comprehensive grammar of the modern language.* Routledge Comprehensive Grammars. London: Routledge.

Horrocks, Geoffrey. 2010. *Greek: A history of the language and its speakers.* Second edition. Chichester, UK: Wiley-Blackwell.

Levinsohn, Stephen H. 2000. *Discourse features of New Testament Greek: A coursebook on the information structure of New Testament Greek.* Dallas, TX: Summer Institute of Linguistics.

Levinsohn, Stephen H., and Mark Dubis. 2019. The use of the Greek article in 1 Peter: A case study. In Daniel King (ed.), *The article in post-Classical Greek*, 102–125. Dallas, TX: SIL International.

Löbner, Sebastian. 1985. Definites. *Journal of Semantics* 4:279–326.

Lombardi Vallauri, Edoardo. 2002. L'articolo greco fra identificabilità ed esclusività del referente. *Studi Italiani di Linguistica Teorica e Applicata* 31:7–33.

Lyons, Christopher. 1999. *Definiteness.* Cambridge Textbooks in Linguistics. Cambridge: University Press.

Manolessou, Io, and Geoffrey Horrocks. 2007. The development of the definite article in Greek. *Studies in Greek Linguistics* 27:224–236. Accessed May 16, 2018. http://www.ins.web.auth.gr/images/MEG_PLIRI/MEG_27_224_236.pdf.

Müth, Angelika. 2011. Categories of definiteness in Classical Armenian. *Oslo Studies in Language* 3(3):11–25.

Napoli, Maria. 2009. Aspects of definiteness in Greek. *Studies in Language* 33:569–611.

Nunn, Henry P. V. 1913 [1912]. *A short syntax of New Testament Greek.* Cambridge: University Press.

Perdicoyianni-Paleologou, Helene. 2014. Noun phrase. In Giannakis, 527–534.

Plank, Frans, and Edith Moravcsik. 1996. The Maltese article: Language particulars and universals. *Rivista di Linguistica* 8:183–212.

Porter, Stanley E. 1994 [1992]. *Idioms of the Greek New Testament.* Biblical Languages: Greek 2. Sheffield, UK: Academic Press.

Quirk, Randolph, Sidney Greenbaum, Geoffrey Leech, and Jan Svartvik. 1985. *A comprehensive grammar of the English language.* General Grammar. London: Longman.

Read-Heimerdinger, Jenny. 2002. *The Bezan text of Acts: A contribution of discourse analysis to textual criticism.* The Library of New Testament Studies 236. Sheffield, UK: Academic Press.

Read-Heimerdinger, Jenny. 2011. The use of the article before names of places: Patterns of use in the book of Acts. In Steven E. Runge (ed.). *Discourse studies and biblical interpretation: A festschrift in honor of Stephen H. Levinsohn,* 371–402. Bellingham, WA: Logos Bible Software.

Read-Heimerdinger, Jenny. 2019. The function of the article with proper names: The New Testament book of Acts as a case study. In Daniel King (ed.), The article in post-Classical Greek, 153–185. Dallas, TX: SIL International.

Robertson, Archibald Thomas. 1914. *A grammar of the Greek New Testament in the light of historical research.* New York: Hodder & Stoughton.

Runge, Steven E. 2019. Towards a unified understanding of the Greek article from a diachronic, cognitive perspective. In Daniel King (ed.), *The article in post-Classical Greek,* 127–152. Dallas, TX: SIL International.

Russell, Bertrand. 1905. On denoting. *Mind* 14:479–493.

Sansone, David. 1993. Towards a new doctrine of the article in Greek: Some observations on the definite article in Plato. *Classical Philology* 88:191–205.

Schroeder, Christoph. 2006. Articles and article systems in some areas of Europe. In Giuliano Bernini and Marcia L. Schwartz (eds.), *Pragmatic organization of discourse in the languages of Europe,* 545–611. Berlin: Mouton de Gruyter.

Stuart, Moses. 1837. *A treatise on the syntax of the New Testament dialect: With an appendix, containing a dissertation on the Greek article.* Edinburgh: Thomas Clark.

Turner, Nigel. 1963. *A grammar of New Testament Greek 3: Syntax.* Edinburgh: T. & T. Clark.

Wallace, Daniel B. 1996. *Greek grammar beyond the basics: An exegetical syntax of the New Testament.* Grand Rapids, MI: Zondervan.

3

The History of Greek Articles: A Syntactic Approach

This chapter proposes a description of some syntactic properties of the definite article (ὁ, ἡ, τό) in Ancient Greek. The framework adopted is based on formal approaches to crosslinguistic variation and on the DP-HYPOTHESIS. Three syntactic contexts are explored: argument nominals where ὁ, ἡ, τό is required, argument nominals where ὁ, ἡ, τό is ungrammatical, and argument nominals where ὁ, ἡ, τό can either be visible or omitted. It will be shown that, with rare exceptions, the distribution of ὁ, ἡ, τό in argument nominal structures in Classical and post-Classical Greek is coherent with the constraints which define crosslinguistic variation in this domain.

3.1 Introduction

This chapter describes some aspects of the syntax of the nominal domain in Ancient Greek.[1]

[1] This chapter sums up the results of my previous research on the syntax of the article-system in the history of Greek, in particular Guardiano 2003, 2006, 2012, 2013, 2016. I am grateful to several colleagues who, in these years, have followed and supported this research with their comments and help. In particular, I want to thank Hilda Koopman, Romano Lazzeroni, Pino Longobardi, Melita Stavrou,

A well-known limit for the study of the syntax of ancient languages is the unavailability of grammaticality judgements elicited from native speakers: formal approaches to the analysis of individual grammars ("I-languages" in Chomsky's 1986 terms)[2] are crucially based on this type of evidence, which is often more revealing than the actual utterances that speakers produce (E-languages). Instead, for very obvious reasons, scholars who want to explore the formal structure of ancient languages can only rely on the empirical evidence provided by textual documentation. This has often been considered a major obstacle for a successful implementation of formal tools to the analysis of ancient grammars. Indeed, written texts contain only a subset of the syntactic structures that speakers are able to produce: thus, it is often impossible to decide whether the absence of a given structure in a corpus is due to its ungrammaticality in the language or to other extemporaneous reasons (stylistic choices, type of register adopted, etc.). Additionally, literary styles are typically the output of complex stylistic processes which might collapse surface structures produced by several different individual grammars. Therefore, one single text often contains structures generated by different I-languages, even at different diachronic stages.

Such limitations can be (at least partially) controlled for through the adoption of a few practical strategies (listed in 1) and of a constrained theory of syntactic variation.

The textual evidence used in the present chapter was selected and analysed on the basis of the following criteria:

(1)   a. *One author at a time.* Texts produced by one and the same author were idealized as the output of a single, internally coherent, I-language. The I-languages of authors belonging to the same diachronic stage were then compared to one another: no significant differences emerged in the domain explored here.

   b. *Simulation of possible (E-)languages.* When possible, texts which are likely to mirror language varieties that could have plausibly been produced by actual speakers, or designed to be accessible to speakers not used to erudite styles, were preferred.

   c. *Systematic survey.* The analysis is based on a systematic scrutiny of the whole amount of nominal structures found in the texts. Such structures were classified in three groups: nominal structures found in argument position (i.e. subjects or direct complements of a verb),

Chiara Bozzone, the members of the Indoeuropean Seminar at UCLA, and two anonymous referees. All mistakes are mine.

[2] The term I-Language (I = internal or internalized) refers to the grammatical (unconscious) internal knowledge of every speaker, i.e. the actual object of theoretical research. The term E-language (E = external or externalized), instead, refers to the observable linguistic output produced by each speaker's I-language; E-languages contain only a subset of the potentially infinite sentences and linguistic expressions that the corresponding I-languages are able to produce.

nominal structures found in non-argument position (i.e. vocatives, predicate nominals, prepositional phrases), and idioms. As we will see below (§3.2), only those in argument position were selected for the purposes of the present study.

The data were collected from the following sources:[3]

(2) a. Homer: *Iliad, Odyssey* (Guardiano 2013, 2016; Bozzone and Guardiano 2015)
     b. Classical Attic: Plato's *Apology, Cratylus* and *Symposium* (Guardiano 2003); Demosthenes' *Philippics* 1–3 and *Olinthiacs* 1–3, Isocrates' *Aegineticus* and *Against the Sophists*, Lysias's *On the murder of Eratosthenes* and *On the refusal of a pension* (Bernasconi 2011)
     c. Hellenistic Koine: Gospels (Guardiano 2003, Manolessou 2000)

It will be shown that the syntactic properties and distribution of definite articles in Classical and post-Classical Greek obey the same rules operating in contemporary languages, e.g. in Standard Modern Greek. This is consistent with the predictions of Roberts' UNIFORMITARIAN HYPOTHESIS: "The languages of the past are not essentially different from the languages of the present. [...] The languages of the past reflect the same Universal Grammar as those of the present" (Roberts 2007:456).

On the diachronic side, it will be shown that the syntactic nature of ὁ, ἡ, τό has not changed from Classical times to the present. The (diachronic) variation in its distribution follows from one major structural change, namely the emergence of a STRONG ARTICLE, whose most visible surface manifestations are the development of an INDEFINITE ARTICLE and the need of an article with proper names.

As far as pre-Classical periods are concerned, Homeric poems are usually described as a diachronic stage at which ὁ, ἡ, τό was embrionically a definite article but not yet generalized.[4] Here, we follow a slightly different proposal, suggested by Bozzone and Guardiano 2015. They hypothesize that the inconsistencies found in the distribution of ὁ, ἡ, τό in Homer are an effect of the composite diachronic stratification of the language of epic, and in particular of the combination of two grammars: a 'conservative' grammar, in which a definite article did not exist, and a more innovative one, in which ὁ, ἡ, τό has the syntactic properties of a grammaticalized (definite) article.

---

[3] Guardiano 2016. The translations of the Greek texts were adapted from the following sources: Vince 1930 (*Demosthenes: Orations*); *World English Bible* (New Testament); Fowler 1921, 1925, 1966 (*Plato*); Murray 1924a (*Iliad*), 1924b (*Odyssey*).

[4] For a summary of the discussion about the nature and functions of the definite article in Ancient Greek (and in Homer in particular), see at least Scott 1910, Smyth 1920:284–298, Chantraine 1953:158–168; 1961, Palmer 1962:136–138 and, more recently, Parenti 1997:49–76 and 77–92, Mendez-Dosuna 1999, Basset 2006, Manolessou and Horrocks 2007, Briulotta 2007, among many others.

The structure of the paper is as follows. Section 3.2 provides a typology of the main syntactic properties crosslinguistically associated with definite articles. Section 3.3 describes the distribution of definite articles in Classical and New Testament Greek. Section 3.4 briefly presents the occurrences of ὁ, ἡ, τό in the Homeric poems. Section 3.5 sums up the conclusions.

3.2 Background

The theoretical background of the present study relies on the DP-HYPOTHESIS.[5] The DP-hypothesis proposes that nominal structures occurring in argument position contain a syntactic category labelled D (determiner) that is responsible for their reading and interpretation. D can either be visible in the linear string (i.e. filled by a dedicated lexical item, for instance an article or a pronoun) or not (i.e. lexically empty, or null). The DP-hypothesis assumes that, independently of whether D is visible or not in the surface form of a nominal structure, all nominal phrases in argument position contain it in their abstract structure.[6] Accordingly, they are called DPs (determiner phrases).

3.2.1 Definiteness

In the formal literature, the DEFINITE READING[7] of (argument) nominal expressions has traditionally been associated to the category D (or to some specialized functional projection directly connected to it).[8] Here, we use a rather conventional broad definition: a nominal expression is DEFINITE when its referent is marked as accessible or identifiable by the hearer on the basis of information available in the extralinguistic or linguistic context (contextual identification [3]) or of general knowledge (4).

(3)   Contextual identification
    a.   The referent is visible in the extralinguistic context: DEIXIS.
    b.   A noun is repeated after first mention: SECOND MENTION (ANAPHORA).
    c.   The referent is mentioned in the discourse: TEXTUAL ANAPHORA.
    d.   The noun is modified by an adjective, a relative clause, a genitive, another complement that identifies the referent: CATAPHORA.
    e.   The referent plays a pivotal role in the discourse: TOPICHOOD.

---

[5] Szabolcsi 1983, 1987; Abney 1987. See also Bernstein 2001, 2008, Longobardi 2001, 2008, Alexiadou et al. 2007, among the others.

[6] This assumption is actually quite controversial. For an overview of the debate, see Boskovic 2008 and literature therein.

[7] See, among many others, at least Krámský 1972, Heim 1982, Hawkins 1991, Laury 1997, Lyons 1999, Abbott 2004, Alexiadou et al. 2007, ch. 1, Schwarz 2012, Napoli in this volume, and references therein.

[8] See, for recent discussion, Alexiadou et al. 2007:53–157, Stark et al. 2007, Gomeshi et al. 2009, Alexiadou 2014, among many others.

f. The existence of the referent can be inferred from pragmatic and/or contextual settings: shared knowledge, situational uses.

(4) General knowledge
    a. ASSOCIATIVE ANAPHORA (Lyons 1999:4)
    b. SITUATIONALLY UNIQUE ENTITIES (*the president of Ghana, the king of France, ...*)
    c. INTRINSICALLY UNIQUE ENTITIES (*sun, moon, sky, equator, ...*)

Crosslinguistically, languages vary according to whether the relationship between D and the definite reading of a nominal expression is overt or not (Longobardi 2001). There are languages (such as for instance Slovene, [5]) where nominal expressions interpreted as definite do not exhibit any visible difference, in their surface form, from nominal expressions interpreted as indefinite: no visible determiner is required.[9]

(5) fant   bere   knjigo
     boy   reads   book
     'A/the boy reads a/the book'

In other languages, instead, the readings in (3) and (4) require a dedicated item in D. The default item used for these purposes is called DEFINITE ARTICLE. Definite articles in D can either be lexically autonomous or enclitic; in the latter case, the noun (or a noun modifier, i.e. an adjective) attaches to D, as for instance in the Romanian examples in (6).

(6) a. D   N
         student-ul   ~~student~~
         student-art.m
         'The student'
     b. D   Adj   N
         bun-ul   ~~bun~~   student
         good-art.m   student
         'The good student'

Certain types of definite articles do not occur in D. For instance, in Scandinavian, there exist two types of definite articles: "PREPOSED FREE ARTICLES (*den, det, de*), similar to the ones of West Germanic, and SUFFIXED ARTICLES (*-en, -et* etc.)" (Dahl 2004:147). Preposed free articles in Germanic are assumed to be in D; Scandinavian suffixed articles, on the other hand, are not D-items. The two types may co-occur in the so-called "DOUBLE

---

[9] For the potential emergence of a definite article in spoken Slovenian and other non-standard varieties of Slavic, see Trovesi 2004.

DETERMINATION" construction, as shown in the following Swedish example from Dahl (2004:148):

(7) D   Adj   N
     det   stora   hus-et
     art   big   house-art
     'The big house'

Technically, a lexical item can be labelled definite article only if it must be visible in order for a nominal phrase to be assigned a definite reading in the absence of other definiteness-assigning strategies:[10] therefore, by definition, definite articles are never optional.

There are languages, such as for instance Gothic or Mauritian Creole (Guillemin 2009), where a D-like item[11] systematically appears with anaphoric argument nominals only (reading 3b), but is not obligatory with other definite readings.

To sum up, languages may be categorized into two major types, as shown in figure 3.1: languages with a GRAMMATICALIZED ARTICLE (Aii), in which nominal structures in argument position with no visible article (BARE NOUNS) do not have any of the definite readings listed in (3) and (4); and languages with no GRAMMATICALIZED ARTICLE (Ai), in which bare nouns may have a definite reading. Among the languages of the latter type, some require a visible item with anaphoric readings (GRAMMATICALIZED TEXTUAL ANAPHORA, [Bi]), while others do not (Bii):

A. Grammaticalized article?
    i.   NO   →   B. Grammaticalized textual anaphora?
                                        i.   YES   (Gothic, Mauritian Creole)
                                        ii. NO   (Slovene, Latin)
    ii. YES (English, Italian)

Figure 3.1. Grammaticalized article and Grammaticalized textual anaphora.

3.2.2 Definite articles and noun modifiers in Modern Greek

In Modern Greek, the item o, η, το is systematically visible in D with all definite noun phrases in argument position.[12] Thus, it behaves as a grammaticalized (definite) article (Aii). In Modern Greek, DPs containing more

---

[10] Such as for instance a demonstrative, a Saxon genitive, a pronominal possessive, etc.

[11] Usually a demonstrative, often the same item that will become a definite article in subsequent diachronic stages of the language.

[12] For a summary of the debate about the nature of o, η, το in Modern Greek, see Alexiadou 2014.

than one definite article are grammatical: this phenomenon is called
DETERMINER (or DEFINITENESS) SPREADING and the noun phrase where
more than one definite article appears is dubbed POLYDEFINITE (Alexiadou,
Haegeman, and Stavrou 2007; Alexiadou 2014). Definiteness spreading is
obligatory with postnominal adjectives, as in example (8):

(8) a. to   kalo   pedi
         the   nice   boy
         'The nice boy'
     b. *to   pedi   kalo
     c. to   pedi   to   kalo
         the   boy   the   nice

In the abstract structure of Modern Greek nominal phrases, adjectival
modifiers of the noun can be placed in two positions, one prenominal and
one postnominal (Androutsopoulou 1994), with different syntactic effects
(postnominal adjectives trigger determiner spreading, prenominal ones
do not) and interpretative properties (postnominal adjectives are interpreted restrictively, intersectively and usually as stage-level predicates,
while prenominal adjectives are not).[13] Such positions are well-visible in
the surface order, as shown in (9). In Modern Greek, (almost) all adjectives can surface both pre- and postnominally (Stavrou 2012, 2015); only
postnominal adjectives, and only in definite DPs, trigger the polydefinite
construction (9c and 9e). In indefinite DPs, determiner spreading does not
take place (9d and 9f).

(9)	D	Adj	N	(art)	Adj
a.	to	kalo	pedi		
	the	nice	boy		
	'the nice boy'				
b.	ena	kalo	pedi		
	a	nice	boy		
	'a nice boy'				
c.	to		pedi	to	kalo
	'the nice boy'				
d.	ena		pedi		kalo
	'a nice boy'				
e.	to	kalo	pedi	to	psilo
	the	nice	boy	the	tall
	'the nice tall boy'				
f.	ena	kalo	pedi		psilo
	a	nice	boy		tall
	'a nice tall boy'				

---

[13] Kolliakou 2004, Campos and Stavrou 2004; see also Cinque 2010.

The label GENITIVE signals the syntactic positions where another class of noun modifiers, namely nominal arguments of the noun, is generated in the crosslinguistic structure of the nominal domain. Modern Greek has a LOW STRUCTURAL GENITIVE (Longobardi 2001), namely a non-prepositional complement of the noun assumed to be originated prenominally, after prenominal adjectives (10a). In Modern Greek, such a genitive appears postnominally in the surface word order (10c) as a consequence of noun movement (10b).

(10) a. D   Adj   Gen   N   (art)   Adj
     b. D   Adj   N   Gen   N̶   (art)   Adj
     c. to   kalo   vivlio   tu Janni   v̶i̶v̶l̶i̶o̶   to   akrivo
        the nice   book   the.gen John   the   expensive
        'John's nice expensive book'
     d. *to kalo   tu Janni   vivlio to   akrivo

3.2.3 "Definite" articles with kind names and proper names

In some languages (e.g. Romance languages), definite articles obligatorily occur with KIND NAMES in argument position (Longobardi 1994, 2005, 2008).

(11) I   dinosauri   sono   estinti.
     the.pl.m   dinosaur.pl.m   are   extinct.pl.m
     'Dinosaurs have become extinct.'

In other languages (e.g. Germanic), kind names in argument position must be bare (12). Articulated nouns never have kind-referring interpretation (Longobardi 1994, 2005, 2008).

(12) Dinosaurs have become extinct.

As shown by Longobardi 1994, 2005, 2008, the crosslinguistic behavior of kind names and that of PROPER NAMES strictly co-vary: languages where kind-referring names need a visible article (in D), also need D to be visible with OBJECT-REFERRING NAMES (i.e. proper names). The difference between proper and kind names is that the former can themselves access the D-position: when a proper name occupies D, no visible article is required, as shown by Longobardi's 1994 (ex. 30, p. 624) well-known examples from Italian, reproduced in (13):

(13)　D　　Adj　N
   a. L'　antica Roma fu　la　città più　importante del　Mediterraneo.
      the　ancientRome was　the　city　most　important　of.the Mediterranean
      'Ancient Rome was the most important city of the Mediterranean.'
   b. Roma antica ~~Roma~~ fu　la　città più　importante del　Mediterraneo.
   c. *　　Antica Roma fu　la　città più　importante del　Mediterraneo.

In Germanic (14), proper names never appear in D:

(14)　　　D　Adj　N
   a. * Rome ancient ~~Rome~~ was the most important city of the Mediterranean.
   b.　　　Ancient Rome was the most important city of the Mediterranean.

In most of the languages where a visible D is obligatory with kind- and object-referring nouns in argument position, the article that occurs in D has the same lexical form as the definite article. Yet, the article that appears in D with referential nouns is not "definite", because it does not signal any of the definite readings reported in (3) and (4). Following Longobardi, we conventionally label it EXPLETIVE.

The contrast between Romance and Germanic is encoded by property C in figure 3.2, OBLIGATORY ARTICLE WITH REFERENTIAL NOUNS.

A.　Grammaticalized article?
   i.　　　NO　→　B.　Grammaticalized textual anaphora?
                i.　YES　(Gothic, Mauritian Creole)
                ii.　NO　(Slovenian, Latin)
   ii.　　YES　→　C.　Obligatory article with referential nouns?
                (or proper names in D)
                i.　YES　(Italian)
                ii.　NO　(English)

Figure 3.2. Grammaticalized article, Grammaticalized textual anaphora, Obligatory article with referential nouns.

Modern Greek obligatorily uses o, η, το with kind names:[14]

(15) a. i　　　　　ðinosavri　　　exun　　eksafanisti.
      the.pl.m　dinosaur.pl.m　have.pl　extinct.pl.m
      'Dinosaurs have become extinct.'
   b. * ðinosavri exun eksafanisti

o, η, το is obligatory with proper names too, which cannot appear in D.[15]

---

[14] See also Panagiotidis 2000.

[15] See Guardiano and Longobardi 2006 and Guardiano and Stavrou 2015 for the relevant literature.

(16)   D   Adj   N
    a. i   arçea   romi   leilatiθice   apo   tus   γotθus
       the   ancient Rome   was ravaged   by   the   Goths
       'Ancient Rome was ravaged by Goths.'
    b. *romi   arçea   ~~romi~~   leilatiθice   apo   tus   γotθus
    c. *   arçea   romi   leilatiθice   apo   tus   γotθus

The impossibility for proper names to access D in Modern Greek is likely to be due to the fact that nouns, in this language, do not have access to any position close to the D-area: as seen above, the noun never precedes, in the linear order, the adjectival modifiers which are generated prenominally.

3.2.4 Indefinite articles

Example (17) shows that, in English, indefinite nominals do not need any visible D: they can be bare.

(17) The teacher left books and pens on the table. I took the books.

In English, the absence of a visible item in D is possible, in argument position, with (non-definite) plural (*books* and *pens* in [17]) and mass nouns (*water* in [18a]), but not with singular count nouns (*dog* in [18b]): the latter can never be bare in argument position.

(18) a. I took water from the fridge
    b. i. * I saw dog in the garden
        ii. I saw a dog in the garden

The need for a visible D with singular count nouns in argument position is described in the literature as one of the (several) consequences of a more abstract property of D, that we conventionally label here STRONG ARTICLE (Crisma 1997, 2011). Languages without a STRONG ARTICLE do not need any visible item in D with count singular arguments (absence of indefinite articles). One such language is Hebrew, where (non-definite) singular count nouns can be bare:

(19)   raiti   kelev
       I.saw   dog
       'I saw a dog'

In Modern Greek, an indefinite article is obligatory with most singular count nouns in argument position.[16]

---

[16] For exceptions, see Alexopoulou et al. 2013.

Figure 3.3 summarizes the properties of the articles introduced in this section:

A. Grammaticalized article?
  i.   NO   →   B. Grammaticalized textual anaphora?
                    i. YES   (Gothic, Mauritian Creole)
                    ii. NO   (Slovenian, Latin)
  ii.   YES   →   C. Obligatory article with referential nouns?
                    i. YES   (Italian, Modern Greek)
                    ii. NO   (English)
             →   D. Strong article?
                    i. YES   (Italian, English, Modern Greek)
                    ii. NO   (Hebrew)

Figure 3.3. Grammaticalized article, Grammaticalized textual anaphora,
Obligatory article with referential nouns, Strong article.

3.2.5 Summary

Two main generalizations emerge from section 3. The first is that the item called DEFINITE ARTICLE collapses different types of syntactic functions, listed in (20):

(20) a. Anaphoric articles: obligatory with nouns that designate entities already explicitly introduced in the previous discourse, but not with other definite nouns.
  b. Definite articles: obligatory with all types of definite nominals.
  c. Semi-expletive articles: obligatory with kind names.
  d. Expletive articles: obligatory with proper names, when proper names do (or can) not occupy the D-position.

The second generalization is that the item usually labeled INDEFINITE ARTICLE is actually a filler of D required with (non-definite) singular count nouns in languages with a STRONG ARTICLE.

Crosslinguistic variation depends on whether a language activates the features of D associated to the different types of articles listed in (20) and to STRONG ARTICLE. The availability of some such options is implicationally constrained:

(21) a. Only languages with no GRAMMATICALIZED ARTICLE can activate type (20a).

b. Only languages with a GRAMMATICALIZED ARTICLE can activate types (20c) and (20d).

c. Only languages with a GRAMMATICALIZED ARTICLE can have STRONG ARTICLE.

3.3 Articles in Classical and New Testament Greek

The development of the article-system in Greek consists of two major events: the creation of a definite article from the DEMONSTRATIVE[17] ὁ, ἡ, τό (Proto-Indoeuropean *so, *seh₂, *tod), that reasonably started during the Archaic period and was already fully accomplished in the Classical era, and the emergence of an indefinite article from the numeral εἷς, μία, ἕνα, presumably started out during the first centuries AD.

According to the literature,[18] adnominal ὁ, ἡ, τό in Ancient Greek is an "optional" definite article, in a "transitional stage" towards full development as an obligatory definiteness marker.

In the present section, we check whether the behaviour of ὁ, ἡ, τό in argument position conforms to the definition of (definite) articles as D-items obligatorily required, in argument position, in order for nominal structures to have a definite reading (3.3.1), and whether it can function as an expletive with kind and proper names (3.3.2).

3.3.1 Definite argument nominals

In order for ὁ, ἡ, τό to be established as a definite article (20b), the following conditions must be satisfied (Guardiano 2016:31):

(22) a. ὁ, ἡ, τό is able to assign a definite reading to the nominal with which it occurs.

b. Bare nominals (i.e. nominal structures that do not contain ὁ, ἡ, τό or any other definite item) in argument position never have a definite reading.

In Classical and New Testament Greek, nominal arguments are preceded by ὁ, ἡ, τό in all the definite contexts listed in (3) and (4), as shown by examples (23) to (31). Condition (22a) is thus satisfied. Additionally, bare argument nouns (with few limited exceptions) never have a definite reading: thus, condition (22b) is satisfied as well. The

---

[17] See Chantraine 1953:158–168 and 1961:123–125, among the others.

[18] See, among recent works, Parenti 1997:49–76, 77–92; Lombardi Vallauri 2002; Manolessou and Horrocks 2007; Bakker 2009:145–213; Napoli 2009, and references therein.

conclusion seems to be that Classical and New Testament Greek have a GRAMMATICALIZED ARTICLE.

Examples (23) to (29) are cases of contextual identification (cf.[3]). Example (23) illustrates second mention (3b): in the anaphoric chain, the first mention of παραλυτικὸν is bare, its second mention has ὁ, ἡ, τὸ.

(23) καὶ ἔρχονται φέροντες πρὸς αὐτὸν **παραλυτικὸν** αἰρόμενον ὑπὸ τεσσάρων [...] καὶ ἰδὼν ὁ Ἰησοῦς τὴν πίστιν αὐτῶν λέγει **τῷ** **παραλυτικῷ**   (Mark 2:3–5)
   'And they came bringing to him a paralytic carried by four men [...] Jesus, seeing their faith, said to the paralytic...'

Example (24) instantiates textual anaphora (3c). The verb λογίζομαι is the head of the anaphoric chain, and the homoradical noun that co-refers with it (λογισμῶν) has ὁ, ἡ, τὸ.

(24) ἵν', εἰ μὲν ὀρθῶς **λογίζομαι**, μετάσχητε **τῶν λογισμῶν**   (Demosthenes, *Philippics* 3.20)
   'In order that, if I am thinking correctly, you may share my reasoning...'

In (25), ὁ, ἡ, τὸ occurs with the noun πόλιν. Its referent (Eretria), previously mentioned in the text, is known from textual information (3c).

(25) ἀλλ' **ἐν Ἐρετρίᾳ**, ἐπειδὴ ἀπαλλαγέντος Πλουτάρχου καὶ τῶν ξένων ὁ δῆμος εἶχε **τὴν πόλιν** καὶ τὸν Πορθμόν (Demosthenes, *Philippics* 3.57)
   'For in Eretria, when Plutarchus and the mercenaries had been removed, the people controlled the city and Porthmus'

Example (26) instantiates cataphoric reading (3d): the noun is modified by a relative clause.

(26) ἐφώνησαν οὖν **τὸν ἄνθρωπον** ἐκ δευτέρου **ὃς** ἦν τυφλός (John 9:24)
   'So they called a second time the man who was blind'

Example (27) contains a topical referent (3e). The noun ἄνθρωπον refers to Philippus, who is not previously mentioned, but is a pivotal character in the text.[19]

(27) ἀλλὰ μείζω γιγνόμενον **τὸν ἄνθρωπον** περιορῶμεν (Demosthenes, *Philippics* 3.29)
   'But we look on the man, who is growing greater'

---

[19] In Classical Greek, ὁ, ἡ, τὸ is obligatory to bring "a key discourse participant back into focus" (Manolessou and Horrocks 2007:5).

Example (28) illustrates situational identification (3f). In the pragmatic settings where the events are taking place, the noun πόλις can only refer to Athens.

(28) καὶ θεοὺς οὓς **ἡ πόλις** νομίζει οὐ νομίζοντα   (Plato, *Apology* 24 b9–c1)
'And (he) does not believe in gods the city believes in'

In (29), a possessive is omitted: δούλους refers to Phylippus' slaves.

(29) κἂν αὐτὸς μὴ παρῇ, **τοὺς δούλους** ἀγωνοθετήσοντας πέμπει;
(Demosthenes, *Philippics* 3.32)
'And if he cannot be present, he sends the slaves to preside in his place?'

Example (30) illustrates associative anaphora (4a).

(30) ἀλλ' ἐν Ἐρετρίᾳ, ἐπειδὴ ἀπαλλαγέντος Πλουτάρχου καὶ τῶν ξένων **ὁ δῆμος** εἶχε τὴν πόλιν καὶ τὸν Πορθμόν   (Demosthenes, *Philippics* 3.57)
'For in Eretria, when Plutarchus and the mercenaries had been removed, the people controlled the city and Porthmus'

In Classical Greek, nouns referring to intrinsically unique objects (4c), such as ἥλιος or σελήνη,[20] do not systematically require ὁ, ἡ, τό (31). These are nouns which refer to entities usually personified as gods or semi-gods. As such, they probably fall within the class of proper names (Guardiano 2003:41–111), and are subject to syntactic constraints different from those acting on definite argument nouns (see 3.3.2 below).

(31) a. οὐδὲ **ἥλιον** οὐδὲ **σελήνην** ἄρα νομίζω θεοὺς εἶναι (Plato, *Apology* 26 d1)
'Do I believe that neither the sun nor et the moon are gods ...?'
b. ἐπεὶ **τὸν μὲν ἥλιον** λίθον φησὶν εἶναι, **τὴν δὲ σελήνην** γῆν (Plato, *Apology* 26 d4–5)
'Since he says that the sun is a stone and the moon earth...'

Notice, finally, that in Classical and New Testament Greek ὁ, ἡ, τό displays a further syntactic function typical of definite articles crosslinguistically: it turns an adjective, a participle or a numeral into the head of a nominal-like structure, i.e. it acts as a "substantivizer," as in (32).

---

[20] See also θάνατος (Guardiano 2003:49, 54, 64–66, 80–81, 84–85), along with a few similar others.

(32) καὶ προσκαλεῖται **τοὺς δώδεκα**   (Mark 6:7)
'And he calls the twelve' (i.e. the apostles)

In Classical and New Testament Greek, non-definite argument singular count nouns can be bare, as in (33):

(33) ἦλθεν **γυνὴ** ἔχουσα **ἀλάβαστρον**   (Mark 14:3)
'A woman came carrying an alabaster jar'

This sets a difference with respect to Modern Greek, and suggests that Classical and New Testament Greek have no STRONG ARTICLE.

3.3.2 Kind names, proper names

In the corpus of Classical and post-Classical texts explored here, there are no instances of bare nouns interpreted as kind names in argument position. ὁ, ἡ, τό is required:

(34) τίνα με λέγουσιν **οἱ ἄνθρωποι** εἶναι;   (Mark 8:27)
'Who do men say that I am?'

Argument bare plurals can only be interpreted as (non-definite) generic, as λίθους in (35):

(35) ἦραν οὖν **λίθους** ἵνα βάλωσιν ἐπὶ αὐτόν   (John 8:59)
'Therefore they took up stones to throw at him'

As it is well-known, in both Classical and New Testament Greek, proper names (of persons [36], places [37] and people [38]) can either have an article or be bare.

(36) a. ὅπου ἦν **ὁ Ἰωάνης** βαπτίζων   (John 1:28)
'...where John was baptizing...'
b. καὶ ἐμαρτύρησεν **Ἰωάνης**   (John 1:32)
'....and John testified...'

(37) a. τῷ Μεγάρων καὶ **τῆς Εὐβοίας** τὸν πολεμοῦνθ' ὑμῖν γενέσθαι κύριον
(Demosthenes, *Philippics* 3.18)
'... the placing of Megara and Euboea in the power of the enemy...'
b. **Εὔβοιαν** δὲ καὶ τὸν Ὠρωπὸν ἀντ' Ἀμφιπόλεως ὑμῖν ἀποδώσει
(Demosthenes, *Philippics* 2.30)
'And would repay you for Amphipolis by restoring Euboea and Oropus to you...'

(38) a. παραδείγμασι χρώμενοι τῇ τότε ῥώμῃ **τῶν Λακεδαιμονίων**
(Demosthenes, *Philippics* 1.3)
'Learn a lesson from the former strength of the Lacedaemonians'
   b. ὁ γὰρ Μεσσήνην **Λακεδαιμονίους** ἀφιέναι κελεύων (Demosthenes,
Philippics 2.13)
'...the one who is ordering the Lacedaemonians to give up Messene...'

This alternation does not correlate with any difference in the syntactic context (e.g. argument vs. non-argument, first vs. second mention, etc.):[21] both options are equally grammatical, regardless of the syntactic configuration in which the proper name occurs.[22]

The alternation between proper names with an article and proper names without any article in argument position could in principle be explained, like in Italian, as the consequence of movement of the proper name itself in D (39b).

(39)   D   N
   a. ὁ   Ἰωάνης
   b. Ἰωάνης   Ἰωάνης

Alternations like that in (39) are impossible in Modern Greek, where proper names do not have access to the D-area (Guardiano 2012:193–194). In order to check whether proper names have access to D (Guardiano and Longobardi 2006) in Classical and New Testament Greek, we observed the surface position of nouns with respect to those modifiers which are assumed to originate prenominally (i.e. structured adjectives and non-prepositional structural genitives). It emerged that the behavior of adjectival modifiers in Ancient Greek is very similar to that of Modern Greek.[23] Virtually all types of adjectives can occur both pre- and postnominally, and the latter require determiner spreading in definite DPs (Guardiano 2003, 2006, 2012):

---

[21] See Guardiano 2003:87–101, 2012:196n35, and references therein.

[22] In Demosthenes, proper names tend to occur with no expletive: Bernasconi (2011:39–43) found 151 instances of proper names with no article (74% of the total) vs. 54 cases of proper names with a visible expletive (26%). Plato's data (Guardiano 2003:106) show a substantial balance (45% of proper names with an article vs. 55% of proper names without an article), while in the Gospels proper names show a stronger tendency to have an article (61%).

[23] With minor differences, not relevant for the present discussion.

(40)   D   Adj   N   (art)   Adj
  a. τὴν   ἀνθρωπίνην   φύσιν
                                          (Plato, *Symposium* 189 d5–6)
      the.f.s.acc. human.f.s.acc   nature.f.s.acc
  b. τὴν   φύσιν   τὴν   ἀνθρωπίνην
                                          (Plato, *Symposium* 191 d3)
  c. *τὴν   φύσιν   ἀνθρωπίνην

As far as genitives are concerned, in New Testament Greek they are inflected, non-iterable and postnominal, as in Standard Modern Greek. Guardiano (2011) proposes that they originate in the same structure as in Modern Greek (shown in 10), i.e. the postnominal postadjectival position called GenO by Longobardi and Silvestri (2013), which is crossed over by the noun. In Classical Greek, the GenO position is also active, but the noun does not move over it, and thus it occurs prenominally in the surface order (Guardiano 2011; Guardiano and Longobardi 2018).

(41) a. D   Gen   N
        ὁ   τῆς Θέτιδος   υἱός   (Plato, *Apology* 28 c2)
        the.s.m.nom   the.s.f.gen Thetis.gen son.s.m.nom
        'The son of Thetis'
  b. D   N   Gen   N̶
      ἡ   μαρτυρία   τοῦ Ἰωάνου   μ̶α̶ρ̶τ̶υ̶ρ̶ί̶α̶   (John 1:19)
      the.f.s.nom testimony.f.s.nom the.s.m.gen John.gen
      'John's testimony'

Such evidence suggests that the noun is not able to access the D-area, as in Modern Greek:[24] in sequences like (42b) D is empty.

(42)   D   N
  a. ὁ   Ἰωάνης
  b.   Ἰωάνης

This seems to violate Longobardi's assumption that the requirement for a visible D with proper names in argument position and the requirement for a visible D with kind names in argument position descend from one single abstract property (STRONG D): in Classical and New Testament Greek, kind names require a visible D while proper names do not. Yet, Guardiano 2012, 2016 has shown that the possibility for proper names to occur without a visible article in Classical and New Testament Greek is a consequence of the absence of a STRONG ARTICLE: this is the property that crucially distinguishes Ancient Greek from Modern Greek in this domain. The absence of a

---

[24] Guardiano 2012:195: "There has never been any possibility, in the history of Greek, for any noun to raise to D."

strong article allows empty Ds both with singular count nouns and in those syntactic configurations where the article does not have any impact on the semantic content of the noun: proper names are one such case, because their intrinsic referential content is non-ambiguous.

The schema in figure 3.4 sums up the behaviour of Classical and New Testament Greek with respect to the properties listed in figure 3.3:

A.	Grammaticalized article?	YES
→ C.	Obligatory article with referential nouns?	YES
→ D.	Strong article?	NO

Figure 3.4. Grammaticalized article, Obligatory article with referential nouns, and Strong article in Classical and New Testament Greek.

To sum up, there are two main surface differences between Ancient and Modern Greek with respect to the syntax of articles. One is that, in Modern Greek, an article is systematically required with singular count nouns in argument position (with few exceptions), while, in Ancient Greek, (non-definite) singular count nouns can be bare. The second is that, in Modern Greek, an article is systematically required with proper names in argument position, while in Ancient Greek it is not.

Both such differences are likely to depend on one single deeper change, namely the emergence of a STRONG ARTICLE (see table 3.1), that introduced stricter constraints on the visibility of the D position in the surface structure of the nominal phrase.

Table 3.1. Syntactic properties of the article in Ancient and Modern Greek

	Classical and New Testament Greek	Modern Greek
A. Grammaticalized article	YES	YES
C. Obligatory article with referential nouns	YES	YES
D. Strong article	NO	YES

3.4 Homeric Greek

In Homeric poems, ὁ, ἡ, τό does not have any of the properties of a fully developed definite article (Guardiano 2016, Bozzone and Guardiano 2015). It is more frequently attested in pronominal[25] rather than adnominal function.

---

[25] Examples (43)–(45) are from Guardiano 2016:38. See also Parenti 1997, Briulotta 2007, for recent surveys. Pronominal uses of ὁ, ἡ, τό are also attested in Classical and

When pronominal, it is frequently used after first mention (43), in cataphoric structures with relative clauses (44), or with adverbs, genitives and prepositional complements (45).

(43) Λητοῦς καὶ Διὸς **υἱός. ὃ γὰρ** βασιλῆϊ χολωθεὶς   (*Iliad* 1.9)
'... son of Leto and Zeus; for he, angered at the king, ...'

(44) λεύσσετε γὰρ **τό γε** πάντες, **ὅ** μοι γέρας ἔρχεται ἄλλη   (*Iliad* 1.120)
'Indeed you all see this, that my prize goes elsewhere'

(45) a. Δηΐφοβ' ἦ μέν μοι **τὸ πάρος** πολὺ φίλτατος ἦσθα   (*Iliad* 22.233–4)
'Deiphobus, in the past you were much dearer to me'
   b. **οἳ δ'ἀμφὶ Πρίαμον** καὶ Πάνθοον ἠδὲ Θυμοίτην   (*Iliad* 3.146)
'And those about Priam and Panthous and Thymoetes ...'

Adnominal occurrences of ὁ, ἡ, τὸ are found in definite DPs only. Yet, the item is not obligatory with any of the definite readings listed in (3) and (4):[26] example (46) instantiates a case of second mention (3b).

(46) στησαμένη **μέγαν ἱστὸν** ἐνὶ μεγάροισιν ὕφαινε [...]
ἔνθα καὶ ἠματίη μὲν ὑφαίνεσκεν **μέγαν ἱστόν**   (*Odyssey* 2.94–104)
'She set up a great web in the palace, [...]
then day by day she weaved at the great web'

The schema in figure 3.5 sums up the behaviour of Homeric Greek with respect to the properties in figure 3.3:

A. Grammaticalized article?   NO[27]
→ B. Grammaticalized textual anaphora?   NO

Figure 3.5. Grammaticalized article and Grammaticalized textual anaphora in Homeric Greek.

New Testament Greek, as shown by the following examples from Guardiano (2003:43):
a. οὓς ἐγὼ μᾶλλον φοβοῦμαι ἢ **τοὺς ἀμφὶ Ἄνυτον** (Plato, *Apology* 18 b2–3)
'I fear them more than Anito's friends'
b. ἐπιχειρῶν ἕκαστον ὑμῶν πείθειν μὴ πρότερον μήτε **τῶν ἑαυτοῦ** μηδενὸς ἐπιμελεῖσθαι (Plato, *Apology* 36 c5–6)
'... attempting to persuade each of you not to care for any of his own things ...'
c. ὑμεῖς **ἐκ τῶν κάτω** ἐστέ, ἐγὼ **ἐκ τῶν ἄνω** εἰμὶ (John 8:23)
'You are from below, I am from above'

[26] See Guardiano 2016:39–40 for a list of further examples.
[27] There is an implicational relation between property A and properties C (OBLIGATORY ARTICLE WITH REFERENTIAL NOUNS) and D (STRONG ARTICLE). Thus C and D cannot be activated in Homeric Greek due the absence of A. For further examples, see Guardiano 2016:40.

In the literature about Homer, ὁ, ἡ, τό is described as a "neutral" (non-deictic, presumably anaphoric) demonstrative, not yet fully developed as a definite article. However, its behavior is not entirely consistent with a demonstrative either (Guardiano 2016:41). First, it can co-occur with other demonstratives; second, it always occurs in one and the same syntactic position (in the leftmost area of the nominal domain), while demonstratives are also found in other positions (after prenominal adjectives and postnominally); third, it can only be preceded by items that, in Greek, typically surface to the left of D, such as universal quantifiers (or demonstratives themselves). Thus, it is probably a D-element, unlike demonstratives. Furthermore, ὁ, ἡ, τό is attested in structures where demonstratives are ungrammatical, for instance with superlative adjectives,[28] or when it acts as a substantivizer with numerals, adjectives, participles, etc.[29] In such cases, it seems to incorporate properties that are typical of, and perhaps peculiar to, definite articles.

Bozzone and Guardiano (2015) suggest that the anomalous behaviour of ὁ, ἡ, τό in Homer, rather than illustrating a "transitional stage" where the definite article is in the process of being developed but not yet established, is a consequence of the overlapping of two different grammars, independently attested at different diachronic stages of the language, and artificially collapsed in the epic style. Indeed, the language of epic was created when definite articles did not exist (no GRAMMATICALIZED ARTICLE). Then, Greek developed a GRAMMATICALIZED ARTICLE, presumably when the textualization of the Homeric poems was not yet concluded. Therefore, at least some generations of the poets who took part in the Homeric tradition spoke a language in which a definite article already existed (Bozzone and Guardiano 2015). Yet, the epic style had frozen the stage with no articles: poets, when learning the epic style, learned to omit the article, against their own natural grammar that, instead, required it (Bozzone 2010). The definite-like uses of ὁ, ἡ, τό attested in the two poems emerged when the 'grammar of epic' (with no articles) and the actual grammar of the poets (where ὁ, ἡ, τό was actually an article) interfered.

3.5 Conclusion

The constraints acting on the occurrences of definite articles with argument nominals in Classical and post-Classical Greek are almost identical to those observable in Modern Greek.

As far as the diachronic perspective is concerned, two major changes have caused a progressive restriction of the syntactic contexts in which an empty D is allowed in argument position. The first is the emergence of a

---

[28] Guardiano 2016:41, ex 37.
[29] Guardiano 2016:41, ex 38.

GRAMMATICALIZED ARTICLE, which has in turn two consequences: the need for a visible item in D in order for a noun to have a definite reading in argument position and the need of a visible D with kind names. The second change is the creation of a STRONG ARTICLE, whose most relevant surface manifestations are the need of a visible article with singular count nouns in argument position and the obligatory article with argument proper names. The schema in figure 3.6 sums up these conclusions:

A. Grammaticalized article?
    i. NO →   B. Grammaticalized textual anaphora?
                NO (Homeric Greek)
    ii. YES →   C. Obligatory article with referential nouns?
                YES (Modern Greek, Classical and New Testament Greek)
      →   D. Strong article?
                YES (Modern Greek)
                NO (Classical and New Testament Greek)

Figure 3.6. Diachronic changes from Homer to Modern Greek.

References

Abbott, Barbara. 2004. Definiteness and indefiniteness. In Laurence Horn and Gregory Ward (eds.), *The handbook of pragmatics,* 122–149. Oxford: Blackwell.

Abney, Steven. 1987. The English noun phrase in its sentential aspect. PhD dissertation. Massachusetts Institute of Technology.

Alexiadou, Artemis. 2014. *Multiple determiners and the structure of DPs.* Linguistik Aktuell/Linguistics Today 211. Amsterdam: Benjamins.

Alexiadou, Artemis, Liliane Haegeman, and Melita Stavrou. 2007. *Noun phrase in the generative perspective.* Studies in Generative Grammar 71. Berlin: Mouton De Gruyter.

Alexopoulou, Theodora, Raffaella Folli, and George Tsoulas. 2013. Bare number. In Raffaella Folli, Christina Sevdali, and Robert Truswell (eds.), *Syntax and its limits,* 300–324. Oxford: University Press.

Androutsopoulou, Antonia. 1994. On adjectives: The licensing of adjectival modification. Ms.

Bakker, Stephanie. 2009. *The noun phrase in Ancient Greek: A functional analysis of the order and articulation of NP constituents in Herodotus.* Amsterdam Studies in Classical Philology 15. Leiden: Brill.

Basset, Louis. 2006. La préfiguration dans l'épopée homérique de l'article défini du grec classique. In Emilio Crespo, Jesus De La Villa, and Antonio R. Revuelta (eds.), *Word classes and related topics in Ancient Greek,* 105–120. Leuven: Peeters.

Bernasconi, Francesco. 2011. Il sintagma nominale in greco classico: Un sondaggio sugli oratori attici. Tesi di Laurea. Università di Trieste.

Bernstein, Judy. 2001. The DP hypothesis: Identifying clausal properties in the nominal domain. In Mark Baltin and Chris Collins (eds.), *The handbook of contemporary syntactic theory*, 536–561. Oxford: Blackwell.

Bernstein, Judy. 2008. Reformulating the determiner phrase analysis. *Language and linguistic compass* 2:1246–1270.

Boskovic, Laszlo. 2008. What will you have? DP or NP? In Emily Elfner and Martin Walkow (eds.), *Proceedings of the North East Linguistic Society 37, University of Illinois at Urbana-Champaign, October 13–15, 2006*, 101–114. Amherst, MA: GLSA, Department of Linguistics, University of Massachusetts.

Bozzone, Chiara. 2010. New perspectives on formularity. In Stephanie W. Jamison, H. Craig Melchert, and Brent Vine (eds.), *Proceedings of the 21st Annual UCLA Indo-European Conference, University of California, Los Angeles, October 30–31, 2009*, 27–44. Bremen: Hempen Verlag.

Bozzone, Chiara, and Cristina Guardiano. 2015. ὁ, ἡ, τό in Homer: Tracking the spread of a syntactic innovation. Paper presented at the International Colloquium on Ancient Greek Linguistics, Rome, March 23–27, 2015.

Briulotta, Renata. 2007. L'articolo determinativo nei poemi omerici. Tesi di Laurea. Università di Palermo.

Campos, Hector, and Melita Stavrou. 2004. Polydefinites in Greek and Aromanian. In Olga Miseska Tomic (ed.), *Balkan syntac and semantics*, 137–173. Amsterdam: John Benjamins.

Chantraine, Pierre. 1953. *Grammaire homérique. Tome II. Syntaxe*. Collection de Philologie Classique 4. Paris: Librairie C. Klincksieck.

Chantraine, Pierre. 1961. *Morphologie historique du grec*. Nouvelle collection à l'usage des classes 34. Paris: Librairie C. Klincksieck.

Chomsky, Noam. 1986. *Knowledge of language: Its nature, origin, and use*. New York: Praeger.

Cinque, Guglielmo. 2010. *The syntax of adjectives: A comparative study*. Linguistic inquiry Monographs 57. Boston: MIT Press.

Crisma, Paola. 1997. L'articolo nella prosa inglese antica e la teoria degli articoli nulli. Tesi di Dottorato. Università di Padova.

Crisma, Paola. 2011. On the so-called "indefinite article." Paper presented at Coloquio de Gramática Generativa XXI, Sevilla, April 2011.

Dahl, Östen. 2004. Definite articles in Scandinavian: Competing grammaticalization processes in standard and non-standard varieties. In Bernd Kortmann (ed.), *Dialectology meets typology: Dialect grammar from a cross-linguistic perspective*, 147–179. Berlin: De Gruyter.

Fowler, Harold N., trans. 1921–1966. *Plato*, 12 vols. Loeb Classical Library. London: Heinemann.

Gomeshi, Jila, Ileana Paul, and Martina Wiltschko, eds. 2009. *Determiners: Universals and variation. Linguistik Aktuell/Linguistics Today 147*. Amsterdam: Benjamins.

Guardiano, Cristina. 2003. Struttura e storia del sintagma nominale nel Greco Antico: Ipotesi parametriche. PhD dissertation. Università di Pisa.

Guardiano, Cristina. 2006. The diachronic evolution of the Greek article: Parametric hypotheses. In Mark Janse, Brian Joseph, and Angela Ralli (eds.), *Proceedings of the 2nd International Conference of Modern Greek Dialects and Linguistic Theory, Mytilene, Greece, September 30–October 3, 2004*, 99–114. Mytilene: University of Patras.

Guardiano, Cristina. 2011. Genitives in the Greek nominal domain: Parametric considerations. In Mark Janse, Brian Joseph, Pavlos Pavlou, Angela Ralli, and Spyros Armosti (eds.), *Studies in Modern Greek dialects and linguistic theory*, 123–134. Nicosia: Research Center of Kykkos Monastery.

Guardiano, Cristina. 2012. Parametric changes in the history of the Greek article. In Dianne Jonas, John Whitman, and Andrew Garrett (eds.), *Grammatical change: Origins, nature, outcomes*, 179–197. Oxford: University Press.

Guardiano, Cristina. 2013. The Greek definite article across time. In *Studies in Greek Linguistics* 33:76–91.

Guardiano, Cristina. 2016. Definite articles in Ancient Greek. In Stephanie W. Jamison, H. Craig Melchert, and Brent Vine (eds.), *Proceedings of the 26th Annual UCLA Indo-European Conference*, 27–46. Bremen: Hempen Verlag.

Guardiano, Cristina, and Giuseppe Longobardi. 2006. Reference and definiteness. Paper presented at the Incontro di Grammatica Generativa XXXII, Firenze, March 2–4, 2006.

Guardiano, Cristina, and Giuseppe Longobardi. 2018. The diachrony of adnominal genitives in Ancient Greek. Paper presented at the workshop On the place of case in Grammar - PlaCiG. Rethymnon, Greece, 18–20 October 2018.

Guardiano, Cristina, and Melita Stavrou. 2015. Adjective-noun combination in Romance and Greek of Southern Italy: Polydefiniteness revisited. Paper presented at the International Conference of Greek Linguistics 12, Freie Universität Berlin, September 16–19, 2015.

Guillemin, Diana. 2009. The Mauritian Creole noun phrase: Its form and function. PhD dissertation. The University of Queensland, Brisbane, Australia.

Hawkins, John A. 1991. On (in)definite articles: Implicatures and (un)grammaticality prediction. *Journal of Linguistics* 27:405–42.

Heim, Irene. 1982. The semantics of definite and indefinite noun phrases. PhD dissertation. University of Massachusetts.

Kolliakou, Dimitra. 2004. Monadic definites and polydefinites: Their form, meaning and use. *Journal of linguistics* 40:263–323.

Krámský, Jiří. 1972. *The article and the concept of definiteness in languages.* Janua Linguarum Series Minor 125. The Hague: Mouton.

Laury, Ritva. 1997. *Demonstratives in interaction: The emergence of a definite article in Finnish.* Studies in Discourse and Grammar 7. Amsterdam: John Benjamins Publishing Company.

Lombardi Vallauri, Edoardo. 2002. L'articolo greco fra identificabilità ad esclusività del referente. *Studi Italiani di Linguistica Teorica e Applicata* 31:7–33.

Longobardi, Giuseppe. 1994. Reference and proper names. *Linguistic Inquiry* 25:609–665.

Longobardi, Giuseppe. 2001. The structure of DPs: Some principles, parameters and problems. In Mark Baltin and Chris Collins (eds.), *The handbook of contemporary syntactic theory*, 562–603. Oxford: Blackwell.

Longobardi, Giuseppe. 2005. Toward a unified grammar of reference. *Zeitschrift für Sprachwissenschaft* 24:5–44.

Longobardi, Giuseppe. 2008. Reference to individuals, person, and the variety of mapping parameters. In Henrik H. Müller and Alex Klinge (eds.), *Essays on nominal determination,* 189–211. Amsterdam: John Benjamins.

Longobardi, Giuseppe, and Giuseppina Silvestri. 2013. The structure of NPs. In Silvia Luraghi and Claudia Parodi (eds.), *The Bloomsbury Companion to Syntax*, 88–117. New York: Continuum.

Lyons, Christopher. 1999. *Definiteness.* Cambridge Textbooks in Linguistics. Cambridge: University Press.

Manolessou, Io. 2000. Greek noun phrase structure: A study in syntactic evolution. PhD dissertation. University of Cambridge.

Manolessou, Io, and Geoffrey Horrocks. 2007. The development of the definite article in Greek. *Studies in Greek Linguistics* 27:224–236.

Mendez-Dosuna, Julien V. 1999. Una nota tipológica sobre el artículo en Homero. In Vincente Bécares Botas, Francisco Romero Cruz, Maria Pilar, and Fernández Álvarez (eds.), *Estudios de Filología clásica e indoeuropeo dedicados a Francisco Romero Cruz,* 153–160. Salamanca: Ediciones Universidad de Salamanca.

Murray, A. T. 1924a. *The Iliad: With an English translation.* Loeb Classical Library. London: Heinemann.

Murray, A. T. 1924b. *The Odyssey: With an English translation.* Loeb Classical Library. London: Heinemann.

Napoli, Maria. 2009. Aspects of definiteness in Greek. *Studies in Language* 33:569–611.

Palmer, Leonard R. 1962. The language of Homer. In Alan J. B. Wace and Frank H. Stubbings (eds.), *A companion to Homer*, 75–178. London-Toronto: MacMillan.

Panagiotidis, Phoevos. 2000. Demonstrative determiners and operators: The case of Greek. *Lingua* 110:717–742.

Parenti, Alessandro. 1997. Aspetti diacronici della definitezza in greco e in rumeno. PhD dissertation. Università di Perugia, Italy.

Roberts, Ian. 2007. *Diachronic syntax. Oxford Textbooks in Linguistics.* Oxford: University Press.

Scott, John A. 1910. Does Homer use the definite article? *Classical Journal* 5:220–223.

Schwarz, Florian. 2012. Different types of definites crosslinguistically. Ms.

Smyth, Herberth W. 1920. *A Greek grammar for colleges.* New York: American Book Company.

Stark, Elisabeth, Elisabeth Leiss, and Werner Abraham, eds. 2007. *Nominal determination: Typology, context constraints and historical emergence. Studies in Language Companion Series 89.* Amsterdam: John Benjamins.

Stavrou, Melita. 2012. Postnominal adjectives in Greek indefinite noun phrases. In Laura Brugè, Anna Cardinaletti, Giuliana Giusti, Nicola Munaro, and Cecilia Poletto (eds.), *Functional heads,* 379–394. New York: Oxford University Press.

Stavrou, Melita. 2015. The fine(r) ingredients of adjectival modification in Greek: The Romance connection. Ms. Aristotle University of Thessaloniki.

Szabolcsi, Anna. 1987. Functional categories in the noun phrase. In Kenesei István (ed.), *Approaches to Hungarian 2: Theories and analyses,* 167–190. Szeged: JATE.

Trovesi, Andrea. 2004. *La genesi degli articoli determinativi: Modalità di espressione della definitezza in ceco, serbo-lusaziano e sloveno.* Materiali linguistici 46. Milano: FrancoAngeli.

Vince, J. H., trans. 1930. *Demosthenes: Orations Olynthiacs, Philippics, Minor Public Speeches, Speech Against Leptines.* Loeb Classical Library 238. London: Heinemann-Harvard.

4

A Discourse-Functional
Approach to the Greek Article

Ronald D. Peters

4.1 Introduction

There is a certain irony that characterizes the Greek article, in that its size (arguably the smallest word in the Greek language) is disproportional to its use (the most frequently used word in the New Testament, by a great margin). Thus, when I began my research into the matter, though there had certainly been movement in grammars over time, a definitive and internally consistent description of its function had yet to be formulated. I provide the following self-quote as justification for such an assessment:

> To date, the first and only comprehensive grammar of the Greek article was Thomas Fanshaw Middleton's *The Doctrine of the Greek Article*, published in 1828. Nearly two centuries later, it is plain to see that our understanding of the article's function has advanced significantly. At its most fundamental level, modern grammarians have been forced to concede, contrary to their predecessors, that the Greek article does not operate in a manner that is analogous to the English definite article. Definiteness and indefiniteness are not established in

83

Greek by the presence or absence of the article. Despite this recognition, grammatical treatments of the Greek article continue to operate on analogy with the English definite article. Though they qualify their explanations by stating that the two articles function differently, they proceed by beginning with the translation equivalent, then explain the Greek article's function as either conformity to or deviation from this norm. Since Middleton, no author has taken up the task of producing a comprehensive grammar of the Greek article based exclusively on descriptions derived from observations of its usage in Koine Greek. (Peters 2014:1)

Hugh James Rose, who later edited Middleton's work, observed that Middleton's treatment of the article differed from others in that it did not consist of "detached and unconnected rules" (Middleton 1828:v). As I took it upon myself to assess that state of research on the article, it was my observation that, though much progress had indeed been made on the grammar of the Greek article, the current grammatical situation was nevertheless still characterized by "detached and unconnected rules." In my research I determined that this was due to one false presupposition and one inadequate methodology. The false presupposition was that the article was a determiner and was primarily akin to the demonstrative pronoun. The inadequate methodology was a continued predilection to address the grammar of the Greek article by means of analogy with the English definite article, first in terms of general correspondence then in terms of deviation from this norm, even when grammarians openly acknowledge the problematic nature of such correspondence.

Were the debate merely a matter of grammar, a minor indulgence in scholarly curiosity, my investigation would have had little to which it could commend itself. However, it is demonstrable that many a discussion of both translation and exegesis has turned on questions regarding the article. Thus, I determined that two hundred years was far too long a time to have passed for the matter to remain unsatisfactorily resolved. I therefore took it upon myself to approach the question of the article's function anew, with the goal of confronting and overturning long held dogmas in the hope that a shift in the paradigm would result in a more satisfactory, and ultimately more useful, description of the article's function. What follows is a summary and moderate expansion of certain elements of the monograph in which I formulated an updated grammar of the Greek article.

The following chapter will be broken into two sections. In the first I will provide a summary of the methodology by which a description of the article's function was formulated through the use of the principles of SYSTEMIC-FUNCTIONAL LINGUISTICS. This will be followed by a summary of the results of this analysis, namely that the Greek article is most closely akin to the relative pronoun, that it orients identification of a referent to the speaker or writer who provides the necessary information for identification, and that items modified by the article are characterized as concrete. The second section will focus on a demonstration of how such a functional grammar of the article may be employed as a tool in discourse analysis of the New Testament and the exegetical value of such an approach.

4.2 A systemic-functional description of the Greek article

4.2.1 A brief grammar of ὁ- items.

The first step in formulating a description of the Greek article was to establish its categorical location within the larger system of Koine Greek. The terminology employed by M.A.K. Halliday provided a useful point to begin. In English, Halliday subdivides deictic elements into two categories, including the definite article:

> In his grammar, Halliday places the English definite article under the general category TH-item. Lexical items in this category share distinctive traits both in morphology and function and consist of demonstrative pronouns and the definite article. Closely related are WH-items, which consist of relative pronouns. Halliday states that each group is part "of a wider set embracing both WH- and TH-forms, which taken together fulfill a DEICTIC or 'pointing out' function." (Peters 2014:71, citing Halliday 2004:86)

In English, the definite article and demonstrative pronoun (TH-items) share certain common traits in terms of morphology and function. However, demonstratives are used to direct the recipient to the information necessary for identifying the referent, whereas the definite article indicates that the recipient already possesses the information or that the information is obvious and recoverable from the situation or context (Halliday 2004:312–314). For example, one may say, *"Please hand me the fork"* if, for the listener, the identity of the utensil is recoverable from the context or obvious from the situation. If not, the statement will direct the listener to the referent in the form of *"Please hand me that fork."* Thus, the keys to identification, with regard to the function of the English definite article, are matters of PROXIMITY and RECOVERABILITY, both of which are readily available to the recipient and require no intervention from the speaker or writer. By contrast, WH-items introduce new information into the discourse, which is either relative to some other entity, as in *who* or *which*, or is used as the identifying characteristic of an extra-linguistic referent and are realized by the use of alternate WH-forms that employ a TH-form, such as *the one who* or *that which*. In such instances, there is a general sense of "identity to be retrieved from elsewhere" (Halliday 2004:86). Thus, while TH-items either direct the recipient to the information necessary for identification or indicate that the information is proximate and/or recoverable, WH-items provide the necessary information. TH-items orient identification to the recipient; WH-items orient identification to the speaker or writer. It is important to note that the use of WH-items does not indicate that the information necessary for identification is not proximate or recoverable; it may very well be. The use of WH-items simply indicates that the speaker or writer is providing this information without further comment.

Turning to the Greek article, historically grammatical treatments have largely proceeded from the assumption that it is most closely related to the demonstrative pronoun. By extension, the Greek article would thus be associated with English TH-items. However, upon closer examination, the Greek article is in fact categorically related most closely to the relative pronoun, not the demonstrative pronoun, both in terms of morphology and function. The morphological similarities are quite obvious. Just as in English one observes the shared traits of TH-items *this, that, the*, so also in Greek one observes the similarities of ὁ ἡ τό when compared to ὅς ἥ ὅ. In addition to this shared morphology, it is also demonstrable that the Greek article and relative pronouns perform similar functions, as will be demonstrated below. Regarding past grammars, it is arguable that the historical categorization with the demonstrative pronoun is one of the primary causes of the "detached and unconnected rules" that too often characterize their treatment of the article. By adapting Halliday's terminology, both the Greek article and relative pronoun may be broadly categorized under the term ὁ- ITEMS. Thus, both are more akin to English WH-items, which are realized as *who* or *which*, as well as the alternate form *the one who* or *that which*.

By employing the term "akin," I am not arguing elements are synonymous. The reader should not assume that the use of English terms is indicative of correspondence in a one-to-one sense. Additionally, it should not be assumed that I am critical of previous scholarship for the use of analogous terms. Instead, my criticism is based first on the analogues employed, and second on the frequently assumed close correspondence between the analogues. It is inevitable that attempts to describe a foreign language will employ analogues from the known language. However, one must use caution in this process. It is my contention that adequate caution has not been employed, resulting in poor and misleading descriptions, a problem I have labored to correct.

In Greek, the article and relative pronoun are used to indicate that the speaker or writer is providing the information necessary for identification. Neither is used to direct the recipient to the information necessary for identification, nor do they indicate that the information is proximate or recoverable from the immediate situation, as is the case with the English demonstrative pronoun and definite article, respectively. That this is the case may be demonstrated by observing how constructions that employ both the Greek relative pronoun and article perform common functions. The following treatment will examine two constructions that support this conclusion: relative clauses and μέν...δέ constructions.

4.2.1.1 Relative clauses

It is often the case that a relative clause functions as a qualifier in a nominal group. In such instances, the relative clause is referred to as a defining relative clause (Halliday 2004:324). In some instances, the relative clause elaborates upon the meaning of another clause "by further specifying or describing it" (Halliday 2004:396). The function may be observed in Greek, as well as English, usage. For example, Paul provides further elaboration on the teaching to which he refers in Rom 16:17:

(1) τὴν διδαχὴν ἣν ὑμεῖς ἐμάθετε
    'the teaching which you learned'

In this example, Paul further specifies τὴν διδαχὴν: it is 'the teaching' ἣν ὑμεῖς ἐμάθετε 'which you learned'. As is the case with English WH-items, when employing Greek ὁ- items, the writer provides this information to the readers, thus orienting identification to himself. The reader must accept this information, based on the writer's "seeing" of the information, for the purpose of identification. As noted above, one should not assume that the relative clause indicates that the recipient does not possess the information. Rather, it makes no comment on this matter and focuses identification on the speaker/writer as the provider of this information.

While this defining function may be accomplished by means of a relative pronoun and a finite verb, a Greek user may perform the same function by means of an article and participle. Using Paul's letter to the Romans again, in 1:18 we observe the following example:

(2) ἀνθρώπων τῶν τὴν ἀλήθειαν ἐν ἀδικίᾳ κατεχόντων
    '[the] people who suppress the truth in unrighteousness'

Just as in the previous example, Paul provides further specification regarding the 'people' ἀνθρώπων, to whom he is referring. However, rather than employ a relative clause, he employs an articular participial clause. Nevertheless, it performs the same function as a defining relative clause. Just as is the case with the relative pronoun, the article indicates that the writer is providing the information necessary for the purpose of identification, thus orienting identification to the writer. Once again, the reader must accept the writer's "seeing" of this information for the purpose of identification.

While relative clauses often function as a qualifier within the nominal group, they may also function as the head of the group. In English, when a relative clause is so employed, the relative pronoun is often realized by means of an alternate form that uses a TH-item as a relative: *the one* (*who*), *that* (*which*) (Halliday 2004:86). In Greek, ὁ- items perform this function as well. Continuing our use of Paul's letter to the Romans, we observe both the article and the relative pronoun being employed in this manner. In 2:21–23, we observe both forms:

(3) ὁ οὖν διδάσκων ἕτερον σεαυτὸν διδάσκεις;
    ὁ κηρύσσων μὴ κλέπτειν κλέπτεις;
    ὁ λέγων μῆ μοιχεύειν μοιχεύεις;
    ὁ βδελυσσόμενος τὰ εἴδωλα ἱεροσυλεῖς;
    ὃς ἐν νόμῳ καυχᾶσαι, διὰ τῆς παραβάσεως τοῦ νομοῦ τὸν θεὸν ἀτιμάζεις;

'Therefore, the one who teaches others, do you teach yourself?
The one who preaches, "Do not steal," do you steal?
The one who says, "Do not commit adultery," do you commit adultery?
The one who despises idols, do you desecrate temples?
The one who has confidence in the law, do you dishonor God by breaking the law?'

In this example, we observe four articular participial clauses that function as the subject of the main clause. In the last line, Paul uses a standard relative clause to perform the same function. In each instance, the ὁ- item indicates that the writer is providing the information necessary for identifying the referent.

Recognition of how ὁ- items function helps us to understand the shortcomings of previous grammatical treatments of the Greek article. As stated above, in English TH-items are employed to direct the recipient to the information necessary for identification (demonstratives) or indicate that the recipient already possesses the information, or that the information is proximate and recoverable (the definite article). Conversely, Greek ὁ- items indicate that this information is being provided by the speaker or the writer. Previous grammatical investigations, failing to fully appreciate this distinction, have been frustrated in their attempts to formulate internally consistent descriptions.

4.2.1.2 μὲν...δὲ constructions

Another characteristic of ὁ- items is that they are the only elements used in μὲν... δὲ constructions. In Luke 23:33 we observe an example that employs the relative pronoun:

(4) ἐκεῖ ἐσταύρωσαν αὐτὸν καὶ τοὺς κακούργους, ὃν μὲν ἐκ δεξιῶν ὃν δὲ ἐξ ἀριστερῶν
    'There they crucified him and the criminals, one on the right and one on the left.'

In this instance, the μὲν... δὲ construction is used the way an English speaker would use a construction such as 'on the one hand... on the other hand'. As may be clearly observed, the author has employed the relative pronoun. However, the Greek article may also be used in such constructions. In Acts 17:32 the author employs such a construction:

(5) Ἀκούσατες δὲ ἀνάστασιν νεκρῶν οἱ μὲν ἐχλεύαζον, οἱ δὲ εἶπαν, ἀκουσόμεθά σου περὶ τούτου καὶ πάλιν.
'Hearing about the resurrection from the dead, some scoffed, while others said, "We will hear you again, regarding this."'

This time, the construction is used in the sense of 'some... others'. For our purposes, it is noteworthy, as stated above, that both the relative pronoun and the article are used in such constructions. This reinforces the conclusion that that both parts of speech share a common function and so should be co-classified.

These are obviously but a few examples. In my published work, *The Greek Article* (2014), I provide a broader and more comprehensive treatment of both the relative pronoun and the article, citing examples from multiple authors and literary genres. Across these spectra, usage is uniform. Thus, I am confident in the co-classification of the relative pronoun and the article, as well as rejection of any classification of the article with demonstratives.

4.2.2 The grammatical function of the Greek article

When a Greek speaker or writer employs the Greek article, it is to indicate that he or she is providing the information necessary for identifying a referent. Thus, the identity of the referent is oriented to the speaker or writer. The article indicates that the information grammaticalized by the head term is to be used for identifying the referent. This is true when any part of speech is employed as the head term: nouns, adjectives, participles, adverbs, numerals, even certain particles. For example, when the article is attached to a participle, it indicates that the action grammaticalized by the participle is to be used as the identifying characteristic of an extra-linguistic referent. This can be observed in Rom 2:21–22, which was also cited in example (3):

(6) ὁ οὖν διδάσκων ἕτερον σεαυτὸν διδάσκεις;
ὁ κηρύσσων μὴ κλέπτειν κλέπτεις;
ὁ λέγων μὴ μοιχεύειν μοιχεύεις;
ὁ βδελυσσόμενος τὰ εἴδωλα ἱεροσυλεῖς;

'Therefore, the one who teaches others, do you teach yourself?
The one who preaches, "do not steal," do you steal?
The one who says, "do not commit adultery," do you commit adultery?
The one who despises idols, do you desecrate temples?'

In each instance, the information grammaticalized by the participles is the identifying characteristic of the extra-linguistic referent: 'the one who teaches', 'the one who preaches', 'the one who says', 'the one who despises'. Additionally, in each instance, the referent is characterized as concrete "in that it is characterized as belonging to immediate experience as an actual thing or event, or is associated with a specific instance" (Peters 2014:186). This should not be confused with definiteness. While an item that is characterized as concrete may or may not correspond with an extra-linguistic referent that exists in reality, the presence of the article does not establish this relationship. Rather, other linguistic elements will indicate such correspondence. Thus, the characterization as concrete produced by the article holds the referent out as such a thing, as something that may be identified and examined, irrespective of whether or not it has a real world referent in view. Using the sample text from Rom 2:21–22, ὁ διδάσκων 'the one who teaches', is characterized as concrete, so that this person may be held out for examination by the reader. Whether or not an actual, real world referent is in view is not indicated. In this instance, ὁ οὖν διδάσκων is held out as such a person. The same is true for each additional person Paul holds out: ὁ κηρύσσων, ὁ λέγων, ὁ βδελυσσόμενος. Each is characterized as concrete, as belonging to immediate experience as an actual person. However, there is no indication that a real world referent is in view.

Virtually any part of speech may be employed as the identifying characteristic of a referent. The use of adjectives in this manner is clearly observed in one of Jesus' well known sayings, recorded in Matt 20:16:

(7) ἔσονται οἱ ἔσχατοι πρῶτοι καὶ οἱ πρῶτοι ἔσχατοι.
    'The last will be first and the first, last.'

In this instance, the article indicates that the information grammaticalized by the adjectives is to be used as the identifying characteristic of the referents. Once again, we observe that οἱ ἔσχατοι and οἱ πρῶτοι are characterized as concrete, as belonging to immediate experience as actual people. This is so that they may be held out for examination by the hearer or reader.

Even adverbs can be employed in this manner, as seen in John 8:23:

(8) ὑμεῖς ἐκ τῶν κάτω ἐστέ, ἐγὼ ἐκ τῶν ἄνω εἰμί
    'You are from below, I am from above.'

In each example cited, the speaker or writer provides information to the recipients, which they are to use for the purpose of identification. The use of the article signals this. There is no indication that the recipients in these instances possess this information. (They may or may not). Thus, the article orients identification to the speaker or writer. Additionally, the referent is characterized as concrete. It is held out as something that may be identified and examined. These factors are critical for understanding the function of the article with its most common head term: nouns.

Based on these factors, I proposed the following description of how nouns are characterized when the article is present and when it is absent: "The presence of the article indicates the speaker or writer's subjective presentation of a noun, which is presented as something concrete, in that it is characterized as belonging to immediate experience as an actual thing or event, or is associated with a specific instance" (Peters 2014:227). This means that the head term is characterized as having a material, perceptible existence, as something that can be perceived by the senses. In addition, the noun is characterized as concrete solely on the basis of the speaker or writer's provision of information:

> The characterization of a noun as concrete is based solely on the fact of the speaker or writer's provision of the information necessary for identification. It gives no indication to the listener or reader of how or where to locate the identity of the noun, or that the identity is proximate in such a way as to be immediately recoverable. The Greek article orients the identification of the head term to the speaker or writer, not the recipient. (Peters 2014:227)

As noted above, it must be remembered that this is a subjective characterization and that "concrete" is not synonymous with "definite." Characterization as concrete may, on occasion, be motivated by correspondence with a real world referent. However, this will be indicated by other linguistic elements and is not indicated by the article. Often, when an element is characterized as concrete, it is characterized as such a thing that may exist or does in fact exist without necessarily indicating correspondence to a real world referent. In such instances, the element so characterized is held out for the recipient's consideration, as if it is something having substance, as having a material, perceptible existence, as something that may be examined. By contrast, in instances when the speaker or writer has the option to employ or not employ the article, which is primarily the case with nouns, the non-articular element is non-concrete or abstract. If the use of the article represents a characterization of the head term, it is arguable that the absence of the article represents a non-characterization. Based on this line of reasoning, I have formulated the following proposal, which is a modification of my published proposal: "The absence of the article indicates the speaker or writer's subjective non-characterisation of a noun, which is left abstract, in that it is not characterised as belonging to immediate experience as an actual thing or event, or associated with a specific instance. The noun has no referent in terms of a class whose identifying characteristic is grammaticalised by the noun."[1]

---

[1] See Peters 2014:227. In my original proposal, I suggested that the absence of the article also constituted a characterisation. I have modified my original position on this and concluded that, instead, the absence of the article reflects a

The categories of concrete and abstract must not be viewed in terms of absolute, polar opposition. Rather, each represents opposite ends of a graded scale or cline, with the potential for elements to be understood as more or less concrete or abstract. Additional linguistic and discourse elements will indicate the degree to which an element is characterized as concrete or abstract (Peters 2014:186). These descriptions will be employed in our analysis in the following section.

4.2.3 The discourse function of the Greek article

In order to understand the motivation behind the choice of characterization, it is essential that one take into account the discourse function of the elements that are modified by the Greek article. This is especially true of nouns and proper nouns, which may or may not be modified by the article and thus operate in a system of binary opposition. Historically, it was concluded that the use of the article was a matter of personal idiom, of personal style. This was due to the fact that grammarians were unable to discern consistent patterns of use and non-use. The approaches employed focused primarily on questions of syntax, rather than characterization motivated by discourse function. As a result, investigators overwhelmingly despaired of discerning any identifiable pattern and concluded that the article, though useful, was employed based on the idiomatic styling of the individual speaker or writer. These grammarians overwhelmingly operated from the presupposition that the article was a demonstrative and functioned as a determiner. Older grammars argued that the article indicated definiteness. Over time, it became apparent that this was not the case. However, grammarians continued to categorize the article as a demonstrative. When this presupposition is jettisoned in favor of the one proposed above, a consistent, useful discourse grammar may be formulated.

Arguably, the most formative and helpful theory for understanding the function of the Greek article is that of discourse grounding, as developed by Stephen Wallace (1982). According to his theory, discourse elements will either be a part of the foreground or the background of the discourse. Foregrounded elements will "stand out" as more salient and are typically

- more important events of a narrative,
- more important steps of a procedure,
- the central points of an exposition, and
- main characters or entities involved in an episode.

Foregrounded elements stand in contrast to backgrounded elements, which are typically

- events of lesser importance;

---

non-characterisation. Thus, the element is non-concrete or abstract. This could also be interpreted as the default or unmarked form, contrasted with the marked, articular form. This would obviously run counter to other treatments of the article, e.g. Heimerdinger and Levinsohn (1992:15–44).

- subsidiary procedures;
- secondary points, descriptions, elaborations, digressions; and
- minor characters or things. (Wallace 1982:208)

The purpose of such linguistic categories is "to differentiate linguistic figure from linguistic ground," in order to "structure an utterance (of one or more sentences) into more or less salient portions" (Wallace 1982:214).

In a given discourse, elements that are more concrete stand out as figures in the discourse and are generally more salient, while elements that are more abstract are generally less salient and function as part of the grounding (Peters 2014:188–191). This is a procedure analogous to the kind of staging employed by photographers and painters. The choice of background has the potential to significantly affect how the well the foregrounded element is perceived as such. For example, when a photographer brings a single element, like a flower, into sharp focus against a blurry background, the flower "pops out." It is clear that this is the photographer's point of focus. Compositional choices indicate salient elements.

Another way to think about this is to use the metaphor of a stage. At certain points during the performance of a play, key characters will move to the front of the stage to deliver their lines. Thus, they are foregrounded because, at least for the moment, they are more salient. At other times, when these or other characters are not salient in the scene, they may move to the back of the stage, in effect becoming part of the background. Staging is often a dynamic, rather than static, affair. Within a single scene, characters may move from foreground to background, then to foreground again.

This kind of staging may also take place in discourse. The characterization of elements within the discourse establishes their position as either background or foreground, as more or less salient. The Greek article performs a key role in characterization, and thus in the staging of a discourse:

> In the case of the article, when a Greek speaker wishes to move a participant to the background of the stage, he or she may do so in part by characterizing the participant as abstract. Conversely, when a speaker wishes to bring a participant to the foreground of the stage, the participant will be characterized as concrete. Thus, even in a single episode, participants will move in and out, to the front and to the back, based on their immediate role. (Peters 2014:190–191)

Historically, it seems that investigations into the function of the Greek article did not take into account the fluid and dynamic nature of participant staging in discourse, which further complicated an already compromised approach. Thus, I stand by my assertion that "when this understanding is applied to the characterization of participants in discourse in the Greek New Testament, it will provide insight into the choices speakers make with regard to the use of the article. It will be seen that the use of the article alone is not a matter of individual style or personal idiom" (Peters 2014:191). Its use and non-use represents a binary system of opposition that produces consistent and uniform characterizations. Additionally, it is only subjective in that its use or non-use is the result of a conscious decision on the part of the speaker to characterize an element of the discourse in a way that performs a function at the discourse level. This view will be particularly helpful in understanding the role of the article with proper nouns. Middleton argued that the article was a symbol "of that which is uppermost in the speaker's mind" (Middleton 1828:25). The analysis of the following examples will demonstrate that Middleton was correct. In addition, when properly applied, this method of analysis has the potential to pay valuable exegetical dividends.

4.3 Matthew 13:44

Jesus' parable of the man who bought a field in which he found treasure provides an opportunity to employ our discourse-functional grammar of the article in order to determine those elements that are more and less salient, those that represent figures, and those that are a part of the grounding of the discourse.

(9) Ὁμοία ἐστὶν ἡ βασιλεία τῶν οὐρανῶν θησαυρῷ κεκρυμμένῳ ἐν τῷ ἀγρῷ, ὃν εὑρὼν ἄνθρωπος ἔκρυψεν, καὶ ἀπὸ τῆς χαρᾶς αὐτοῦ ὑπάγει καὶ πωλεῖ πάντα ὅσα ἔχει καὶ ἀγοράζει τὸν ἀγρὸν ἐκεῖνον.
'The kingdom of heaven is like a treasure hidden in a field, which a man, having found, hides. And because of his joy, he goes and sells all that he has and buys that field.'

The first articular element of the discourse is ἡ βασιλεία τῶν οὐρανῶν. According to older theories that emphasized definiteness, the interpreter might conclude that the choice to characterize this element as concrete was motivated by a presumption that there is a real world referent that corresponds to the linguistic sign. The kingdom of heaven is a real place, thus it should be characterized not merely as concrete, but as definite. While correspondence to a real world referent is certainly possible, according to the grammar formulated above, the article does not indicate this. Thus, the interpreter must postulate another reason for the speaker or writer's choice of characterization. From a discourse perspective, ἡ βασιλεία τῶν οὐρανῶν 'the kingdom of heaven' is more salient because it is what the discourse is about. Everything that comes after is exposition on the nature or character of ἡ βασιλεία τῶν οὐρανῶν. Therefore, the choice of characterization was motivated by the saliency of this element. Because it is more salient, it is characterized as concrete so that it will stand out as a figure in the discourse.

Next, we observe θησαυρῷ. As a noun, this element enjoys a relationship with the article of binary opposition, it may or may not be articular (as was the case with ἡ βασιλεία τῶν οὐρανῶν). In this instance, θησαυρῷ is characterized as more abstract. One might first respond with surprise, assuming that θησαυρῷ is also salient. However, a closer reading suggests otherwise. The speaker is more interested in θησαυρῷ as an abstract quality than as something that may be characterized as belonging to experience as an actual thing or specific instance, as having material, perceptible existence. In this instance, treasure appears to be a necessary element for establishing the ground against which the next articular element, τῷ ἀγρῷ is seen. This raises an important consideration. Background should not be interpreted as unimportant or unnecessary. Without background elements, there can be no foreground. Thus, less salient does not mean unimportant. Rather, recognition of discourse grounding and matters of saliency provides the necessary information by which the interpreter identifies the roles of discourse elements.

The discourse ends with the man selling all he has in order to buy τὸν ἀγρὸν ἐκεῖνον. Since both instances of this element are articular, we may conclude that 'the field' is more salient; it has been given greater prominence by characterizing it as having material, perceptible existence. While the presence of the treasure is necessary for understanding the importance, the value of the field, and therefore provides grounding for the discourse, ultimately it is 'the field' that is specifically identified as the thing the man purchases. Thus, it is characterized as concrete, as more salient, as a figure in the discourse. Interestingly, this analysis strongly suggests that the element that 'the kingdom of heaven' is compared to is in fact 'the field', not 'the treasure'.

It is also interesting to note that the man is not characterized as concrete, he is merely ἄνθρωπος, *a man* as we would say in English. His abstract characterization establishes him as part of the grounding of the discourse. He is necessary to the discourse in that someone must be identified as the buyer of the field, but ultimately he is not salient. The discourse is concerned solely with the kingdom of heaven and how a field may serve as a metaphor to describe it. The man plays an important role. However, he is not a salient element; it's not about him.

Lastly, we observe that τῆς χαρᾶς αὐτοῦ is also articular. This suggests that it, too, is more salient. Once again, the presence of θησαυρῷ is necessary for establishing the ground against which τῆς χαρᾶς αὐτοῦ is seen. The joy of the man is predicated on his discovery of the treasure and represents his motive for buying the field. However, the choice of characterization places greater salience on the motive of joy than the acquisition of the treasure as the motivating factor.

At this point we may rightly ask about the exegetical payoff. In his commentary on the Greek text of Matthew, with regard to τῷ ἀγρῷ, John

Nolland writes: "It is unclear how the definite article should be taken" (Nolland 2005:563). I hope that the analysis above has provided the clarification. Nolland's commentary on the passage devotes considerable space to the treasure. If our analysis is correct, he has focused on the background element. The story is not about the treasure, but about the kingdom of heaven, the field, and joy. These, to use Middleton's words, are the elements uppermost in the speaker's mind. Nolland asks, "So what does the story relate to the kingdom of heaven? The value to the individual of discovering the kingdom of heaven is clearly important" (Nolland 2005:564). This suggests that he interprets treasure as analogous to the kingdom of the heavens. Our analysis suggests something different. The kingdom of heaven is not the treasure; it is the field in which the treasure is found. Just as one might sell all of his belongings in order to acquire a field that contains treasure, how much more should he sell all to acquire the kingdom of heaven, in which one finds the greatest treasure of all and the accompanying joy.[2]

This analysis should not be interpreted as suggesting that the speaker or the writer place little value on θησαυρῷ. Quite the contrary, if it did not have value its role in the discourse would have little meaning. Clearly the whole reason for purchasing the field was to acquire the treasure hidden therein. Greater salience is not a comment on the perceived inherent value of any element. In this instance, the discourse is not about the treasure, but about the kingdom, the field, and the joy. θησαυρῷ provides a necessary grounding element against which these other things can rightly be viewed and understood.

In conclusion, the kingdom of heaven is like a field. The field's value is based on the treasure hidden in it. So too, the value of the kingdom of heaven is found in the treasure it contains. If one would sell all he possesses to purchase a field that contains material treasure, how much more should he surrender all to acquire the kingdom and thus take possession of the treasure it contains.

4.4 Acts 5:1–11

Arguably, no other use of the use of the Greek article has frustrated attempts to formulate a consistent and uniform grammatical description more than its presence with proper nouns. However, when characterization is understood as a matter of discourse grounding, discourse staging, to use the play metaphor, it is possible to formulate a description of its function that is indeed uniform. The key consideration is, as stated above, that one see such staging as dynamic, rather than static. The following narrative will illustrate this.

---

[2] My first instinct is to equate the treasure with the message of the Gospel. Thus, the value of the kingdom is predicated on the fact that it is the repository of the Gospel of Jesus Christ.

In the story of Ananias and Sapphira, Luke employs articular and non-articular forms of the participants' names to indicate greater or lesser salience at certain, strategic points in the narrative.

(10)Ἀνὴρ δέ τις Ἀνανίας ὀνόματι σὺν Σαπφίρῃ τῇ γυναικὶ αὐτοῦ ἐπώλησεν κτῆμα ² καὶ ἐνοσφίσατο ἀπὸ τῆς τιμῆς, συνειδυίης καὶ τῆς γυναικός, καὶ ἐνέγκας μέρος τι παρὰ τοὺς πόδας τῶν ἀποστόλων ἔθηκεν. ³ εἶπεν δὲ ὁ Πέτρος· Ἀνανία, διὰ τί ἐπλήρωσεν ὁ σατανᾶς τὴν καρδίαν σου, ψεύσασθαί σε τὸ πνεῦμα τὸ ἅγιον καὶ νοσφίσασθαι ἀπὸ τῆς τιμῆς τοῦ χωρίου; ⁴ οὐχὶ μένον σοὶ ἔμενεν καὶ πραθὲν ἐν τῇ σῇ ἐξουσίᾳ ὑπῆρχεν; τί ὅτι ἔθου ἐν τῇ καρδίᾳ σου τὸ πρᾶγμα τοῦτο; οὐκ ἐψεύσω ἀνθρώποις ἀλλὰ τῷ θεῷ. ⁵ ἀκούων δὲ ὁ Ἀνανίας τοὺς λόγους τούτους πεσὼν ἐξέψυξεν, καὶ ἐγένετο φόβος μέγας ἐπὶ πάντας τοὺς ἀκούοντας. ⁶ ἀναστάντες δὲ οἱ νεώτεροι συνέστειλαν αὐτὸν καὶ ἐξενέγκαντες ἔθαψαν.

⁷ Ἐγένετο δὲ ὡς ὡρῶν τριῶν διάστημα καὶ ἡ γυνὴ αὐτοῦ μὴ εἰδυῖα τὸ γεγονὸς εἰσῆλθεν. ⁸ ἀπεκρίθη δὲ πρὸς αὐτὴν Πέτρος· εἰπέ μοι, εἰ τοσούτου τὸ χωρίον ἀπέδοσθε; ἡ δὲ εἶπεν· ναί, τοσούτου. ⁹ ὁ δὲ Πέτρος πρὸς αὐτήν· τί ὅτι συνεφωνήθη ὑμῖν πειράσαι τὸ πνεῦμα κυρίου; ἰδοὺ οἱ πόδες τῶν θαψάντων τὸν ἄνδρα σου ἐπὶ τῇ θύρᾳ καὶ ἐξοίσουσίν σε. ¹⁰ ἔπεσεν δὲ παραχρῆμα πρὸς τοὺς πόδας αὐτοῦ καὶ ἐξέψυξεν εἰσελθόντες δὲ οἱ νεανίσκοι εὗρον αὐτὴν νεκρὰν καὶ ἐξενέγκαντες· ἔθαψαν πρὸς τὸν ἄνδρα αὐτῆς, ¹¹ καὶ ἐγένετο φόβος μέγας ἐφ' ὅλην τὴν ἐκκλησίαν καὶ ἐπὶ πάντας τοὺς ἀκούοντας ταῦτα.

When Ananias and Sapphira are introduced, their names lack the article, suggesting that their introduction is part of the grounding of the discourse. At this point, Luke is setting the scene. The events recorded in verses 1–2 establish the background, which is necessary to understand latter events. These verses establish context. Thus, as background they are necessary. However, they are not the most place names.

In verse 3, Peter is marked with the article, suggesting greater prominence or salience. Contextually, this is the point where Peter confronts Ananias with his deception. When Ananias is identified by name in verse 5, his name is articular as well. This suggests that, for Luke, Peter's confrontation of Ananias and Ananias' subsequent death are meant to be seen as peaks in the narrative. His staging may be analogous to the stage director who instructs actors to step to the front of the stage to deliver their lines or perform their actions. In verse 8, Peter's name lacks the article, but this changes in verse 9 when, as before, he confronts Sapphira for sharing in her husband's deception. This may again be interpreted as another peak or front stage moment.

Taking these factors into consideration, the interpreter should look to these stage front occurrences to identify salient elements. The lines delivered in these instances and the actions that take place are decisive moments that the author, acting as stage director, has deliberately chosen to highlight. He has recorded this story for a reason and his characterization choices provide insight into the significance, the message, he attached to the story, especially at certain decisive points.

Though not a direct participant in the narrative, Satan is also marked with the article, making him more salient. This may be have been motivated by a desire to draw attention to the fact that the act of deception perpetrated by Ananias and Sapphira is to be interpreted a direct association with the work of Satan. This adds greater weight to the wickedness of their motives and activity in this matter.

Exegetically, our analysis of the text should focus on these instances of confrontation over the matter of deception as key moments, which the author himself has identified as salient. While the sale of the field and the conspiracy are necessary for setting the scene, the reader is meant to draw meaning from the moments of confrontation for deception and subsequent judgment. It is possible that the author sees an analogue in the actions of Nadab and Abihu, recorded in Lev 10:1–11. If so, we may conclude that Luke uses this episode to draw a parallel between the new community (the Church) and the old one (Israel). For both, holiness before God is a necessary characteristic. Violation of this results in swift and severe judgment.

4.5 1 Timothy 4:11–14

In this passage, we observe two clusters of elements, the first are non-articular, the second articular. A discourse interpretation based on the characterization of these two groupings will provide insight into what is uppermost in the writer's mind.

(11)[11] Παράγγελλε ταῦτα καὶ δίδασκε. [12] Μηδείς σου τῆς νεότητος καταφρονείτω, ἀλλὰ τύπος γίνου τῶν πιστῶν ἐν λόγῳ, ἐν ἀναστροφῇ, ἐν ἀγάπῃ, ἐν πίστει, ἐν ἁγνείᾳ. [13] ἕως ἔρχομαι πρόσεχε τῇ ἀναγνώσει, τῇ παρακλήσει, τῇ διδασκαλίᾳ. [14] μὴ ἀμέλει τοῦ ἐν σοὶ χαρίσματος, ὃ ἐδόθη σοι διὰ προφητείας μετὰ ἐπιθέσεως τῶν χειρῶν τοῦ πρεσβυτερίου.

The first, non-articular cluster is observed in verse 12. Timothy is to be an example to the believers ἐν λόγῳ, ἐν ἀναστροφῇ, ἐν ἀγάπῃ, ἐν πίστει, ἐν ἁγνείᾳ. A discourse reading based on the theory outlined above must conclude that, since these elements are characterized as abstract, they must be interpreted as a part of the grounding of the discourse, they are less salient. Initially, such an interpretation will likely face resistance since many would assume that these characteristics are, by their very nature, too important to be considered less salient. However, it must be remembered that discourse salience is not a matter of the perceived value or importance of the elements themselves. It is rather a matter of the role they play in the discourse.

The second, articular cluster is observed in verse 13, where Paul instructs Timothy to give attention τῇ ἀναγνώσει, τῇ παρακλήσει, τῇ διδασκαλίᾳ. The choice to characterize these elements as concrete indicates that the author considers them more salient, that these elements represent what is uppermost in his mind. At this point, it is imperative that we take into account the first clause of this section, found in verse 11. Paul instructs Timothy παράγγελλε ταῦτα καὶ δίδασκε. These two imperatives provide priming for what follows, which is a discourse on instruction and teaching. Thus, the imperatives combined with the second cluster serve to identify what is uppermost in the writer's mind. The present discourse is primarily concerned with corporate worship and Timothy's responsibilities in these gatherings. This interpretation is affirmed again in verse 16 were the author writes, ἔπεχε σεαυτῷ καὶ τῇ διδασκαλίᾳ. Once again we note that articular τῇ διδασκαλίᾳ.

There is a potential obstacle to Timothy's success in these matters, σου τῆς νεότητος. By characterizing this element as concrete, the author indicates that it too is more salient. The solution to this is for Timothy to be an example, τύπος, which is non-articular. This, along with the traits that are to characterize Timothy's example, is all a part of the grounding of the discourse. They are necessary in that they provide the ground against which the other elements are seen. However, they are not the point of the discourse. Based on our analysis, we must conclude that, while the character traits Timothy is to exemplify are certainly important, in terms of the present discourse, what is uppermost in Paul's mind is Timothy's execution of his duties relating to the service of teaching.

4.6 Conclusion

I have argued that the Greek article has been largely misunderstood due to faulty categorization as a demonstrative, as a determiner, combined with faulty methodology that tries to account for its function by means of analogy with the English definite article. In addition to this, and due largely to it, the discourse function of the Greek article has not been fully appreciated. By combining a functional grammatical description of the Greek article with a corresponding functional discourse description we are able to engage in a robust linguistic analysis of articular and non-articular structures that yields valuable exegetical insights.

References

Halliday, M. A. K. 2013. *An introduction to functional grammar.* Third edition. Revised by Christian M. I. M. Matthiessen. Abingdon, UK: Routledge.

[Read-]Heimerdinger, Jenny, and Stephen H. Levinsohn. 1992. The use of the definite article before names of people in the Greek text of Acts with particular reference to Codex Bezae. *Filología Neotestamentaria* 5: 15–44.

Middleton, Thomas Fanshaw. 1828. *The doctrine of the Greek article applied to the criticism and the illustration of the New Testament.* Eugene, OR: Wipf and Stock.

Nolland, John. 2005. *The Gospel of Matthew: A commentary on the Greek text.* The New International Greek Testament Commentary. Grand Rapids, MI: Eerdmans.

Peters, Ronald D. 2014. *The Greek article: A functional grammar of ὁ-items in the Greek New Testament with special emphasis on the Greek article.* Linguistic Biblical Studies 9. Leiden: Brill.

Wallace, Stephen. 1982. Figure and ground: The interrelationships of linguistic categories. In Paul J. Hopper (ed.), *Tense-aspect: Between semantics and pragmatics,* 201–223. Amsterdam: John Benjamins.

5

The Use of the Greek Article in 1 Peter: A Case Study

Stephen H. Levinsohn and Mark Dubis

5.1 Preliminaries

The year 2013 saw a plethora of material on the article in New Testament Greek. Not only was it the theme of a Greek Language and Exegesis session of the Evangelical Theological Society (ETS) in November, but the year also saw the completion of two doctoral dissertations on the topic: Stephen Janssen's "The Greek Article in Pauline Literature: Traditional Grammar and Discourse Perspectives" at Dallas Theological Seminary and Ronald D. Peters' "The Greek Article: A Functional Grammar of ὁ-items in the Greek New Testament with Special Emphasis on the Greek Article" at McMaster University.[1]

The consensus today is that the presence of the article has to do with cognitive identifiability rather than definiteness. Runge (chapter 6 in this volume) describes the grammaticalization path by which articles are believed to develop in a language, as originally hypothesized by Joseph Greenberg (1978:47–82). Runge states, "Demonstratives seem to be the 'stem cells'

---

[1] Now published as *The Greek Article: A Functional Grammar of ὁ-items in the Greek New Testament with Special Emphasis on the Greek Article* (Peters 2014).

from which adnominals like articles and relative pronouns arise" (§6.1.1 in this volume). Stage I in the development involves the article becoming a marker of definiteness rather than solely referring to items in the real world. Stage II sees a bleaching of this function so that the article indicates simply that the referent is "cognitively identifiable." By Stage III, its use has spread to new contexts, where it functions as a marker of nominalization (e.g. in participial and infinitival clauses) (Runge, §6.1.1).[2]

A significant part of Peters' monograph is devoted to arguing that the Greek article should be related more to the relative pronoun than to demonstratives (2014:69–178), and the grammaticalization path described by Runge explains why this might be so: both articles and relative pronouns appear to have reached Stage II through a similar bleaching process.

Runge explains the difference between definiteness and identifiability as follows: "Definiteness is a binary grammatical category; something is either definite or not. Identifiability is a cognitive category concerned with the degree of shared knowledge between a speaker and a hearer. There are many instances where a grammatically indefinite entity is cognitively identifiable" (Runge, §6.1.1.1). In Luke 8:8, for instance, the intended referent of Ὁ ἔχων ὦτα ἀκούειν[3] is grammatically indefinite (it does not refer to a specific person), but it is cognitively identifiable from the context as being anyone who has just heard what was said.

In his discussion of the difference between the English definite article and the Greek article, Peters claims that "while the English definite article assumes information that both the speaker and recipient share in common, the Greek article orients this information to the speaker" (2014:271). We dispute this claim. Lambrecht insists that identifiability "has to do with a speaker's assessment of whether a discourse representation of a particular referent is already stored in the hearer's mind or not" (1994:76). In other words, identifiability is oriented to the hearer instead of the speaker. Further, the presence of the article in Greek may be likened to an instruction from the speaker or writer (hereafter, the author) to the hearers or readers (hereafter, the recipients) to process the information provided in such a way that the identity of the referent is unambiguous.[4]

---

[2] Peters (2014:69) also writes that, by the Koine period, "the article and relative pronoun had both separated themselves from the historic demonstrative," though he does not suggest that, at an earlier stage in its development, the article might have been a marker of definiteness.

[3] Throughout this paper, the Greek text is taken from the *Nestle-Aland Novum Testamentum Graece* (28th rev. ed.; Münster: Institute for New Testament Textual Research, 2013). Peters (2014:130) points out that the parallel passage in Mark 4:9 has a relative pronoun instead of the article.

[4] Similarly, the presence of the definite article in English may be likened to an instruction from the author to the recipients to process the information provided in such a way that the referent is definite.

How is the recipient to unambiguously identify the referent that the author has in mind? Lambrecht's list includes anaphora, deixis and encyclopedic knowledge, among others (Lambrecht 1994:87–92). Anaphoric reference is a form of cohesion (Thompson 2004:181), whereas Peters' desire to orient the Greek article exclusively to the speaker leads him to imply that it is not a marker of cohesion (Peters 2014:233).

Runge distinguishes the prototypical function of the article with "identifiable noun phrases" from less prototypical uses with nominalized forms such as infinitives and participles (Runge, §6.1.2). These latter entities are still cognitively identifiable but are "less likely to have a discourse anaphor" (Runge, §6.2.1.1).[5] With such forms, identifiability is "more likely to derive from encyclopedic knowledge or pragmatic bootstrapping" (Runge, §6.2.1.1). So, although Peters cites Matt 13:3 (ἰδοὺ ἐξῆλθεν ὁ σπείρων τοῦ σπείρειν) as evidence that "the article does not indicate to the recipients, 'You know who I am talking about' (Peters 2014:194)," it follows from Runge's prediction that the identifiability of participial ὁ σπείρων will rather derive from the encyclopedic knowledge shared by speaker and audience as to how sowers of that period sowed their seed.[6]

Notwithstanding the above differences, there is a consensus among the authors cited that the Greek article indicates that the referent is identifiable. As such, it is the marked member of a pair, in opposition to the absence of the article. This marking may be expressed as +Identifiable.

At this point, it is appropriate to remind the reader that "when a certain marker is present, the feature implied by the marker is present. However, when the marker is absent, nothing is said about the presence or absence of the feature. The sentence is simply unmarked for that feature. In other words, it is not necessarily true that the function of the unmarked form is the opposite of that of the marked form" (Levinsohn 2000:ix). In the case of Greek, this means that, whereas entities with the article such as ὁ Ἰησοῦς are +Identifiable, it does not follow that the absence of the article (Ἰησοῦς) means that the referent is not identifiable.

Because the Greek article is the marked member of a "privative opposition" (Crystal 1991:307), Peters follows Porter in assigning prominence to that member,[7] which means that he considers the article to be both +Identifiable and +Salient (Peters 2014:272). Such a claim is linguistically suspect, as one would not expect two features to distinguish the members of

---

[5] It appears that this proviso is unnecessary for 1 Peter. In §5.3.4, for instance, we argue that the presence of the article with infinitives instructs the recipients to relate them to something in the prior context (a "discourse anaphor").

[6] "[T]he tale Jesus narrates seems quite ordinary as it provides the beginning, middle, and end of the yearly cycle experienced by farmers" (Green 1997:324).

[7] "Markedness is one of the most important means by which prominence is established for a given element" (Porter 2009:56).

a closed set with only two members. This is because underspecification is a characteristic of natural languages.[8]

Furthermore, Runge demonstrates that Porter has confused symmetrical and asymmetrical markedness and "derives a symmetrical theoretical framework of markedness from their asymmetrical claims."[9] This means that, although the presence versus absence of the article may be presented as a privative opposition, it does not follow that the marked member will be more prominent than the unmarked member.

Finally, consider the presence versus absence of the article with proper names in Acts 15:39–40 (ἐγένετο δὲ παροξυσμὸς ὥστε ἀποχωρισθῆναι αὐτοὺς ἀπ᾽ ἀλλήλων, τόν τε Βαρναβᾶν παραλαβόντα τὸν Μᾶρκον ἐκπλεῦσαι εἰς Κύπρον, Παῦλος δὲ ἐπιλεξάμενος Σιλᾶν ἐξῆλθεν παραδοθεὶς τῇ χάριτι τοῦ κυρίου ὑπὸ τῶν ἀδελφῶν). The references to Barnabas and Mark are articular at the point at which they cease to be salient, whereas the references to Paul and Silas, who continue to be salient, are anarthrous. The presence of the article therefore cannot indicate that the referent is salient (Levinsohn 2000:156–157).

Levinsohn has argued elsewhere for the importance of "distinguishing between the 'meaning' of a [feature], which remains basically unchanged, and the 'overtones' associated with it, which vary with the context," as this "results in an approach to prominence that is intuitively more satisfying than one in which a fixed degree of prominence" is assigned to each feature (Levinsohn 2010:170). We return to this topic in the next section.

5.2 Thematic prominence (salience) versus focal prominence

Any discussion of the Greek article needs to account not only for its presence but also for those occasions when an entity is identifiable yet the reference to it is anarthrous. We now consider three circumstances when an anarthrous reference to an identifiable entity is found.

- Anarthrous references to identifiable entities at the beginning of a letter.

  For example, 1 Pet 1:1–2 (Πέτρος ἀπόστολος Ἰησοῦ Χριστοῦ ἐκλεκτοῖς παρεπιδήμοις διασπορᾶς Πόντου, Γαλατίας, Καππαδοκίας, Ἀσίας καὶ Βιθυνίας, κατὰ πρόγνωσιν θεοῦ πατρὸς ἐν ἁγιασμῷ πνεύματος εἰς ὑπακοὴν καὶ ῥαντισμὸν αἵματος Ἰησοῦ Χριστοῦ) contains anarthrous references to God and to the Holy Spirit even though both are cognitively identifiable to both Peter and the recipients of the letter.

---

[8] See Rooryck 1994:208.

[9] "Asymmetrical markedness *organizes* sets of data based on the presence or absence of certain qualities, i.e. linguistic features. Symmetrical markedness *ranks* a set based on the quantity of a particular shared feature, e.g. semantic weight or prominence" (Runge 2016).

- Anarthrous references to named participants or other entities, in a passage in which they have already been referred to with the article.

  For example, in the exchange between Cornelius and Peter that is recorded in Acts 10:24–43, articular references to Cornelius (24b, 25b, 30) and Peter (25a, 26) are followed by an anarthrous reference to Peter (34) in the introduction to the key speech of 10:34–43.[10]

- Instances of Colwell's construction in which "A definite predicate nominative ... does not have the article when it precedes the verb" even though it has it when it follows the verb (Colwell 1933:13).

  In this regard, John 1:49 (Ῥαββί, σὺ εἶ ὁ υἱὸς τοῦ θεοῦ, σὺ βασιλεὺς εἶ τοῦ Ἰσραήλ NA28) is particularly noteworthy, because of the variant σὺ εἶ ὁ βασιλεὺς τοῦ Ἰσραήλ.

  We discuss these three circumstances in turn.

5.2.1 Anarthrous references to identifiable entities at the beginning of a letter

Although Peters insists that the orientation of the Greek article is with respect to the speaker/writer rather than the recipients,[11] the absence of the article at the beginning of a letter such as 1 Peter suggests that the writer assumes that the mental representation of the recipients vis-à-vis the contents of the letter is empty (a *tabula rasa*).[12] It is not the case, though, that every reference to an entity at the beginning of a letter is anarthrous. For example, in 1 Thess 1:1 (Παῦλος καὶ Σιλουανὸς καὶ Τιμόθεος τῇ ἐκκλησίᾳ Θεσσαλονικέων ἐν θεῷ πατρὶ καὶ κυρίῳ Ἰησοῦ Χριστῷ), the reference to the gathering of the Thessalonians (τῇ ἐκκλησίᾳ Θεσσαλονικέων) is articular. This suggests that Paul, Silvanus and Timothy envisage the gathering of Thessalonians as something that is happening when the letter is to be read, and so identifiable as far as the Thessalonians are concerned.[13]

---

[10] For discussion of this example, see Heimerdinger and Levinsohn 1992:28, and Levinsohn 2000:§8.3.

[11] Contrast Janssen 2013:139: "identifiability on the part of the reader: article is generally used."

[12] When writers or addressees are identified by name at the beginning of a NT letter, the reference is always anarthrous.

[13] The reference to the Thessalonians is anarthrous because the writers assume simply that *some* Thessalonians will be present. When writers or addressees are identified with a common noun at the beginning of a NT letter, then the article is usually present. In 2 John 1 and 3 John 1, for instance, Ὁ πρεσβύτερος is articular because the author expects the recipients to be able to identify "the elder" from their encyclopedic knowledge of who would be writing such a letter to them. As Jackman (1988:175) notes, "The definite form of the title ('the elder') shows that it was quite sufficient to identify the author to his readers."

In line with the above observations, Heimerdinger and Levinsohn proposed as a default rule that references by name to participants who are being activated are anarthrous, whereas subsequent references are articular (Heimerdinger and Levinsohn 1992:18; Levinsohn 2000:150). The same principle can be proposed as a default rule for all entities.

Exceptions to the above default rule are significant and, particularly when a subsequent reference to an identifiable entity is anarthrous, may well give prominence to the entity (see the following sections).

5.2.2 Anarthrous references to active, identifiable entities that are thematic

Levinsohn suggested that, because subsequent reference to active participants are normally articular, "[a]narthrous references to active participants are therefore of particular significance. In particular, they make the participant and/or his or her initiative or speech PROMINENT, because of its particular importance" (Levinsohn 2000:155–156).[14] So the anarthrous reference to Peter in Acts 10:34 gives prominence to his following speech, in contrast to the previous speeches of his conversation with Cornelius.

In her discussion of prominence, Kathleen Callow distinguishes between THEMATIC PROMINENCE ("what I'm talking about") and FOCAL PROMINENCE (prominence given to constituents of the comment about a propositional topic) (Callow 1974:52). Such a distinction parallels Halliday's division of sentences into THEME and RHEME (Halliday 2004:64) and recognizes the potential for both the theme (the topical subject) and a constituent of the rheme (the "dominant focal element") (Heimerdinger 1999:167) to be prominent.[15]

So, in Acts 10:34, the anarthrous reference to Peter marks him as thematically prominent or "salient," where "[s]alience has to do with attention being drawn to a specific participant" (Heimerdinger and Levinsohn 1992:20). Other devices that NT Greek uses for thematic prominence include the intensive pronoun αὐτός "to emphasize identity" (Dana and Mantey 1927:129), the proximal demonstrative οὗτος (Levinsohn 2009:210–212) and "the postposing of a topical subject when the event concerned is in chronological sequence with the last one described" (Levinsohn 2014b:1). The article, in contrast, does not give thematic prominence to its referent, since the default way of referring to a topical subject is with the article (see §5.2.1).[16]

---

[14] See also Heimerdinger and Levinsohn 1992:23.

[15] Contrast Peters' (2014:230) analysis of Matt 3:4c (ἡ δὲ τροφὴ ἦν αὐτοῦ ἀκρίδες καὶ μέλι ἄγριον) which classifies John's food as "more salient, while the specific things that he ate are less salient."

[16] Of the 30 nominal subjects in 1 Peter (excluding those found in quotes from the LXX), 21 are articular, 7 are anarthrous, and 2 have articular and anarthrous

5.2.3 Anarthrous references to active, identifiable constituents that are focal

Whereas anarthrous references to topical subjects make them thematically prominent, Colwell's construction concerns anarthrous references to active, identifiable constituents of the predicate, that is, to focal constituents. In John 1:49, the topical subject (theme) is σύ, while the predicates are εἶ ὁ υἱὸς τοῦ θεοῦ (49a) and βασιλεὺς εἶ τοῦ Ἰσραήλ (49b) or, if the variant is followed, εἶ ὁ βασιλεὺς τοῦ Ἰσραήλ. As Colwell notes, when the predicate nominative precedes the verb, it is often anarthrous (Colwell 1933:13).

The placement of focal constituents before the verb is captured in Simon Dik's template for languages such as NT Greek that often place topical subjects before the verb in narrative (Dik 1989:363). His template is: P1 P2 V X, where

- position 1 (P1) can be occupied by one or more TOPIC constituents,[17]
- position 2 (P2) can be occupied by a FOCUS constituent,
- V is the verb, and
- X is any other constituent. (Levinsohn 2006:3)[18]

Placing a focal constituent in P2 gives it prominence and, if the entity concerned is active and identifiable, the omission of the article adds to that prominence.

So, in John 1:49b, the articular variant σὺ εἶ ὁ βασιλεὺς τοῦ Ἰσραήλ suggests that βασιλεὺς τοῦ Ἰσραήλ is active and identifiable.[19] Placing βασιλεὺς before the verb (σὺ βασιλεὺς εἶ τοῦ Ἰσραήλ) gives it prominence and omitting the article adds to that prominence.

---

variants. We find no instance in 1 Peter in which the article has been omitted in order to mark the referent as thematically prominent.

[17] The TOPIC of a clause or sentence is usually its subject, and is the constituent about which a comment is made (Levinsohn 2000:95). Compare the terms SUBJECT – PREDICATE in traditional grammar.

[18] The focus is "the information in the sentence that is assumed by the speaker not to be shared by him [or her] and the hearer" (Jackendoff 1972:230). In a sentence that makes a comment about a topic, the focus is all the information about the topic that is "new" as far as the immediate context is concerned.

[19] It seems unlikely that the article with ὁ υἱὸς τοῦ θεοῦ or the variant ὁ βασιλεὺς τοῦ Ἰσραήλ relates the expressions to something said during the conversation between Jesus and Nathanael. Rather, Philip's reference to Jesus in John 1:45 as ὃν ἔγραψεν Μωϋσῆς ἐν τῷ νόμῳ καὶ οἱ προφῆται εὑρήκαμεν had probably made them accessible to Nathanael's mind. Further evidence that the expressions are to be related back to the conversation between Philip and Nathanael is Jesus' use of the article in 1:48 with the infinitival expression πρὸ τοῦ σε Φίλιππον φωνῆσαι ὄντα ὑπὸ τὴν συκῆν to refer to that occasion (articular infinitives are discussed in §5.3.4).

5.3 Application to 1 Peter

We now discuss the implications of the presence versus absence of the article in different environments in 1 Peter. We begin with a verse-by-verse scrutiny of its use and non-use with nominals and adjectivals[20] in 1:3–12. We then examine its use and non-use with all instances of πνεῦμα and Χριστός in the letter, before concluding with a brief discussion of articular infinitivals.

5.3.1 1 Peter 1:3–12

Although space prohibits walking verse by verse through the entire letter of 1 Peter, it will be beneficial to work through a selected passage in detail. The opening of the book is especially appropriate since many entities are activated within the first dozen verses.

In order to facilitate the following discussion, we have constructed a diagram of the text of 1 Pet 1:1–12 (see table 5.1). Curly brackets appear around phrases, whether noun phrases (e.g. ἐκλεκτοῖς παρεπιδήμοις in 1b) or adjectival phrases (e.g. τοὺς ἐν δυνάμει θεοῦ φρουρουμένους in 5a).[21] We have placed the null symbol (ø) in front of any nominal or adjectival that appears without the article (e.g. Πέτρος in 1a). We have also underlined phrases that have the article, excluding modifiers other than the article (e.g. τῆς...χάριτος in 10b). Doubled curly brackets indicate that one phrase appears embedded within another (see 3b).

Table 5.1. 1 Peter 1:1–12

Verse	Biblical Text
1:1a	ø Πέτρος ø ἀπόστολος ø {Ἰησοῦ Χριστοῦ}
1:1b	ø {ἐκλεκτοῖς παρεπιδήμοις} ø διασπορᾶς
1:1c	ø Πόντου, ø Γαλατίας, ø Καππαδοκίας, ø Ἀσίας καὶ ø Βιθυνίας
1:2a	κατὰ ø πρόγνωσιν ø θεοῦ ø πατρὸς
1:2b	ἐν ø ἁγιασμῷ ø πνεύματος
1:2c	εἰς ø ὑπακοὴν καὶ ø ῥαντισμὸν ø αἵματος ø {Ἰησοῦ Χριστοῦ}
1:2d	ø χάρις ὑμῖν καὶ ø εἰρήνη πληθυνθείη.
1:3a	ø Εὐλογητὸς {ὁ θεὸς καὶ πατὴρ} {τοῦ κυρίου} ἡμῶν ø {Ἰησοῦ Χριστοῦ}

---

[20] Throughout this chapter, we use the label NOMINAL to refer to both individual nouns and noun phrases. Similarly, we use the label ADJECTIVAL to refer to both individual adjectives and adjectival phrases, and the label INFINITIVAL to refer to both individual infinitives and infinitival phrases or clauses.

[21] PHRASE in this paper always refers to a related group of words and never to a single word.

1:3b	{{ὁ κατὰ {τὸ πολὺ αὐτοῦ ἔλεος} ἀναγεννήσας}} ἡμᾶς
1:3c	εἰς ø {ἐλπίδα ζῶσαν}
1:3d	δι' ø ἀναστάσεως ø {Ἰησοῦ Χριστοῦ} ἐκ ø νεκρῶν,
1:4	εἰς ø {κληρονομίαν ἄφθαρτον καὶ ἀμίαντον καὶ ἀμάραντον τετηρημένην ἐν ø οὐρανοῖς εἰς ὑμᾶς}
1:5a	{τοὺς ἐν ø δυνάμει ø θεοῦ φρουρουμένους} διὰ ø πίστεως
1:5b	εἰς ø {σωτηρίαν ἑτοίμην ἀποκαλυφθῆναι} ἐν ø {καιρῷ ἐσχάτῳ}
1:6a	ἐν ᾧ ἀγαλλιᾶσθε,
1:6b	ὀλίγον ἄρτι, εἰ δέον ἐστίν, λυπηθέντας ἐν ø {ποικίλοις πειρασμοῖς},
1:7a	ἵνα {τὸ δοκίμιον} ὑμῶν {τῆς πίστεως}
1:7b	ø {πολυτιμότερον ø χρυσίου}
1:7c	{τοῦ ἀπολλυμένου, διὰ ø πυρὸς δὲ δοκιμαζομένου}
1:7d	εὑρεθῇ εἰς ø ἔπαινον καὶ ø δόξαν καὶ ø τιμὴν
1:7e	ἐν ø ἀποκαλύψει ø {Ἰησοῦ Χριστοῦ}
1:8a	ὃν οὐκ ἰδόντες ἀγαπᾶτε,
1:8b	εἰς ὃν ἄρτι μὴ ὁρῶντες, πιστεύοντες δὲ ἀγαλλιᾶσθε
1:8c	ø {χαρᾷ ἀνεκλαλήτῳ καὶ δεδοξασμένῃ}
1:9a	κομιζόμενοι {τὸ τέλος} {τῆς πίστεως} ὑμῶν
1:9b	ø σωτηρίαν ø ψυχῶν.
1:10a	περὶ ἧς σωτηρίας ἐξεζήτησαν καὶ ἐξηραύνησαν ø προφῆται
1:10b	{{οἱ περὶ {τῆς εἰς ὑμᾶς χάριτος} προφητεύσαντες}}
1:11a	ἐραυνῶντες
1:11b	εἰς τίνα ἢ ø {ποῖον καιρὸν} ἐδήλου {τὸ ἐν αὐτοῖς πνεῦμα} ø Χριστοῦ
1:11c	προμαρτυρόμενον {τὰ εἰς ø Χριστὸν παθήματα}
1:11d	καὶ {τὰς μετὰ ταῦτα δόξας}.
1:12a	οἷς ἀπεκαλύφθη ὅτι οὐχ ἑαυτοῖς, ὑμῖν δὲ διηκόνουν αὐτά,
1:12b	ἃ νῦν ἀνηγγέλη ὑμῖν διὰ {τῶν εὐαγγελισαμένων} ὑμᾶς
1:12c	ἐν ø {πνεύματι ἁγίῳ ἀποσταλέντι ἀπ' ø οὐρανοῦ}
1:12d	εἰς ἃ ἐπιθυμοῦσιν ø ἄγγελοι παρακύψαι.

In order to simplify our presentation, we analyze the use and non-use of the article in 1 Pet 1:1–12 in three stages. First, we discuss the use of the article with nominals. Second, we turn our attention to the non-use of the article with nominals. Finally, we address both the use and non-use of the article with adjectivals.[22]

5.3.1.1 Use of the article with nominals

The first article in 1 Pet 1:1–12 appears in 3a in the nominal ὁ θεὸς καὶ πατήρ, where the article does double duty to modify both θεὸς and πατήρ. Both of these entities have already been activated in the letter (see the anarthrous mention of God the Father in 2a in the phrase κατὰ πρόγνωσιν θεοῦ πατρός), so it is predictable that the subsequent mention of both θεός and πατήρ in 3a would be articular.

Somewhat different is the articular appearance of τοῦ κυρίου in 3a since, unlike θεός and πατήρ, the term κύριος has not yet appeared in the letter. The article attached to κυρίου instructs the recipients to treat κύριος as identifiable, and the first suitable referent in the prior context[23] is Ἰησοῦ Χριστοῦ, which last appeared in 2c.[24] Another way of describing what is happening here is that the writer regards κύριος as accessible[25] to the recipients because of the prior mention of Ἰησοῦ Χριστοῦ. The presence of an article with a nominal does not require the exact same nominal to have already appeared. If the same nominal does appear earlier with the same referent, it is easy to see what the article is pointing to. Otherwise, we must carefully consider the preceding literary context (or perhaps the recipients' situational context) to understand what the article instructs the recipients to relate the nominal to.

The nominal τὸ...ἔλεος in 3b is articular, even though this is the first time that ἔλεος has appeared in 1 Peter. Again, the article is the author's way of instructing the recipients to relate ἔλεος to something in the prior context. To discern what it is that activated ἔλεος 'mercy', we note that this term connotes both a person's distress and the positive action of someone else who moves to alleviate the first person's distress. Already the letter has metaphorically identified the recipients as marginalized 'exiles' who are in the distressing circumstance of being 'scattered' in an alien land (1b). Positively, though, the recipients have been 'chosen' (ἐκλεκτοῖς) according

---

[22] For an analysis of other elements of the syntax of 1 Pet 1:1–12, see Dubis 2010:1–22.

[23] Here and in what follows, "prior context" refers to the prior *literary* context (the reference earlier in 1 Peter to which the article is to be related).

[24] This view of the article corresponds with the assertion of Relevance Theory that the first referent that is judged to be OPTIMALLY RELEVANT is the one that will be taken as the intended referent: "Stop when your expectations of relevance are satisfied" (Wilson et al. 2012:282).

[25] "[W]hen an entity is introduced, other items that the culture associates with the entity are also **accessed**.... What is accessed is **culture specific**. In Biblical Jewish culture, for instance, mention of a town such as *Antioch in Pisidia* (Acts 13:14) accesses *the synagogue*, which in turn makes *the officials of the synagogue* accessible (15)." (Levinsohn 2015:141)

to God the Father's foreknowledge (1b–2a). Since this expression of the merciful action of God the Father has already been mentioned, it is not surprising that 3b regards the mercy of God the Father, now expressed in his regenerating work, to already be accessible to the recipients.

The article is next used with δοκίμιον in 7a, thereby instructing the recipients to relate δοκίμιον to something in the prior context. Although this is the first use of δοκίμιον in 1 Peter, we need look no further than πειρασμοῖς in 6b to explain the article. The terms δοκίμιον and πειρασμός and their cognates frequently appear together in contexts of testing/assaying (e.g. 2 Cor 13:5; Heb 3:9; Jas 1:12). So it is not surprising that δοκίμιον (which refers to that which emerges authenticated from a metallurgical test, here metaphorically identified with the recipients' faith) can be related to the preceding use of πειρασμός, which refers to the 'tests' that the recipients have experienced because of their Christian identity.[26]

Articular τῆς πίστεως in 7a is easily analyzed since this noun was activated (anarthrously) in 5a and both uses of πίστις have the same referent. We can say the same for the articular reappearance of this noun in 9a—now that the recipients' faith is firmly established information, the use of the article in the phrase τῆς πίστεως is expected. The head noun of τῆς πίστεως is the also articular τὸ τέλος ("end, outcome"). The article instructs the recipients to relate τέλος to something in the prior context. Since verse 7 has already expressed the author's desire that the recipients' faith might result in their acclamation at the Parousia (ἵνα τὸ δοκίμιον ὑμῶν τῆς πίστεως... εὑρεθῇ εἰς ἔπαινον καὶ δόξαν καὶ τιμὴν ἐν ἀποκαλύψει Ἰησοῦ Χριστοῦ), the article on τέλος likely instructs the recipients to relate the 'outcome' of faith in 9a to the description in verse 7 of what their faith will lead to at the second coming of Christ (which is further related to their 'salvation' in the following appositive). In other words, the eschatological 'outcome' of the recipients' faith should already be accessible to the recipients because of the contents of verse 7.

The next articular noun is τῆς...χάριτος in 10b. The noun χάρις appeared in the letter opening (see the anarthrous occurrence χάρις ὑμῖν καὶ εἰρήνη πληθυνθείη in 2d), but it seems unlikely that τῆς...χάριτος in 10b is activated by that initial (and more generic) use. Instead, the articular expression in 10b seems more likely to relate to the various gracious manifestations of God's favor mentioned in verses 3–9 (e.g. their regeneration in 3, enduring inheritance in 4, divine protection in 5a, coming acclamation in 7, and salvation in 5b and 9). In other words, when the writer places an article on χάριτος in 10b, he is instructing his recipients to associate this 'grace' or 'gift' with something that is readily identifiable, and the most suitable referent is the various facets of God's salvation just elaborated upon in verses 3–9.

Verse 11b has an articular mention of the Spirit (τὸ...πνεῦμα), which is not surprising since the Spirit of God was introduced (anarthrously) in 2b.

---

[26] For further discussion of the meaning of δοκίμιον, see Dubis 2002:12.

Next in 11c and 11d we have the articular use of the paired expressions τὰ...παθήματα and τὰς...δόξας. Some commentators view this as an exclusive reference to Jesus' passion and resurrection/exaltation (Goppelt 1993:100; Davids 1990:63). If this is the correct interpretation, then the 'sufferings' (τὰ...παθήματα) of Jesus would be accessible to the recipients because of the reference to Jesus' blood in 2c, and the 'glories' (τὰς...δόξας) of Jesus could well be accessible because of the reference to Jesus' resurrection in 3d. The plural number of παθήματα and δόξας, however, raises questions as to whether the referent of this pair might extend beyond Jesus to include the 'sufferings' and 'glories' of those united to him. Indeed, the force of the entire eulogy section in 1:3–12 is to establish the suffering/glory theme that will characterize the rest of 1 Peter. Already the preceding verses have established both the recipients' current sufferings (5a, 6b–7c) and their future glories, in which they have already begun to share (3b–4, 5b, 7d–e, 9a–b). Given the prominence of this theme in the preceding verses, it is likely that the articles modifying τὰ...παθήματα and τὰς...δόξας are pointing to these sufferings and glories in the recipients' experience, which they undergo in union with Christ (who has established this paradigm in his own experience). This understanding corresponds to a macrolevel theme of the OT prophets, namely, that after Israel's 'sufferings', Israel will experience 'glory' (or to put a finer point on it, after exile, they will experience a glorious return from exile). Indeed, 1 Peter begins with the recipients' identity as 'exiles' (ἐκλεκτοῖς παρεπιδήμοις διασπορᾶς in 1b–c) and continues to build on this motif throughout the book, suggesting that the long-awaited return from exile has now begun in Christ (e.g. the use of Isaiah 40 in 1:24–25).[27]

The final articular nominal in 1:1–12 appears in 12b with τῶν εὐαγγελισαμένων ὑμᾶς ('the ones who announced the good news to you'). We offer two explanations for the presence of the article. It may instruct the recipients to relate those who evangelized them to something in the prior context. Thus the article in τῶν εὐαγγελισαμένων ὑμᾶς may make a connection between the description of the recipients' salvific blessings in 1b–12a and the evangelists whose gospel message enabled the recipients to enter into those blessings. Or to put it another way, the reference to the evangelists who first opened the door to the recipients' Christian faith may be accessible because of the description in 1b–12a of the results of the recipients' Christian faith. Alternatively, the article may be present because the author assumes that the different groups of recipients across Asia Minor will be able to identify the various referents of τῶν εὐαγγελισαμένων ὑμᾶς from their extra-linguistic knowledge of who

---

[27] For a detailed defense of this identification of τὰ...παθήματα and τὰς...δόξας in 11c–d, see Dubis 2002:110–117. On the restoration from exile theme in 1 Peter, see especially Dubis 2002, chapter 3.

evangelized them, even though the author himself would not necessarily be able to do so.

5.3.1.2 Non-use of the article with nominals

We now discuss nominals that do not appear with the article. We have already indicated that it is common for a Greek author to initially activate a referent via an anarthrous noun. So, as already noted in section 5.2.1, it is not surprising that we do not find a single article in the first two verses of 1 Peter. That is, of the twenty-one nominals that appear in 1:1–2, none of them bear the article.[28] All of these entities appear anarthrously in order to activate them in the recipients' minds. Thereafter we expect that any references to these same entities will be articular unless they are marked as focally prominent.[29]

None of the anarthrous nouns in 1:3–4 (with the exception of the formulaic Ἰησοῦ Χριστοῦ) have been mentioned earlier in the book. So, again, it is not surprising that ἐλπίδα in 3c, ἀναστάσεως and νεκρῶν in 3d, and κληρονομίαν and οὐρανοῖς in 4 are all anarthrous. The author is not instructing the recipients to relate these entities to something in the prior context. Instead, these entities are presented as altogether new.

In 1:5 we find some more anarthrous nouns that have not previously appeared in 1 Peter: δυνάμει and πίστεως in 5a and σωτηρίαν and καιρῷ ἐσχάτῳ in 5b. Their anarthrous nature is again consistent with all of these entities being activated. The appearance of θεοῦ in 5a, however, needs explanation. The referent θεός was initially activated by its anarthrous appearance in 2a. Then, once activated, a predictable articular use of θεός appeared in 3a. Since God is already activated (and the referent is most certainly the same as in 3a), it is appropriate to ask why the next reference to God in 5a is anarthrous. The answer is that θεοῦ in 5a is focally prominent.[30]

---

[28] These entities are as follows: Πέτρος, ἀπόστολος, Ἰησοῦ Χριστοῦ [bis], ἐκλεκτοῖς παρεπιδήμοις, διασπορᾶς, Πόντου, Γαλατίας, Καππαδοκίας, Ἀσίας, Βιθυνίας, πρόγνωσιν, θεοῦ, πατρός, ἁγιασμῷ, πνεύματος, ὑπακοὴν, ῥαντισμὸν, αἵματος, χάρις, εἰρήνη.

[29] The only item that is perhaps unexpected in 1:1–2 is the second appearance of Ἰησοῦ Χριστοῦ in 2c. Since Ἰησοῦ Χριστοῦ was activated in 1a, we might expect the reference in 2c to be articular. Nevertheless, the phrase Ἰησοῦς Χριστός (along with the reversed Χριστὸς Ἰησοῦς) has become a frozen expression through its repeated use within the Christian community, routinely appearing anarthrously, as the 220 appearances of these phrases within the Greek NT testify, including the 8 tokens in 1 Peter (all with the order Ἰησοῦς Χριστός). We have bracketed Ἰησοῦς Χριστός as a noun phrase.

[30] In addition to the focal prominence of θεοῦ itself (due to its anarthrous nature), we note that θεοῦ is also part of a focally prominent prepositional phrase (Dubis 2010:8).

Thus we could translate it, with italics to mark emphasis, as 'who are being guarded by the *power of God*'.

In 1:6b ποικίλοις πειρασμοῖς is activated anarthrously, as is χρυσίου in 7b. The same is true of πυρὸς in 7c, the triplet of ἔπαινον, δόξαν, τιμὴν in 7d, ἀποκαλύψει in 7e,[31] and χαρᾷ in 8c.[32]

In 1:9b we find σωτηρίαν, a noun which has already appeared in 5b. The reference appears to be quite similar and we might therefore expect σωτηρίαν in 9b to be articular. The same could be said for ψυχῶν since the 'lives' of the recipients could easily be accessible by association with the recipients themselves. Since the entire appositional phrase σωτηρίαν ψυχῶν is focal, however, both nouns are likely to be anarthrous in order to give the phrase focal prominence. The noun σωτηρία appears again in 10a as an embedded antecedent in περὶ ἧς σωτηρίας, and the modifying relative pronoun ('which salvation') marks it as identifiable.[33]

Much has been made of anarthrous προφῆται in 10a, particularly Selwyn's claim that the prophets here are Christian prophets rather than Old Testament prophets. Selwyn's argument is based in part on the anarthrous nature of προφῆται, which, according to him, "is more natural if the reference were to men whose activities were well known to the readers" (1947:263). However, we would expect προφῆται to be anarthrous, anyway, because the prophets (who are almost certainly Old Testament prophets) are here being activated for the first time.[34]

---

[31] With respect to ἀποκαλύψει in 1:7e, one might wonder whether this term should have been accessible because of the use of the cognate ἀποκαλυφθῆναι in 5b, but the referents are different.

[32] It can be difficult at times to determine whether a noun is anarthrous because it is being activated or because it is focal. For example, πυρὸς in 7c could be anarthrous because it is being activated. But what if it were activated by its association with the metallurgical term δοκίμιον in 7a? Then πυρὸς would be anarthrous not because it is being activated but because it is marked as focally prominent (an argument for the latter is that πυρὸς appears within the focal constituent διὰ πυρός, which is already marked for focal prominence by being fronted with respect to δοκιμαζομένου). Rather than debate such examples, it is more fruitful to focus one's exegetical energies on anarthrous entities that are already *clearly* activated (and therefore marked for focal prominence by their anarthrous nature).

[33] For discussion of the historical relationship between the article and the relative pronoun, see §5.1 of the present paper and Runge, §6.1 (in the present volume).

[34] A critical objection to Selwyn's position is the contrast between the prophets and the recipients in 1:12 (οὐχ ἑαυτοῖς, ὑμῖν δὲ) alongside the contrast between an (implicit) 'then' and (explicit) 'now' (νῦν), suggesting that the prophets stand in a different redemptive era than the recipients, thus implying that the prophets are Old Testament prophets. For further discussion (though without his current understanding of the article), see Dubis 2002:108–110.

In 11b we find anarthrous καιρὸν. Although we might have expected this noun to be articular since the same noun appeared earlier in 5b, the author apparently does not want to instruct the recipients to relate the καιρὸν in 11b to the καιρῷ ἐσχάτῳ in 5b, probably because, from the perspective of the prophets of old, the time in 11b was uncertain. On the anarthrous use of Χριστός in 11b and 11c and of πνεῦμα in 12c, see sections 5.3.3 and 5.3.2 below.

In 12c we find anarthrous οὐρανοῦ, a noun which also appeared earlier in 4; here it is anarthrous because it is focally prominent. In 12d ἄγγελοι is anarthrous because 'angels' are being activated.

5.3.1.3 Use and non-use of the article with adjectivals

We now consider the use and non-use of the article in 1:1–12 with adjectivals. The key principle involved is as follows: the presence of an article with an adjectival instructs the recipients to anchor[35] the adjectival to an identifiable nominal (or to express this in more traditional terms, the article instructs the recipients to interpret the adjectival as an attributive modifier of the nominal).[36]

If an articular nominal is modified by an anarthrous adjectival (e.g. ὁ ἄνθρωπος ἀγαθός), in contrast, then the adjectival is FLOATING (i.e. not anchored to the articular nominal), thus signaling that it should be read as a predicate adjective. When both the nominal and the adjectival are anarthrous, the recipient has the option of interpreting the adjectival in one of the two following ways: (1) as a floating constituent (i.e. as a predicate adjective); (2) as an anchored constituent (i.e. as an attributive adjective). In such instances, the literary context must be one's guide.

We now examine the adjectivals in 1 Pet 1:1–12 in greater detail, working verse by verse through the passage. The first adjective appears in 1b in the anarthrous phrase ἐκλεκτοῖς παρεπιδήμοις, where ἐκλεκτοῖς is best understood as attributively modifying contiguous παρεπιδήμοις.

In 1:3a, the adjectival εὐλογητὸς is anarthrous, whereas the following noun phrase ὁ θεὸς καὶ πατὴρ is articular. εὐλογητὸς is therefore unanchored from ὁ θεὸς καὶ πατὴρ, and thus should be read as a predicate adjective. In 3b the presence of the article in the phrase ὁ...ἀναγεννήσας instructs the

---

[35] "A discourse entity is Anchored if the NP representing it is LINKED, by means of another NP, or 'Anchor', properly contained in it, to some other discourse entity" (Prince 1981:236). See also Crystal's (1991:20) definition of an anchor in phonology, which can also be applied to the article: "a segment to which another segment ASSOCIATES is said to be its 'anchor'. A unit which is not 'anchored' may be said to be FLOATING."

[36] This principle is most relevant to those constructions that are traditionally described as involving the second attributive position (e.g. ὁ ἄνθρωπος ὁ ἀγαθός) and the third attributive position (ἄνθρωπος ὁ ἀγαθός). In the first attributive position (e.g. ὁ ἀγαθὸς ἄνθρωπος), the initial article marks the entire adjective-noun constituent as identifiable.

recipients to anchor this adjectival participle to an identifiable nominal, and the most relevant nominal (as determined by agreement, proximity and semantics) is the articular noun phrase ὁ θεὸς καὶ πατήρ. In 3c in the anarthrous phrase ἐλπίδα ζῶσαν, ζῶσαν is best understood as attributive to contiguous ἐλπίδα. A similar situation applies in 1:4, where the series of anarthrous adjectivals ἄφθαρτον, ἀμίαντον, ἀμάραντον and τετηρημένην ἐν οὐρανοῖς εἰς ὑμᾶς are all best understood as attributive to anarthrous and contiguous κληρονομίαν.

In 1:5a the articular adjectival participle τοὺς...φρουρουμένους modifies the pronoun ὑμᾶς at the end of verse 4. Although pronouns do not take an article, they are by their very nature always identifiable since they point to a specific referent, and thus we expect adjectivals that modify pronouns to take the article. This explains why τοὺς...φρουρουμένους is articular, namely, because it modifies a pronoun (ὑμᾶς).

In 1:5b the anarthrous adjectival ἑτοίμην ἀποκαλυφθῆναι is best understood as attributive to σωτηρίαν, and similarly ἐσχάτῳ is best understood as attributive to καιρῷ (with both σωτηρίαν and καιρῷ being anarthrous because they are being activated). The same argument applies in 6b to the anarthrous adjective ποικίλοις, which modifies πειρασμοῖς, and in 8c to the compound anarthrous adjectival ἀνεκλαλήτῳ καὶ δεδοξασμένῃ that modifies χαρᾷ.

In 1:7b the adjective πολυτιμότερον is anarthrous despite the fact that it agrees with articular τὸ δοκίμιον in 7a. πολυτιμότερον is thereby unanchored or floating with respect to τὸ δοκίμιον, which in turn indicates that πολυτιμότερον should be read as a predicate adjective.

In 1:7c the compound adjectival participial phrase τοῦ ἀπολλυμένου... δὲ δοκιμαζομένου is articular, with the article τοῦ doing double duty and instructing the recipients to anchor the phrase to an identifiable nominal. The article agrees with χρυσίου (7b) in case, gender, and number, with χρυσίου being anarthrous since it is being activated. At first sight, this construction (traditionally called the "third attributive position" by Greek grammarians) seems to break our rule that articular adjectivals will be anchored to an identifiable nominal. What happens in fact is that, after the nominal has been introduced, it becomes identifiable as it is now in the mental representation of the recipients. This is not far from Robertson's affirmation regarding the third attributive position: "the substantive is indefinite and general, while the attribute makes a particular application" (Robertson 1919:777).[37]

---

[37] Wallace 1995:307 appropriately modifies Robertson's quote by inserting "often" in brackets: "the substantive is [often] indefinite and general." The substantive in third attributive constructions, as Wallace understands, is certainly not always indefinite (or, better, not always "unidentifiable"). As an example, see εἰς θεὸν τὸν ἐγείραντα αὐτὸν ἐκ νεκρῶν καὶ δόξαν αὐτῷ δόντα in 1 Pet 1:21, where the already activated and thus identifiable θεὸν is modified by the following articular compound adjectival participial construction. By way of contrast (and more similar

So, in the case of χρυσίου τοῦ ἀπολλυμένου, διὰ πυρὸς δὲ δοκιμαζομένου (7b–c), χρυσίου enters the recipients' mental representation in 7b. It is now identifiable in 7c, so the adjectival participial phrase can be anchored to it. Third attributive constructions are sometimes translated with a relative clause, which helps to make the point that the nominal is first introduced and then commented upon by the following adjectival.

Another third attributive construction is found in 10a–b, where the adjectival participial phrase οἱ περὶ τῆς εἰς ὑμᾶς χάριτος προφητεύσαντες in 10b modifies προφῆται in 10a. Once προφῆται has been activated anarthrously in 10a and is in the recipients' mental representation, προφῆται becomes identifiable in 10b, which allows the following articular participial phrase to be anchored to it.

Finally, consider the phrase πνεύματι ἁγίῳ ἀποσταλέντι ἀπ' οὐρανοῦ in 1:12c. One might expect πνεύματι to be articular since the Holy Spirit was activated anarthrously in 2b and mentioned again in 11b. Since πνεύματι here is identifiable, it must therefore be anarthrous for focal prominence (see further in §5.3.2). Now we need to make one last point. If an article is removed from a nominal for the sake of focal prominence, we expect attributive modifiers to similarly be anarthrous (although this does not apply to third attributive constructions, such as that in 1:21, confirming that the adjectival in these constructions is treated as a somewhat separate component). Thus ἁγίῳ is anarthrous. Similarly, since the adjectival ἀποσταλέντι ἀπ' οὐρανοῦ in 12c is anarthrous, we understand it to also be an attributive adjectival that is anarthrous because it modifies a noun that is anarthrously marked for focal prominence. Since both ἁγίῳ and ἀποσταλέντι ἀπ' οὐρανοῦ modify πνεύματι attributively, we could woodenly translate πνεύματι ἁγίῳ ἀποσταλέντι ἀπ' οὐρανοῦ as 'the sent-from-heaven Holy Spirit.'

5.3.2 πνεῦμα

We now discuss the significance of the presence versus absence of the article with reference to the eight instances of πνεῦμα in 1 Peter, as they illustrate the introduction of an entity without the article (1:2), the presence of the article with an entity to mark it as cognitively identifiable and to be related to something in the context (1:11, 3:4, 3:19, 4:14), and the absence of the article when the entity is focally prominent (1:12, 3:18, 4:6). We discuss each reference in turn.

As is usual at the beginning of a letter (see §5.2.1), the introductory reference to the Holy Spirit in 1:2 is anarthrous (κατὰ πρόγνωσιν θεοῦ πατρὸς ἐν ἁγιασμῷ πνεύματος).

---

to 1:7b–c), see Διὰ Σιλουανοῦ ὑμῖν τοῦ πιστοῦ ἀδελφοῦ in 5:12. Here Silvanus is first activated anarthrously and then, now identifiable, modified by an articular adjectival: 'Through Silvanus, who is a faithful brother with respect to you'. On this understanding of 5:12, see further in Dubis 2002:173–174.

The second instance of πνεῦμα is found in 1:11 (εἰς τίνα ἢ ποῖον καιρὸν ἐδήλου τὸ ἐν αὐτοῖς πνεῦμα Χριστοῦ) and is articular; it is part of the clausal topic τὸ ἐν αὐτοῖς πνεῦμα Χριστοῦ. The final reference in 4:14 (ὅτι τὸ τῆς δόξης καὶ τὸ τοῦ θεοῦ πνεῦμα ἐφ' ὑμᾶς ἀναπαύεται) is similar. It is not surprising that both of these tokens are articular since πνεῦμα was activated in 1:2.

The reference in 1:12 is anarthrous (ἃ νῦν ἀνηγγέλη ὑμῖν διὰ τῶν εὐαγγελισαμένων ὑμᾶς [ἐν] πνεύματι ἁγίῳ ἀποσταλέντι ἀπ' οὐρανοῦ). This is significant since πνεῦμα was activated in 1:2, so it is anarthrous here in order to give focal prominence to πνεύματι ἁγίῳ. This emphasis upon the Holy Spirit may be present because Peter is stressing that "the same Spirit who inspired the prophets has been sent from heaven to inspire the messengers" (Davids 1990:64). A less likely alternative is that Peter omits the article to avoid instructing the recipients to connect his mention of the Spirit in 1:12 to the previous reference in 1:11 because he does not wish them to identify "the full effusion of the Spirit now...with His limited working in the prophets" (Mason 1884:20).

The articular reference to πνεῦμα in 3:4 (ἀλλ' ὁ κρυπτὸς τῆς καρδίας ἄνθρωπος ἐν τῷ ἀφθάρτῳ τοῦ πραέως καὶ ἡσυχίου πνεύματος) is not to the Holy Spirit but to the spirits of the wives that Peter addresses.[38] The article indicates that this entity ('the humble and quiet spirit') is to be related to something in the context, probably the submissiveness to which the wives are exhorted in 3:1, which is also reflected in the 'purity and reverence' of their lives in 3:2.

In 3:18 (ζωοποιηθεὶς δὲ πνεύματι), πνεύματι is focally prominent in light of the contrast with σαρκὶ in the previous clause. So, even if the entity is cognitively identifiable because it refers to 'his spirit' (Barclay) or 'the Spirit' (NIV), we would expect the reference to be anarthrous (see also 4:6). However, πνεύματι could be anarthrous because it is not identifiable. Whichever interpretation is preferred, it must be consistent with the articular reference in 3:19 (ἐν ᾧ καὶ τοῖς ἐν φυλακῇ πνεύμασιν πορευθεὶς). Since these spirits have not previously been mentioned, the presence of the article indicates that the entity is to be related to something in the context, and the only candidate seems to be πνεύματι in 3:18. Levinsohn therefore takes πνεύματι to mean "in the sphere of 'the spirit'" (cf. Beare 1947:169). Such an interpretation makes 'the spirits in prison' accessible, in line with the extra-Biblical Jewish literature of the time.[39]

Dubis disagrees. He translates θανατωθεὶς μὲν σαρκί, ζωοποιηθεὶς δὲ πνεύματι as 'by being put to death in the flesh but being made alive by the Spirit', referring to the crucifixion and resurrection of Jesus (Dubis

---

[38] Davids 1990:119 identifies the πνεῦμα here as "the character of the human spirit or the human spirit as influenced by God's grace."

[39] See, for example, chapter 7 ("Light from the book of Enoch") of Dalton 1989:165–176.

2002:105), with πνεύματι referring to the Holy Spirit. He also interprets τοῖς ἐν φυλακῇ πνεύμασιν in 3:19 as a reference to "demonic spirits to whom Christ proclaimed his victory...during his ascension to heaven" (2002:120). Since no specific reference to demonic spirits has previously been made in the letter, the article attached to this phrase suggests that the entity is identifiable by some other means than its prior activation. In other words, something has made it accessible to the recipients. Given the widespread appearance of the story of the 'watchers' in ancient Jewish literature (e.g. 1 Enoch), it is possible that τοῖς ἐν φυλακῇ πνεύμασιν is identifiable via the encyclopaedic knowledge of the recipients. Alternatively, the macro-level theme of persecution and suffering has perhaps made these demonic spirits accessible because the readers know that evil spiritual forces are the ultimate source of their hardships (Achtemeier 1996:261, 274).[40]

5.3.3 Χριστός

Although most nouns behave like πνεῦμα when it comes to the presence versus absence of the article, Χριστός does not. The combination Ἰησοῦς Χριστός is always anarthrous in 1 Peter,[41] and Χριστός by itself is only articular in 3:15, 4:13 and 5:1 (discussed later in this section). So the norm is for Χριστός to be anarthrous even when it is the topic of a clause, as in the genitive absolute Χριστοῦ οὖν παθόντος σαρκὶ (4:1a). It is also anarthrous within an articular phrase, as in τὸ ἐν αὐτοῖς πνεῦμα Χριστοῦ (1:11). Why, then, is it articular on three occasions? What is the effect in these passages of indicating that the reference to Christ is identifiable and to be related to something in the context?

The exhortation κύριον δὲ τὸν Χριστὸν ἁγιάσατε ἐν ταῖς καρδίαις ὑμῶν (3:15) is an adaptation of Isa 8:13 (LXX), with τὸν Χριστὸν replacing αὐτόν. Although Χριστὸν is not an adjective, we may think of it as being in third attributive position. We have already noted that Peters closely relates the article to the relative pronoun, and this is one place where that insight is particularly helpful, as Peters's desire is to identify the κύριον of the quote from Isaiah as the Messiah. In other words, the sense of κύριον...τὸν Χριστὸν is '[the] Lord who is Christ.'[42]

The motivation for the presence of the article in 4:13 (τοῖς τοῦ Χριστοῦ παθήμασιν) and 5:1 (ὁ συμπρεσβύτερος καὶ μάρτυς τῶν τοῦ Χριστοῦ παθημάτων) is different. In both passages, a contrast is being made between Christ's sufferings and his glory (e.g. in 4:13: καθὸ κοινωνεῖτε τοῖς τοῦ Χριστοῦ παθήμασιν, χαίρετε, ἵνα καὶ ἐν τῇ

---

[40] This perspective appears in the description of Satan as a source of Christian suffering in 5:8–9.

[41] The reverse order (ἐν Χριστῷ [Ἰησοῦ]) is found only in 5:10.

[42] Goppelt (1993:242) comments, "thus 'Lord,' which stands in the LXX for Yahweh, the name of God, is interpretively applied to the exalted Christ."

ἀποκαλύψει τῆς δόξης αὐτοῦ χαρῆτε ἀγαλλιώμενοι). In most NT books, the norm is for genitival modifiers to follow their head noun (Porter 1995:291; Peters 2014:259). Placing an anarthrous genitive before the noun gives it greater prominence.[43] So, τοῖς Χριστοῦ παθήμασιν would have given greater prominence to anarthrous Χριστοῦ. The pragmatic effect of making the reference articular, then, is to direct attention more to the head noun παθήμασιν.[44]

To substantiate this understanding of the articular forms of Χριστός, consider the following additional instances in 1 Peter in which an articular genitive modifier precedes its head noun. In each, the information expressed by the genitive is more established than that of the head noun:

- 1:17 τὸν τῆς παροικίας ὑμῶν χρόνον—'exile' was activated in 1:1
- 3:1 διὰ τῆς τῶν γυναικῶν ἀναστροφῆς—'wives' was activated earlier in the verse
- 3:20 ἡ τοῦ θεοῦ μακροθυμία—the last reference to 'God' was in 3:17
- 4:4 εἰς τὴν αὐτὴν τῆς ἀσωτίας ἀνάχυσιν—any one of the vices in 4:3 is sufficient to make ἀσωτίας accessible
- 4:14 τὸ τῆς δόξης καὶ τὸ τοῦ θεοῦ πνεῦμα—'glory' and 'God' were both referred to in 4:10, whereas the last time πνεῦμα was used was in 4:6 and the last definite reference to the Holy Spirit was in 1:12.

In each of the above passages, the pragmatic effect of making the genitive articular is again to direct attention to the head noun itself.

This suggests that 2:15 (τὴν τῶν ἀφρόνων ἀνθρώπων ἀγνωσίαν) should be interpreted in the same way as 4:13 and 5:1 above, with 'foolish men' used to describe the people in 2:12 and attention being directed rather to their 'ignorance' (ἀγνωσίαν).

5.3.4 With infinitival expressions

We argue in this section that the presence of the article with infinitival expressions (hereafter, INFINITIVALS) marks them as identifiable and instructs the recipients to relate them to something in the prior context.[45]

We start with anarthrous and articular infinitivals following intransitive verbs of motion. In his sections on infinitivals of purpose and of result, Wallace lists "[s]imple or 'naked' infinitives (usually following an [intransitive] verb of motion)" (1995:591, 593) as in Luke 1:59 (ἐν τῇ ἡμέρᾳ τῇ ὀγδόῃ

---

[43] See Peters 2014:261.

[44] See Levinsohn 2011:6–7 (§3.3), for discussion of occasions when an adjective precedes its head noun yet is not emphasized.

[45] Peters 2014:209 begins his discussion of articular infinitivals with a reference to their identifiable nature ("When the article modifies a participle, the verbal element of the participle is used as the identifying feature of a class. With an infinitive, this is also true"). However, his emphasis then seems to switch to "the substantive, or nominal, aspect of the infinitive," whereas "it is arguable that when an infinitive does not have the article, the verbal quality is in view" (ibid.).

ἦλθον περιτεμεῖν τὸ παιδίον) and Luke 3:7 (ἔλεγεν οὖν τοῖς ἐκπορευομένοις ὄχλοις βαπτισθῆναι ὑπ' αὐτοῦ). However, intransitive verbs of motion may be followed by "τοῦ + infinitive" (Wallace 1995:591, 593) when the prior context allows the author to mark the infinitival as identifiable. See, for example, Matt 3:13 (τότε παραγίνεται ὁ Ἰησοῦς ἀπὸ τῆς Γαλιλαίας ἐπὶ τὸν Ἰορδάνην πρὸς τὸν Ἰωάννην τοῦ βαπτισθῆναι ὑπ' αὐτοῦ), which occurs in a pericope that has already described other people coming to John to be baptised by him.[46] The presence of τοῦ instructs the recipients to relate βαπτισθῆναι ὑπ' αὐτοῦ to something in the prior context—a context that includes the arrival of other participants with the same purpose (3:5–7).

Four articular infinitivals occur in 1 Peter: two with τοῦ and two with εἰς το. We discuss them in turn, beginning with those with τοῦ, since, as we have just noted, they contrast with anarthrous, "naked" infinitivals.

In 3:10 (ὁ γὰρ θέλων ζωὴν ἀγαπᾶν καὶ ἰδεῖν ἡμέρας ἀγαθὰς παυσάτω τὴν γλῶσσαν ἀπὸ κακοῦ καὶ χείλη[47] τοῦ μὴ λαλῆσαι δόλον) a quotation appears from the LXX of Ps 33:14 (MT 34:14), with parallelism between the two parts. The article with μὴ λαλῆσαι δόλον instructs the recipients to relate its referent to something in the context; namely, the parallel clause παυσάτω τὴν γλῶσσαν ἀπὸ κακοῦ.

In 4:17 (ὅτι [ὁ] καιρὸς τοῦ ἄρξασθαι τὸ κρίμα ἀπὸ τοῦ οἴκου τοῦ θεοῦ), the presence of the article with the infinitival also instructs the recipients to relate its referent to something in the context. Earlier references to "the eschatological judgment" (Dubis 2002:153) include πάντων δὲ τὸ τέλος ἤγγικεν in 4:7 and, possibly, τῇ ἐν ὑμῖν πυρώσει πρὸς πειρασμὸν ὑμῖν γινομένῃ in 4:12.[48]

Since infinitivals with εἰς are always articular, it is unwise to read too much into the presence of the article with them. Given that infinitivals with ὥστε are always anarthrous, though, it is not unreasonable to perceive of the article following εἰς as an instruction to relate the infinitival to something in the prior context; namely, to the clauses to which it is subordinated.

Prior to 3:7 (εἰς τὸ μὴ ἐγκόπτεσθαι τὰς προσευχὰς ὑμῶν), there has been no mention of prayers, so the article with προσευχὰς ὑμῶν presumably relates 'your prayers' to οἱ ἄνδρες and then to the underlying assumption that Christian husbands will pray. Similarly, the article with the infinitival

---

[46] In Luke 1:76–77 (προπορεύσῃ γὰρ ἐνώπιον κυρίου ἑτοιμάσαι ὁδοὺς αὐτοῦ, τοῦ δοῦναι γνῶσιν σωτηρίας τῷ λαῷ αὐτοῦ), the first infinitival following the verb of motion is anarthrous, whereas the next one is articular, thereby instructing the recipients to relate it to something in the prior context such as the previous infinitival. In other words, ἑτοιμάσαι ὁδοὺς αὐτοῦ makes τοῦ δοῦναι γνῶσιν σωτηρίας accessible. See also Luke 1:78–79 and Ac 26:18.

[47] Both the verb and the article with χείλη are elided.

[48] "Paralleling the 'time of the crucible' at Qumran, πυρώσει refers to the anticipated eschatological ordeal" (Dubis 2002:146).

would be consistent with the assumption that they would wish their prayers to be effective.

Dubis suggests that 4:2 (εἰς τὸ μηκέτι ἀνθρώπων ἐπιθυμίαις ἀλλὰ θελήματι θεοῦ τὸν ἐπίλοιπον ἐν σαρκὶ βιῶσαι χρόνον) "probably modifies ... the immediately preceding πέπαυται ἁμαρτίας" and "represents the ultimate intention of ὁ παθὼν σαρκὶ in forsaking sin: he turns from sin in order to devote himself to doing the will of God for the rest of his life" (2002:132). The prior context to which the articular infinitival is to relate would therefore appear to be πέπαυται ἁμαρτίας.

Finally, a comment about why infinitivals with ὥστε are always anarthrous (the only example in 1 Peter is in 1:20–21: φανερωθέντος δὲ ἐπ' ἐσχάτου τῶν χρόνων δι' ὑμᾶς τοὺς δι' αὐτοῦ πιστοὺς εἰς θεὸν τὸν ἐγείραντα αὐτὸν ἐκ νεκρῶν καὶ δόξαν αὐτῷ δόντα, ὥστε τὴν πίστιν ὑμῶν καὶ ἐλπίδα εἶναι εἰς θεόν). Levinsohn found that, when ὥστε is used as an inter-sentential connective, "the logical relation with the context is less direct and, quite often, the input for the result introduced by ὥστε is more than one proposition" (2014a:335). The absence of the article when an infinitival is introduced with ὥστε would also be consistent with the logical relation between it and its context being "less direct" than with εἰς τό.

In the case of 1 Pet 1:20b–21 (cited in previous paragraph), Dubis takes the infinitival "to indicate the result of the preceding compound participial phrase" and writes, "the emphasis here seems to be ... on the recipients' faith and hope as the effect of Christ's resurrection and glorification" (2002:35). Many intervening events will have taken place before "Christ's resurrection and glorification" results in the recipients of 1 Peter setting their faith and hope on God, so it is indeed the case that, at least in this passage, "the logical relation with the context is less direct."[49]

We conclude, then, that the presence of the article with infinitivals (including those introduced with τοῦ and εἰς τό), and its absence when an infinitival is introduced with ὥστε, is consistent with its function elsewhere in 1 Peter as a marker of cognitive identifiability.

5.4 Conclusions

This chapter has confirmed that the Greek article indicates that the entity concerned is cognitively identifiable rather than definite, even when it is participial or infinitival. It has also argued that the presence of the article with a nominal instructs the recipients to process the information provided in such a way that the identity of the referent is unambiguous. Similarly, its presence with an adjectival instructs the recipients to anchor the adjectival to an identifiable entity. Recipients are to achieve identifiability by relating

---

[49] See also Matt 10:1, 15:33 and 27:1. In contrast, both Luke 4:29 and 20:20 have εἰς τό as a variant.

the entity to something in the context; this will usually be the textual context but will sometimes be what the writer assumes about the immediate situational context of the recipients or their encyclopedic knowledge.

We have noted that the norm in 1 Peter is for entities to be introduced for the first time without the article, which suggests that the writer assumes that the mental representation of the recipients vis-à-vis the contents of the letter is empty (a *tabula rasa*). Once an entity has been activated, however, the writer may remove the article from a nominal in order to mark it as focally prominent.

References

Achtemeier, Paul J. 1996. *1 Peter: A commentary on First Peter.* Hermeneia: A Critical and Historical Commentary on the Bible 74. Minneapolis, MN: Fortress.

Beare, Francis Wright. 1947. *The First epistle of Peter: The Greek text with introduction and notes.* Oxford: Basil Blackwell.

Callow, Kathleen. 1974. *Discourse considerations in translating the Word of God.* Grand Rapids, MI: Zondervan.

Colwell, E. C. 1933. A definite rule for the use of the article in the Greek New Testament. *Journal of Biblical Literature* 52(1):12–21.

Crystal, David. 1991. *A dictionary of linguistics and phonetics.* Third edition. Oxford: Basil Blackwell.

Dalton, William J. 1989. *Christ's proclamation to the spirits: A study of 1 Peter 3:18–4:6.* Second edition. Analecta Biblica 23. Rome: Pontifical Biblical Institute.

Dana, Harvey E., and Julius R. Mantey. 1927. *A manual grammar of the Greek New Testament.* Toronto: Macmillan.

Davids, Peter H. 1990. *The First epistle of Peter.* The New International Commentary on the New Testament. Grand Rapids, MI: Eerdmans.

Dik, Simon. 1989. *The theory of functional grammar 1: The structure of the clause.* Functional Grammar Series 20. Providence, RI: Foris.

Dubis, Mark. 2002. Messianic woes in First Peter: Suffering and eschatology in 1 Peter 4:12–19. *Society of Biblical Literature* 33. New York: Lang.

Dubis, Mark. 2010. *1 Peter: A handbook on the Greek text.* Baylor Handbook on the Greek New Testament. Waco, TX: Baylor University Press.

Goppelt, Leonhard. 1993. *A commentary on 1 Peter.* Translated by J. E. Alsup. Grand Rapids, MI: Eerdmans.

Green, Joel B. 1997. *The gospel of Luke.* The New International Commentary on the New Testament. Grand Rapids, MI: Eerdmans.

Greenberg, Joseph H. 1978. How does a language acquire gender markers? In Joseph H. Greenberg (ed), *Universals of human language: Word structure,* 47–82. Stanford, CA: University Press.

Halliday, M. A. K. 2013. *An introduction to functional grammar*. Third edition. Revised by Christian M. I. M. Matthiessen. Abingdon, UK: Routledge.

Heimerdinger, Jean-Marc. 1999. *Topic, focus and foreground in Ancient Hebrew narratives*. The Library of Hebrew Bible/Old Testament Studies 295. Sheffield, UK: Academic Press.

[Read-]Heimerdinger, Jenny, and Stephen H. Levinsohn. 1992. The use of the definite article before names of people in the Greek text of Acts, with particular reference to Codex Bezae. *Filología Neotestamentaria* 5:15–44.

Jackendoff, Ray S. 1972. *Semantic interpretation in generative grammar*. Studies in linguistics series. Cambridge, MA: MIT Press.

Jackman, David. 1988. *The message of John's letters*. Bible Speaks Today Series 122. Leicester, UK: Inter-Varsity Press.

Janssen, Stephen. 2013. *The Greek article in Pauline literature: Traditional grammar and discourse perspectives*. Dallas, TX: Dallas Theological Seminary.

Lambrecht, Knud. 1994. *Information structure and sentence form: Topic, focus, and the mental representations of discourse referents*. Cambridge Studies in Linguistics 71. Cambridge: University Press.

Levinsohn, Stephen H. 2000. *Discourse features of New Testament Greek: A coursebook on its information structure and other devices*. Second edition. Dallas, TX: SIL International.

Levinsohn, Stephen H. 2006. The relevance of Greek discourse studies to exegesis. *Journal of Translation* 2(2):11–21. Accessed May 16, 2018. https://www.sil.org/resources/publications/entry/40248.

Levinsohn, Stephen H. 2009. Towards a unified linguistic description of οὗτος and ἐκεῖνος. In Stanley E. Porter and Matthew Brook O'Donnell (eds.), *The linguist as pedagogue: Trends in the teaching and linguistic analysis of the Greek New Testament*, 204–216. Sheffield, UK: Phoenix Press.

Levinsohn, Stephen H. 2010. Aspect and prominence in the synoptic accounts of Jesus' entry into Jerusalem. *Filología Neotestamentaria* 23:161–174.

Levinsohn, Stephen H. 2011. A fresh look at adjective-noun ordering in articular noun phrases. Paper presented at the International Conference of the Society of Biblical Literature, London, England, July 2011. Accessed May 16, 2018. www.sil.org/resources/archives/68397.

Levinsohn, Stephen H. 2015. Self-instruction materials on narrative discourse analysis. SIL International, 2011. Accessed May 16, 2018. www.sil.org/resources/archives/68643.

Levinsohn, Stephen H. 2014a. "Therefore" or "wherefore": What's the difference? In Richard A. Taylor and Craig E. Morrison (eds.), *Reflections on lexicography: Explorations in Ancient Syriac, Hebrew and Greek sources*. Perspectives on Linguistics and Ancient Languages 4, 325–343. Piscataway, NJ: Gorgias Press.

Levinsohn, Stephen H. 2014b. The postposing of topical subjects in Luke-Acts and John. Paper presented at the International Conference of the Society of Biblical Literature, Vienna, Austria, July 2014. Accessed May 16, 2018. www.sil.org/resources/archives/68388.

Mason, A. J. 1884. The First epistle of St. Peter. In Charles John Ellicot (ed.), *Ephesians to Revelation*. A Bible commentary for English readers 8. London: Cassell.

Peters, Ronald D. 2014. *The Greek article: A functional grammar of ὁ-items in the Greek New Testament with special emphasis on the Greek article.* Linguistic Biblical Studies 9. Leiden: Brill.

Porter, Stanley E. 2009. Prominence: A theoretical overview. In Stanley E. Porter and Matthew Brook O'Donnell (eds.), *The linguist as pedagogue: Trends in the teaching and linguistic analysis of the Greek New Testament*, 45–74. Sheffield, UK: Phoenix Press.

Porter, Stanley E. 1995. *Idioms of the Greek New Testament.* Second edition. Vol. 2 of Biblical Languages: Greek. Sheffield, UK: Academic Press.

Prince, Ellen F. 1981. Toward a taxonomy of given-new information. In Peter Cole (ed.), *Radical pragmatics*, 223–255. New York: Academic Press.

Robertson, Archibald T. 1919. *A grammar of the Greek New Testament in the light of historical research.* Third edition. London: Hodder & Stoughton.

Rooryck, Johan. 1994. On two types of underspecification: Towards a feature theory shared by syntax and phonology. *Probus* 6:207–233.

Runge, Steven E. 2016. Markedness: Contrasting Porter's model with the linguists cited as support. *Bulletin for Biblical Research* 26(1):43–56.

Selwyn, Edward G. 1947. *The First epistle of St. Peter: The Greek text with introduction, notes, and essays.* Second edition. Thornapple Commentaries. London: Macmillan.

Thompson, Geoff. 2004. *Introducing functional grammar.* Second edition. London: Hodder & Stoughton.

Wallace, Daniel B. 1995. *Greek grammar beyond the basics: An exegetical syntax of the New Testament.* Grand Rapids, MI: Zondervan.

Wilson, Deirdre, and Dan Sperber. 2012. *Meaning and Relevance.* Cambridge: University Press.

6

Towards a Unified Understanding of the Greek Article from a Diachronic, Cognitive Perspective

Steven E. Runge

6.1 Introduction

6.1.1 Grammaticalization

The article did not spontaneously arise out of a vacuum; it developed in Ancient Greek along the same lines as in other languages.[1] Understanding the diachronic development of languages enhances our understanding of a synchronic snapshot at any given point in time. The article's development in Indo-European and African languages has followed certain cross-linguistic patterns, the most notable of which is a development from demonstrative pronouns (Givón 1984:354; Diessel 1999:25; De Mulder and Carlier 2011:523). Demonstratives seem to be the "stem cells" from which adnominals like articles and relative pronouns arise, only to have new demonstrative forms arise to take their place. The path of development that Bauer

---

[1] I wish to thank Daniel King for his thought-provoking questions and comments throughout the editorial process. His engagement and tenacious attention to detail have strengthened my work, though any remaining deficiencies are my own.

traces for Ancient Greek, beginning with Homer, is consistent with the claims regularly found in biblical studies (Bauer 2007:105–106.).[2]

In terms of the grammaticalization path by which the article is believed to develop in a language, there are four stages hypothesized by Greenberg.[3] Grammatical devices like the article arise to formally mark some language feature that would otherwise have been only implicit. The function comes first, then a form develops to mark its presence. A demonstrative marker is the form typically used for explicitly marking the noun phrase. This early article-as-demonstrative usage (Stage 0) indicates "that the identity of the referent should be established by making reference to the speech situation or the immediate context of utterance" (De Mulder and Carlier 2011:526). It refers to entities outside the text-world in the real world, typically new, non-topical entities rather than topical entities (Diessel 1999:25). It marked a noun as more salient than another in the context not unlike the prototypical use of demonstratives as modifiers.

By Greenberg's Stage I the article has become a marker of definiteness. Diessel notes that "when anaphoric demonstratives develop into definite articles, their use is gradually extended from non-topical antecedents to all kinds of referents in the preceding discourse. In the course of this development, demonstratives lose their referential function and turn into formal markers of definiteness" (1999:25). Although the use as a marker of definiteness supplants the demonstrative use, vestiges of the earlier function will nevertheless remain. The deixis associated with pointing outside the text world becomes deixis within the text world, whether anaphoric or cataphoric. The Greek article has thus developed within the language rather than being a feature borrowed from Proto-Indo-European. This means that the article in Greek has a much longer history of grammatical development compared to other modern European languages, such as English (De Mulder and Carlier 2011:522–523). This disparity in the historical development of the article in Greek versus English partially explains the numerous mismatches in use between the two languages.

Stage II of the development is typified by an ever-widening use with noun phrases besides only those that are definite. This leads to a watering down or "bleaching" of the narrower semantic meaning of its Stage I function. Instead of marking the more specific semantic feature of definiteness, the Stage II article simply indicates that it is cognitively identifiable.[4] Identifiability "has to do with a speaker's assessment of whether a discourse representation of a particular referent is already stored in the hearer's mind

---

[2] See also Blass 1898:145; Robertson 1923:755; Wallace 1996:208.

[3] These were first outlined in Greenberg 1978:47–82. For a recent overview of the current state of discussion, see De Mulder and Carlier 2011.

[4] Claims like Wallace's that the article does not definitize, but instead that it conceptualizes, indicate an awareness that it serves a cognitive rather than purely grammatical function. See Wallace 1996:209–210.

or not" (Lambrecht 1996:76).[5] Although there is some overlap between the grammatical notion of definiteness and the cognitive notion of identifiability, the latter is broader and less restricted than the former. Hence the shift of the Greek article from Stage I (definiteness marker) to Stage II (identifiability marker) represents a bleaching of the article's semantic specificity.

The final stage that Greenberg has identified on the grammaticalization path is Stage III, where the article serves as a simple nominal marker. "Whereas the semantic dimension is predominant in the first stages of the grammaticalization process, it can progressively fade out, which is reflected in a spread to new contexts where the articles convey neither definiteness nor specificity" (De Mulder and Carlier 2011:525). Use of the article with verbal forms like participles and infinitives, with adverbs, and with adjectives would be characteristic of Stage III. The article marks the form as nominalized in some way, that is, that it is not serving its prototypical function (Bauer 2007:109–111). In Koine Greek this usage is reflected in the traditional distinction between adjectival and adverbial participles, or between articular and anarthrous infinitives, principally based on the presence or absence of the article (Porter 1995:182–183, 194; Robertson 1923:154–157, 764–766; Blass 1898:233–235, 242–244; Wallace 1996:610–611, 617–621). Similarly, the article with an adjective marks the phrase as substantive rather than as a qualitative attribute.

6.1.1.1 Identifiability

Because identifiability is constrained by the knowledge shared between a speaker and hearer, it is necessarily contextually constrained. This means a referent construed as unidentifiable in one discourse context might be identifiable in another, based upon differences in the degree of shared knowledge. Furthermore, since it is the *referent* that is activated by the previous mention rather than the specific expression used (e.g. a proper name), alias expressions with an article can be used to refer to the same referent. Wallace (1996:219) cites the example of a certain official introduced as τις βασιλικός but subsequently referred to as ὁ ἄνθρωπος (John 4:46, 50). The presence of the article here indicates that this referent should be uniquely identifiable to the reader, and hence understood as referring to the same official introduced in verse 46.

So what exactly is the difference between definiteness and identifiability? Definiteness is a binary grammatical category; something is either definite or it is not. Identifiability is a cognitive category concerned with the degree of shared knowledge between a speaker and a hearer. In many instances a cognitively identifiable entity also will be marked as grammatically definite.

---

[5] More specifically, he states: "The referent of a noun phrase may be considered identifiable because in the universe of discourse of the interlocutors or of the speech community as a whole there exists only ONE referent which can be appropriately designated with that noun phrase" (1996:87).

But identifiability is scalar rather than binary. There are many instances where a grammatically *indefinite* entity is cognitively identifiable. In the clause, ὁ Ἰωάννης καὶ ἐκ τῶν μαθητῶν αὐτοῦ δύο (John 1:35),[6] John's two disciples are grammatically indefinite, but they are cognitively identifiable based on their anchoring relation to John, αὐτοῦ.[7]

Since identifiability is scalar we find gradations of identifiability, such as the "referential indefinite" (Gundel, Hedberg, and Zacharski 1993:275–277).[8] This level implies that the hearer is not able to identify the referent, but it is accessible enough to process additional information about the referent. "This" is often used in English to mark something as referentially indefinite, such as the set expression "This guy walks into a bar...." You may not be able to pick the guy out of a police lineup (and perhaps neither can I), but it is sufficiently referential for you to process the rest of the anecdote. In Greek the indefinite pronoun τις is used, for example καὶ ἦν τις βασιλικὸς οὗ ὁ υἱὸς ἠσθένει ἐν Καφαρναούμ (John 4:46). Note that once 'a certain ruler' is introduced, the reference to his son is articular, based on the fact that he is anchored to his father. The scalar notion of cognitive identifiability appears to be universal across languages, but is "imperfectly and non-universally matched by the grammatical category of definiteness" (Lambrecht 1996:87).

Lambrecht describes several means by which a referent may become identifiable, which overlap significantly with the functions claimed by grammarians: anaphora, deixis, encyclopedic knowledge, and what Lambrecht calls "pragmatic bootstrapping" (1996:87–92). Anaphora refers to the previous mention of a referent in a discourse, such as "an upcoming meeting."[9] Regardless of whether I supply you with any other semantic detail about the timing or nature of the meeting, I am nevertheless obligated to use definite reference to it.[10] The persistence of an anaphoric referent in our short-term memory is influenced by various factors, such as distance from the last reference, its salience within the discourse, the presence or absence of competing referents, among other things. Thus, the reference in Matt

---

[6] All Greek texts are taken from the *Greek New Testament: SBL edition* (Holmes 2010). Unless otherwise specified, all English translations are taken from the Lexham English Bible (Harris et al. 2012).

[7] Prince states, "A discourse entity is Anchored if the NP representing it is LINKED, by means of another NP, or 'Anchor,' properly contained in it, to some other discourse entity" (Prince 1981:236).

[8] For a discussion of referential indefinites in the Greek NT, see Runge 2010:372–374.

[9] See Wallace 1996:217–218.

[10] Lambrecht states: "The fact that identifiability can be created through mere mention of a reference in the discourse, without any further semantic specification, confirms our observation that identifiability of a referent (and corresponding definite coding in English) does not necessarily entail familiarity with, or knowledge about, the referent" (Lambrecht 1996:89).

13:35 to τὴν οἰκίαν is reasonably understood to be an anaphoric reference back to 13:1 since there has been no other competing referent, such as a different house.[11]

Previous reference is not the only method by which information can be shared between speakers and hearers. A referent may be identifiable based on its presence in the physical context. In the text-world of Scripture, participants can use articular reference for entities that are present in the context. This use may represent a fossilized vestige of Stage 0 of the article, where it served as a demonstrative marker on the noun phrase.[12] However in most cases where an articular reference declares something to be present in the text-world, it is reasonable to construe this as simply identifiable, where the writer expects the reader to accept that the entity is present. Consider John the Baptist's declaration as Jesus approaches him to be baptized, ἴδε ὁ ἀμνὸς τοῦ θεοῦ ὁ αἴρων τὴν ἁμαρτίαν τοῦ κόσμου (John 1:29). John's intended referent is ostensibly identified as the one approaching him based on a gesture or eye contact. The salient point is that Jesus is uniquely identifiable.

Another means by which something may become identifiable is a reader's knowledge of the world around them. Each of us has a great deal of encyclopedic knowledge about the world and how it works. If there are entities for which there is only one possible referent, such as celestial bodies (e.g. the moon), deities (e.g. the devil), government officials (the Queen of England), then there is no need to introduce the referent; the initial reference in the discourse may be articular. This correlates to Wallace's categories of monadic (one of a kind) and well-known uses of the article, where there is only one possible referent for the referring expression (Wallace 1996:223–225). The introduction of Sergius Paulus in Acts 13:7 illustrates this. Immediately after "a certain magician" Bar-Jesus is introduced using a conventional approach, he is said to be σὺν τῷ ἀνθυπάτῳ Σεργίῳ Παύλῳ. Use of the article is appropriate based on the shared expectation that there exist proconsuls in government service. The title is sufficient to mark his identifiability with the article.

Shared encyclopedic knowledge can be just as subject to change from context to context as that derived from anaphoric reference. A reference to "the president" while watching the State of the Union speech in America would undoubtedly refer to the country's president. However, mention of "the president" at a board meeting of my fly fishing club or at a company meeting at work may have a referent other than the President of the United

---

[11] Wallace recognizes this is the most logical solution, yet seems reluctant to accept that a referent could persist so long anaphorically (Wallace 1996:216).

[12] Wallace uses a demonstrative pronoun in his translation of the article in several examples: Acts 19:15 (this Paul), under the deictic use of the article, Matt 14:15; Luke 17:6; Rev 1:3 (1996:219, 221). This may indicate that he interprets the article as doing something more than simply marking identifiability in these contexts.

States. We find the same kind of differentiation made in Matthew, where the same expression is used for the initial reference to different entities. In Matt 26:41 the referent of τό πνεῦμα is the inner person that is willing, contrasted with the flesh that is weak. In Matt 27:50 τό πνεῦμα also refers to that which Jesus gave up as he died. In contrast, there is an anarthrous reference in Matt 22:43 to David ἐν πνεύματι calling the Christ "Lord." In each case the writer is depending on the reader's encyclopedic knowledge to select the appropriate referent, based on contextual factors.

There are also contexts that rely upon schemas or frames to establish identifiability, where mention of one member of a set cognitively activates other related members.[13] The classic illustration used is a restaurant, the mention of which allows me to speak about other entities as uniquely identifiable (e.g. the waiter, the menu, and the food). I can depend on your knowledge about such things and thus avoid the need for introducing every last detail as though it was brand new to you. The initial articular reference to Jesus entering εἰς τὴν συναγωγὴν on the Sabbath in Nazareth is reliant on the reader's acceptance that Nazareth had a synagogue, even if they had never visited it. The same principle explains Jesus handing the book τῷ ὑπηρέτῃ after he had finished reading. This shared encyclopedic knowledge—even that which exists within a specialized community context—enables articular references to be made without previous mention within the discourse.[14] This utilization of encyclopedic knowledge to establish identifiability is captured by Wallace's category of simple identification (Wallace 1996:216–217).

The final means by which a referent may become identifiable is what Lambrecht calls PRAGMATIC BOOTSTRAPPING or PRAGMATIC ACCOMMODATION. The introduction of the centurion's slave (Luke 7:2) offers a good example, where neither the slave nor the centurion have been previously mentioned. But by anchoring τινος δοῦλος to ἑκατοντάρχου, the centurion is able to be anaphorically referred to in the following relative clause. This represents one extreme of bootstrapping, where neither referent is identifiable. More commonly we find brand new entities introduced as identifiable topics by anchoring the new participant to another that is already established in the discourse. The anchoring relation is often established by a possessive relation, such as τὸν τοῦ ἀρχιερέως δοῦλον (John 18:10), or ἡ μήτηρ τῶν υἱῶν Ζεβεδαίου (Matt 20:20). In neither case has there been previous mention

---

[13] See Lambrecht 1996:90.

[14] This role of shared encyclopedic knowledge highlights the importance of examining what this may have entailed for early readers of the NT. The key component is what the writer would have reasonably expected the reader to be able to identify. Obviously this would differ between a letter meant for general circulation and a letter meant only for a specific context, but underscores the critical importance of considering Second Temple and Greco-Roman encyclopedic knowledge the reader or writer would have had.

of the slave or the mother, but the connection to an identifiable referent sufficiently anchors them to the discourse, allowing for articular reference.

One final class of referents that are typically articular in Greek is identifiable abstract referents. The Greek article's broader semantic range is what enables it to be used with identifiable qualities or abstract concepts, where English would demand a much higher degree of concreteness. Consider the numerous articular noun phrases in Paul's exposition of love in 1 Cor 13, illustrated from verse 4: ἡ ἀγάπη μακροθυμεῖ, χρηστεύεται ἡ ἀγάπη, οὐ ζηλοῖ ἡ ἀγάπη, οὐ περπερεύεται, οὐ φυσιοῦται. Wallace states, "In translating such nouns, the article should rarely be used (typically, only when the article also fits under some other individualizing category, such as anaphoric)" (1996:226). Porter attributes the presence of articles with abstract substantives in Greek to "performing its particularizing function" (1995:107). In terms of cognitive linguistics, it moves the referent from the abstract to the uniquely identifiable.

6.1.2 Summary

The prototypical function of the Greek article in the Koine period is as a marker of identifiability, what Greenberg has described as Stage II. The presence of the article on a noun phrase reflects the writer's belief that the reader is able to uniquely identify the intended referent. This identifiability may come about through previous mention (discourse anaphora), presence in the physical context (deixis), activation as part of a larger set (schema or related entities), or a shared encyclopedic knowledge of the world, or simple pragmatic accommodation (pragmatic bootstrapping).

Identifiability must not be confused with definiteness. The former is a cognitive, scalar notion, whereas the latter is a grammatical and binary notion. The disagreement we find in both linguistic and grammatical discussions about the article stems from attempts to describe the grammatical or syntactic function of the article without reference to its cognitive function. It plays a key role in the referential system, and is thus best understood and described in this context, against the backdrop of referential semantics. Just as there are various ways of making something grammatically definite, so too are there different ways of indicating cognitive identifiability.

Another factor that has led to confusion is the attempt to capture all uses of the article under one broad function. There are core, prototypical functions that the article serves; these may rightly be called the default function of the article. But there are other, less-prototypical uses of the article in Greek that represents developments beyond the core, prototypical function of marking identifiability. If we take identifiability as the core semantic meaning of the article and its use with identifiable noun phrases as its prototypical function, then we are in a position to explain the less prototypical uses, which is the topic of the next section.

6.2 Less prototypical uses:
Stage III development of the article

6.2.1 Use to nominalize

There are several different uses of the article that might seem at odds with the view I am arguing for, in which the article marks a referent as cognitively identifiable. These uses include the article with non-nominal entities like verb forms, adverbs and adjectives, and its use as a substitute pronoun. After providing a brief overview of these issues, I will move on to reconcile the pragmatic uses of the article that appear to run counter to what is claimed above.

6.2.1.1 Use with adverbs, adjectives, and verbs

The section above on grammaticalization ended with a discussion of Stage III, where the article has become ubiquitous enough that its usage extends to serving as a nominalizing marker. The various stages of the grammaticalization process do not discretely begin and end, nor is there only ever one stage or semantic meaning present at any given time. The use of the article to nominalize participles (substantival participles), adjectives and adverbs matches the linguistic profile of Stage III. The increasing use of the article with infinitives in Classical and Koine periods may also be viewed as a nominalizing of sorts, in that it compensates for the infinitive's loss of case endings earlier in its history "to restore the balance between the substantival and verbal aspects of the inf[initive] now that tense and voice had come in" (Robertson 1923:1054). This use of the article with these forms should not be construed as changing their morphology, but rather as constraining readers *not* to construe the usage as prototypical of the specific form. Such a view is consistent with what we find claimed in Greek grammars. Wallace describes the article's use as a substantizer as the ability to "turn almost any part of speech into a noun;" it individualizes or categorizes (Wallace 1996:231). Similarly Porter (1995:108) states that by adding the article "many words can be made to function in the same way that a noun does;" it particularizes or categorizes. Blass treats this usage more as a case of the noun having been elided or omitted (Blass 1898:154).

If indeed the function of the article with non-nominal entities is to constrain them to function as nouns, then we cannot necessarily draw the same kinds of exegetical conclusions as with the prototypical use with nouns. Stage III usage evokes a different set of interpretive constraints than Stage I or II. Consider the standard anarthrous introduction of new entities in Stage

I or II. Anarthrous reference typically signals that the writer does not expect the reader to be able to uniquely identify the intended referent, whereas articular reference carries this expectation. Use as a nominalizer precludes anarthrous reference based on the fact that the article's function is to nominalize. Anarthrous activation is not a possibility in these cases because the form to be nominalized could be misconstrued as being the more prototypical use of the form. In other words, trying to have a nominalized adjective, participle or infinitive recognized as such without the article being present would be no mean feat. This is not to say it cannot be done; Wallace notes instances where it indeed occurs, hence his caveats that the substantival use of an infinitive (as subject or object) "may or may not have the article" (1996:600, 602).[15] In the case of the adjective he states, "usually, though not always, such a substantival adjective will have the article" (Wallace 1996:294). Porter (1995:121) would seem to agree based on his anarthrous substantival adverbial examples (Matt 5:45; 11:5; Rom 1:4).

Knowledge of the grammaticalization process—and what is entailed by Stage III in particular—demands that two distinctions be made. From the standpoint of human cognition, the presence of the article, even with a non-nominal entity, still constrains the entity to be understood as uniquely identifiable to the reader, as far as the writer is concerned. In this sense the article still accomplishes the same prototypical function as with nouns. However, the improbability (impossibility?) of activating the referent through a standard initial anarthrous reference like a noun phrase means that the referent is less likely to have a discourse anaphor compared to a standard articular noun. The identifiability is more likely to derive from encyclopedic knowledge or pragmatic bootstrapping. This is not to say there cannot be an anaphor; referential identification is a cognitive process constrained by the semantics of the discourse context.

From the standpoint of conventional grammar, the nominalizing use of the article represents a less prototypical usage. The semantic bleaching expected from grammaticalization is reflected in the article's use with morphological entities other than nouns. Its role, marking first definiteness of noun phrases (Stage I) and then identifiability (Stage II), enables its role to be extended quite naturally to the nominalizing function (Stage III). The presence of the article enables what is morphologically not a noun from the standpoint of morphology, to be understood to function as a noun in terms of both grammar and syntax.

Based on the fact that discourse anaphora is the least likely means by which these nominalized entities have become identifiable, the presence of the article cannot be used as a basis for claiming co-referentiality with something in the preceding context. Connecting subsequent references to previously mentioned anaphors is a cognitive process informed by grammatical and linguistic markers in the context. Thus, Burk's caution about

---

[15] There are no similar caveats for substantival participles or adjectives.

what he terms the conventional view of the anaphoric reference of articular infinitives, as represented by section 399 in Blass, Debrunner, and Funk (1961:205), is important (Burk 2004:258). Blass, Debrunner, and Funk state that "in general the anaphoric significance of the article, i.e. its reference to something previously mentioned or *otherwise well known,* is more or less evident. Without this anaphoric reference, an infinitive as subject or object is usually anarthrous" (1961:205).[16] This statement places an unfortunate stress on the role of anaphora, a shift in the wrong direction from Blass's original statement.[17] It would be more accurate to place the stress on the "otherwise well known" part, that is, what is already identifiable.

6.2.1.2 *Use as a substitute pronoun*

Greenberg observes that articles can evolve to serve as subject and object pronouns rather than demonstratives:

> This does not exclude the diachronic possibility that they come from earlier demonstratives which, on the one hand developed into pronouns and on the other, into articles.... It is not excluded that the article should arise from what is ultimately a demonstrative, but come more directly from a third person pronoun.... Where a deleted pronoun has no modifier [i.e. all that is left is the article], we have a pronominal substitute. Where the noun has modifiers, there may be a substitute, e.g. "one" in English "the good one." (Greenberg 1990:264–265)

Grammarians have treated the use of the article as a substitute pronoun as fundamentally different usage than its use with a noun. Wallace states, "The use of the article for the *personal* and *alternating* pronouns comes the closest to an actual independent use in which the article no longer functions in its normal capacity. There is no noun that it modifies; normally, such an article involves no other force" (1996:211). Blass makes an important observation about the referential role these articles play, which serves as a point of departure for this section:

> Every part of speech which is joined to a substantive as its attribute or in apposition to it—adjective, pronoun, participle, adverb, prepositional expression, the same case or the genitive of another substantive etc.—may in this connection, and without the substantive being actually

---

[16] Italics mine.

[17] Articular infinitives in the nominative and accusative "are generally used in such a way that the anaphoric meaning of the article, with reference to something previously mentioned or otherwise well known, is more or less clearly marked" (Blass 1898:233).

> expressed, be accompanied by the article, which in the
> case of the omission of the substantive often takes its place
> and indicates the substantive to be supplied: thus οἱ τότε
> *sc.* ἄνθρωποι, where *the omission of οἱ is impossible*. (Blass
> 1898:154) [18]

Greek is a PRO-DROP language, whereby overt references to cognitively active subjects may be omitted, typically based on the amount of morphological encoding present on finite verbs.[19] This means that where an entity persists in the syntactic role of subject, the only morphological marking needed for subsequent references is that which is found on finite verbs; an independent pronoun would be the minimum for non-subjects, though in some cases they can be completely elided and remain implicit. Grice's maxim of quantity captures this tendency not to use more morphological marking than is necessary to maintain reference (Huang 2000:207). The one exception to this expectation of zero subject implying same subject is following verbs of speaking. There the default expectation is that the speaker and hearer will switch roles. Thus, where the conversation unfolds as expected with regular switches between speaker and hearer, these switches may also use minimum encoding.

Blass' recognition of the pivotal role played by the article in a noun phrase is corroborated by the pro-drop principle of MORPHOLOGICAL REDUCTION. One may omit the noun, but omitting the article would impact judgments about identifiability, or—in the case of articular pronouns—lead to a zero reference.[20] But this begs the question, why is the articular pronoun present in the first place? If the referent is so identifiable that the noun can be omitted then why not just drop the entire overt reference, as we see happening so often in Greek with zero subjects and implied non-subjects? What exegetical significance does the pronominal article have? The answer to this question lies in observing the apparent restrictions on the distribution of pronominal articles.

Based on a search of the *Cascadia Syntax Graphs of the Greek New Testament: SBL Edition* (Wu and Tan 2012), there are 252 instances where a bare determiner (i.e. an article) serves as a clause function (e.g. subject, object or indirect object) on its own without any other elements present

---

[18] Italics mine.

[19] See Huang 2000:53–54.

[20] An important exception in the case of anarthrous references to active participants, as described by Levinsohn: "According to the principle of §9.2.1, further references to activated participants are normally articular. Anarthrous references to activated participants are therefore of particular significance. In particular, they make the participant and/or his or her initiative or speech *prominent*, because it is of particular importance" (Levinsohn 2000:155–156). See also [Read-]Heimerdinger and Levinsohn 1992:15–44; Read-Heimerdinger 2002:116–144; Read-Heimerdinger 2011:371–412.

(e.g. nouns, adjectives, or relative clauses). In every instance the article is in the nominative and Cascadia analyzes the clause function of the articular pronoun as "subject." Every articular pronoun is clause-initial, placed in a position of prominence before the verb.[21] There are other instances of articular pronouns occurring in the oblique cases, such as in the double accusative or predicate accusative construction, which appear to undermine the association of articular pronouns with nominative subjects, such as the accusative arguments of ἔδωκεν in Eph 4:11. Here τούς serves as the subject of a secondary predication about the role that each group is given, i.e. apostles, prophets, evangelists, pastors and teachers. This apparent exception further supports the apparent restriction of articular pronouns to the subject role, with the case being determined by the relationship of the noun phrase to the verb.[22] Unfortunately, these predicate accusative constructions are annotated in the same way as simple articular noun phrases in the Cascadia and OpenText syntactic databases and are therefore unsearchable (Porter, O'Donnell, Reed, and Tan:2006).[23]

There are two basic uses of articular pronouns, each apparently restricted to a certain text-type.[24] The first use introduces one or more entities that are a subset of some identifiable set in the context. These subset entities often form the basis of a comparison, and represent the predominant function of articular pronouns in non-narrative. Each serves as what has traditionally been called a CONTRASTIVE TOPIC, as in 1 Cor 7:7:

(1) θέλω δὲ πάντας ἀνθρώπους εἶναι   Yet I wish that all men were even
     ὡς καὶ ἐμαυτόν• ἀλλὰ ἕκαστος   as I myself am. However, each
     ἴδιον ἔχει χάρισμα ἐκ θεοῦ, **ὁ** μὲν   man has his own gift from God,
     οὕτως, **ὁ** δὲ οὕτως.   **one** in this manner, and **another**
                                            in that. (NASB)

The other general function is found in narrative proper, where the articular pronoun also serves a contrastive topic. It most often occurs following direct speech where the subject has changed. From a cognitive standpoint, the change in subject is already expected as described

---

[21] For a discussion of the role information status plays in the analysis of fronted clause constituents, see Runge 2010:189–195.

[22] I thank the editor for drawing my attention to the non-nominative uses of articular pronouns, which I had previously overlooked.

[23] Searching syntax databases is a powerful research tool, but also constrained by the design of the database. The Cascadia search I constructed eliminates most of the chaff, but not all of it. Col 2:8, Heb 12:25 and 1 Pet 2:10 show up as hits based on complexities of the syntax graph, but each is a case where the article governs a participle, ὁ συλαγωγῶν, τὸν χρηματίζοντα, and οἱ οὐκ ἠλεημένοι respectively.

[24] Wallace treats each separately, noting that "it is probably best to consider this [the alternative use] a subset of the personal pronoun use" (Wallace 1996:212–213).

above.[25] In fact, continuing with the same subject is what typically requires overt encoding; switches following a speech are often achieved in Koine Greek without an explicit subject based on verb morphology in contrast to the Classical period where an article would be expected.[26] This is illustrated in Matt 9:28–29:

(2) ἐλθόντι δὲ εἰς τὴν οἰκίαν προσῆλθον αὐτῷ οἱ τυφλοί,

And after He had come into the house, the blind men came up to Him,

καὶ λέγει αὐτοῖς ὁ Ἰησοῦς· Πιστεύετε ὅτι δύναμαι τοῦτο ποιῆσαι;

and Jesus *said to them, "Do you believe that I am able to do this?"

Ø λέγουσιν αὐτῷ· Ναί, κύριε.

They *said to Him, "Yes, Lord."

[29] τότε Ø ἥψατο τῶν ὀφθαλμῶν αὐτῶν λέγων· Κατὰ τὴν πίστιν ὑμῶν γενηθήτω ὑμῖν.

[29] Then **He** touched their eyes, saying, "Be it done to you according to your faith."

Thus, use of an articular pronoun in narrative represents more morphological encoding than is necessary to maintain reference. In order to understand the pragmatic motivation for this usage, we need to understand the principles by which they operate.

All the articular pronouns identified in the *Cascadia* syntax search are fronted topics, what I have termed a FRAME OF REFERENCE (Runge 2010:193–195) and what Levinsohn calls a POINT OF DEPARTURE (2000:8). Fronting a topic serves a dual function according to Levinsohn: "It provides a starting point for the communication; and it 'cohesively anchors the subsequent clause(s) to something which is already in the context (i.e. to something accessible in the hearer's mental representation)'" (2000:8). So while these fronted articular pronouns instruct the reader on how to relate the topic that precedes to the one that follows (typically changed), this shift in topic also creates some level of discontinuity. This is where the second function comes into play: cohesion. The instructions for connecting what precedes to what follows (e.g. change in topic) simultaneously link the potentially disconnected chunks together, bridging a potential break in the discourse. The amount of morphological encoding that is used for the topical frame of reference affects the degree of contrast perceived. This means that use of a full nominal expression to switch to a highly identifiable referent is perceived as more contrastive than use of a pronoun, which is more contrastive than the use of an articular pronoun (Dooley and Levinsohn 2001:134). The absence of an overt subject is construed as the unmarked option as there is no marker of discontinuity. There is still a change in subject, but the author

---

[25] For an introduction to the default encoding expectation in various narrative contexts see Runge 2007:112–140.

[26] I thank the editor for bringing this diachronic shift in usage to my attention.

has utilized no more encoding than is necessary to represent the change; the morphology of finite verbs is sufficient.

The convention of using articular pronouns in the NT as a reduced, "frontable" form provides a morphologically reduced and thus less contrastive topical frame of reference compared to using a full noun phrase. The fronted element always provides cohesive linkage to what precedes, but can vary in the degree of perceived contrast depending on the amount of encoding used. Coining a member of a subset requires some explicit marker to activate it as illustrated in example (1), whereas articular pronouns following a reported speech refer to highly identifiable entities. In either case the articular pronoun represents the minimum level of movable encoding available. Compare the different encoding levels in Mark 10:36–40:

(3)   ³⁶ ὁ δὲ εἶπεν αὐτοῖς· Τί θέλετε ποιήσω ὑμῖν;

³ And **he** said to them, "What do you want that I [do] for you?"

³⁷ οἱ δὲ εἶπαν αὐτῷ· Δὸς ἡμῖν ἵνα εἷς σου ἐκ δεξιῶν καὶ εἷς ἐξ ἀριστερῶν καθίσωμεν ἐν τῇ δόξῃ σου.

³⁷ So **they** said to him, "Grant to us that we may [sit] one at your right hand and one at *your* left in your glory."

³⁸ ὁ δὲ Ἰησοῦς εἶπεν αὐτοῖς· Οὐκ οἴδατε τί αἰτεῖσθε· δύνασθε πιεῖν τὸ ποτήριον ὃ ἐγὼ πίνω, ἢ τὸ βάπτισμα ὃ ἐγὼ βαπτίζομαι βαπτισθῆναι;

³⁸ But **Jesus** said to them, "You do not know what you are asking! Are you able to drink the cup that I drink, or to be baptized with the baptism that I am baptized with?"

³⁹ οἱ δὲ εἶπαν αὐτῷ· Δυνάμεθα.

³⁹ And **they** said to him, "We are able."

ὁ δὲ Ἰησοῦς εἶπεν αὐτοῖς· Τὸ ποτήριον ὃ ἐγὼ πίνω πίεσθε καὶ τὸ βάπτισμα ὃ ἐγὼ βαπτίζομαι βαπτισθήσεσθε, ⁴⁰ τὸ δὲ καθίσαι ἐκ δεξιῶν μου ἢ ἐξ εὐωνύμων οὐκ ἔστιν ἐμὸν δοῦναι, ἀλλ᾽ οἷς ἡτοίμασται.

So **Jesus** said to them, "You will drink the cup that I drink, and you will be baptized with the baptism that I am baptized with, ⁴⁰ but to sit at my right hand or at *my* left is not mine to grant, but *is* for those for whom it has been prepared."

The conversation advances using articular pronouns, except in the two instances where Jesus redirects the conversation from where James and John had intended. Such redirection or countering is often marked in languages by overencoding.[27] The use of a full noun phrase instead of either a zero subject or an articular pronoun results in greater contrast. In verse

---

[27] For a typological introduction to the pragmatic function of using full NPs for active participants see Stephen H. Levinsohn 2000:1–13; for an application to the Greek NT see Levinsohn 2000:135–136, 140–142.

38 Jesus asks whether they can drink from the cup without addressing the issue of whether he will grant their request. It is only after the two have affirmed their willingness to drink that Jesus tells them it is not his to grant, another redirection from where they intended things to go.

6.2.2 Articles in the midst of a noun phrase

Another less prototypical use of the article is to create what Wallace classifies as second and third attributive constructions, which are identified by the presence of an extra article, that is, article-noun-article-modifier or noun-article-modifier, respectively (Wallace 1996:214; Porter 1995:116). This is not to say that these constructions are uncommon, but simply to note that the use of an article in the midst of a single noun phrase is not semantically required. Prototypically articles begin a noun phrase, which means the presence of a mid-phrasal article must be intended to accomplish some other discourse function than signaling a new noun phrase. After all, the mid-phrasal article is what defines the construction, and it does not actually begin a new noun phrase; rather it divides what would otherwise have been a more cohesive phrase into two parts. What then is the exegetical significance of including what appears to be an extra article? To answer this question we need to consider the role that packaging information into manageable chunks plays in our processing of discourse.

Despite the fact that we may process huge amounts of text or speech, they are not monolithic. Instead, they are structured into chunks, which are composed of recursively smaller chunks. Conventions like paragraphing and punctuation in print, guide readers in how to chunk the discourse into smaller thought-units. In spoken discourse, pauses and intonational contours can convey similar information. Constructions like left- and right-dislocations (a.k.a. hanging nominatives or *pendens* constructions) prototypically enable introduction of complex entities in stages: a generic reference inside the clause boundaries, additional information outside the main clause in the dislocation (Runge 2010:297–301, 321–326). Thus, second and third attributive constructions may well serve a processing function, breaking what might otherwise be a complex noun phrase down into two more-manageable chunks, as in John 3:29:

(4) ὁ ἔχων τὴν νύμφην νυμφίος ἐστίν   The one who has the bride is the
     ὁ δὲ φίλος τοῦ νυμφίου ὁ ἑστηκὼς   bridegroom. But **the friend of**
     καὶ ἀκούων αὐτοῦ χαρᾷ χαίρει   **the bridegroom, who stands**
     διὰ τὴν φωνὴν τοῦ νυμφίου   **and hears him**, rejoices greatly
     because of the bridegroom's voice.

There has been no mention of bridal party members in the preceding context, so the bride, the bridegroom and the friend are all being introduced into the discourse. The description of the friend is complex, and the second attributive construction enables the entity to be introduced using two smaller chunks. In English we prefer to use a relative clause in such cases, as Wallace suggests for translating the second article (Wallace 1996:214). However, as we have said (§6.1.2), that introduction of one member of a set—a schema—like a bridal party makes the others identifiable. This explains why we see the articular references. So although this phrase appears to be complex at first blush, it is actually quite identifiable. The information about the friend standing and hearing could just as easily have been conveyed in a subsequent clause. It is not restrictive; rather it is a comment about him that might have required a second clause had the second article not been present (i.e. "But the friend of the bridegroom stands and hears him. He rejoices greatly...") The desire to focus on a single action—rejoicing—necessitated packaging the other activity in something other than a main clause. The second attributive position discloses the information in its own separate package for processing, figuratively speaking as essentially a second noun phrase in apposition. The effect is to relegate the actions of standing and listening to the noun phrase rather than to a second clause. The latter would have placed the action on a par with the main clausal action of rejoicing. The extra article enables there to be only one assertion: this complex entity rejoicing over the bridegroom's voice.

Third attributives also introduce complex entities in stages, though most often the nominal element is the name of a place or a person.[28] Consider the example from Eph 6:21-22:

(5) Ἵνα δὲ εἰδῆτε καὶ ὑμεῖς τὰ κατ'   Now, so that you also may
     ἐμέ τί πράσσω πάντα γνωρίσει   know my circumstances, what
     ὑμῖν **Τυχικὸς ὁ ἀγαπητὸς ἀδελφὸς**   I am doing, **Tychicus, my dear**
     καὶ πιστὸς διάκονος ἐν κυρίῳ   **brother and faithful servant in**
     ὃν ἔπεμψα πρὸς ὑμᾶς εἰς αὐτὸ   **the Lord**, will make known to you
     τοῦτο ἵνα γνῶτε τὰ περὶ ἡμῶν καὶ   all things, whom I have sent to
     παρακαλέσῃ τὰς καρδίας ὑμῶν   you for this very reason, that you
                                           may know our circumstances, and
                                           he may encourage your hearts.

But the question arises of whether the attributive information is restrictive and thus semantically required to pick out the intended referent (i.e. *this* Tychicus and not some other one). If we examine a selection of second and third attributive constructions—those in John's gospel—we find that the vast majority of these noun phrases are not complex, but rather very identifiable from the standpoint of cognitive processing and identifiability. Even examples (4) and (5) are not very complex in contrast to the more widely used first attributive constructions. Compare the uses of ἴδιος bolded in the following

---

[28] See John 14:27, Rom 8:23 and Eph 4:16 for examples of third attributives used without proper nouns.

examples from John in (6), where it is found in both first and second attributive positions. Compare its use in opposition to αὐτός, which is *italicized*.

(6)	John 10:3 1st Attr.	τούτῳ ὁ θυρωρὸς ἀνοίγει, καὶ τὰ πρόβατα *τῆς φωνῆς αὐτοῦ* ἀκούει καὶ **τὰ ἴδια πρόβατα** φωνεῖ κατ᾽ ὄνομα καὶ ἐξάγει αὐτά.	For this one the doorkeeper opens, and the sheep hear *his voice*, and he calls **his own sheep** by name and leads them out.
	John 10:4 1st Attr.	ὅταν **τὰ ἴδια πάντα** ἐκβάλῃ, ἔμπροσθεν αὐτῶν πορεύεται, καὶ τὰ πρόβατα αὐτῷ ἀκολουθεῖ, ὅτι οἴδασιν *τὴν φωνὴν αὐτοῦ*	Whenever he [sends] out **all his own**, he goes before them, and the sheep follow him because they know *his voice*.
	John 10:12 1st Attr.	ὁ μισθωτὸς καὶ οὐκ ὢν ποιμήν, οὗ οὐκ ἔστιν **τὰ πρόβατα ἴδια**, θεωρεῖ τὸν λύκον ἐρχόμενον καὶ ἀφίησιν τὰ πρόβατα καὶ φεύγει—καὶ ὁ λύκος ἁρπάζει αὐτὰ καὶ σκορπίζει	The hired hand, who is not the shepherd, whose **own the sheep** are not, sees the wolf approaching and abandons the sheep and runs away—and the wolf seizes them and scatters them.
	John 1:41 2nd Attr.	εὑρίσκει οὗτος πρῶτον **τὸν ἀδελφὸν τὸν ἴδιον** Σίμωνα καὶ λέγει αὐτῷ Εὑρήκαμεν τὸν Μεσσίαν ὅ ἐστιν μεθερμηνευόμενον Χριστός	This one first found **his own brother Simon** and said to him, "We have found the Messiah!" (which is translated "Christ").
	John 7:18 2nd Attr.	ὁ ἀφ᾽ ἑαυτοῦ λαλῶν **τὴν δόξαν τὴν ἰδίαν** ζητεῖ ὁ δὲ ζητῶν τὴν δόξαν τοῦ πέμψαντος αὐτὸν οὗτος ἀληθής ἐστιν καὶ ἀδικία ἐν αὐτῷ οὐκ ἔστιν	The one who speaks from himself seeks **his own glory**. But the one who seeks the glory of the one who sent him—this one is true, and there is no unrighteousness in him.

In John 1:41 it would be expected that the brother whom Andrew found was his own, based on the typical referent of ἀδελφός being a male sibling in narrative proper. There is a meaningful distinction made in the use of ἴδιος versus αὐτός in 10:3–4, whereas in 1:41 and 7:18 ἴδιος occurs without such an opposition. Nevertheless, placing it in the second position has the effect of singling out that bit of information unlike the first position or the use of αὐτός.

Another factor to consider besides complexity is the nature of the information typically found in second and third position. Is it restrictive or non-restrictive? I have proposed elsewhere that there is a processing hierarchy that explains how seemingly polysemous uses of the same construction can be differentiated (Runge 2007:39).[29] The default expectation is that the information provided is semantically required, i.e. restrictive and thus necessary to identify the intended referent. However this only accounts for a portion of the data found in John. Most of the second and third attributive modifiers are *non-restrictive*. Of the twenty-five third attributive constructions in John, only nine of them are clearly restrictive.[30] Another five might be construed as restrictive, but not necessarily.[31] The remaining nine are clearly not restrictive; the attributive modifier conveys thematically salient information.[32] Consider the description of Judas in 12:4:

(7) λέγει δὲ Ἰούδας ὁ Ἰσκαριώτης εἷς   But Judas Iscariot, **one of his**
     ἐκ τῶν μαθητῶν αὐτοῦ ὁ μέλλων   **disciples (the one who was**
     αὐτὸν παραδιδόναι   **going to betray him)** said,

The patronym 'Iscariot' would have been sufficient to restrict the possible referents to 'the Judas' last mentioned in John 6:70–71. There he was identified as 'the son of Simon Iscariot', 'one of the twelve', 'the devil who would betray Jesus'. Rather than restricting the referent's identity in 12:4, the attributive information reiterates thematically salient information characterizing Judas as the betrayer, which John reiterates again in 13:2, 21–26; 18:2, and 5.

We find a similar distribution of restrictive vs. non-restrictive information in John's use of second attributive constructions, where thematically salient information is segmented off by the second article. Of the nine occurrences of the lemma ἀληθινός in John, only four are attributive modifiers. Three of these four place the attributive in the second attributive position (1:9; 6:32, 15:1 vs. 17:3). Similarly, the three references to the good shepherd (10:11,14) feature καλός in second position. The possessive pronoun ἐμός is found in second or third position twenty-four of the thirty-one times it serves as an attributive.[33] One cannot explain this usage based on its being too complex to process in one chunk, or as always being restrictive. Instead, these positions quite often appear to be used for the pragmatic purpose of thematic highlighting, setting a particularly salient bit of information apart for extra attention. The attention is not

---

[29] For an application to the polysemous functions of the historical present see Runge 2010:128–134.

[30] John 1:23, 40, 45; 11:1; 18:5; 19:25, 38; 20:1; 21:2.

[31] John 6:8; 8:56; 12:21, 38; 19:19.

[32] John 1:42; 6:42; 7:42; 11:11, 28; 12:4; 18:7, 24; 20:18.

[33] John 5:30 (2x), 43; 6:38; 7:6 (2x), 18; 8:16, 17, 31, 37, 43 (2x), 56; 10:26, 27; 12:26; 13:1; 14:15; 15:9, 11, 12; 17:13, 17, 24; 18:35, 36 (4x); 14:27.

based on it being the most important part of the utterance, i.e. being focal or emphatic.[34] Rather, the prominence it is assigned is based on its thematic salience to the context, (re)shaping how we view the referent in the particular context.

John's style has sometimes been criticized for its improper use of Greek conventions. This raises the question of how John's use of these attributive constructions compares to that of Paul, an author praised for his style. Syntax queries for these constructions in Romans through Colossians revealed remarkable similarities to John's style. All but one instance of third position attributives involved a proper name. The names were predominantly found in the greetings sections of his letters, at the opening or at the conclusion. In 1 Cor 1:1, 2 Cor 1:1, and Col. 1:1, attributives modifying Sosthenes and Timothy are in the third position. The majority of the other twenty-eight occurrences are found in the greetings sections at the end of the letters.[35]

But despite the location in the letter, only a very few could be construed as restrictive, intended to eliminate possible referents. Rather, the information in this prototypically restrictive construction served the non-restrictive purpose of characterizing the participant. In other words, just as restrictive information anchors newly activated participants to the discourse, so this non-restrictive information activates a different, thematically salient profile of an already identifiable referent. Consider the attributive information from Romans 16, where all of the referents are members of the Roman church:

---

[34] For a discussion on the meaningful distinction between accessible versus non-accessible, focal information see Runge 2010:188–193.

[35] Rom 16:1, 5, 8, 9, 10, 11, 12, 23; Col 4:7, 9, 10, 14.

(8) Rom 16:5	καὶ τὴν κατ' οἶκον αὐτῶν ἐκκλησίαν ἀσπάσασθε Ἐπαίνετον τὸν ἀγαπητόν μου ὅς ἐστιν ἀπαρχὴ τῆς Ἀσίας εἰς Χριστόν	also greet the church in their house. Greet **Epenetus my dear friend**, who is the first convert of Asia for Christ.
Rom 16:8	ἀσπάσασθε Ἀμπλιᾶτον τὸν ἀγαπητόν μου ἐν κυρίῳ	Greet **Ampliatus, my dear friend in the Lord.**
Rom 16:9	ἀσπάσασθε Οὐρβανὸν τὸν συνεργὸν ἡμῶν ἐν Χριστῷ καὶ Στάχυν τὸν ἀγαπητόν μου	Greet **Urbanus, our fellow worker in Christ**, and **my dear friend Stachys.**
Rom 16:10	ἀσπάσασθε Ἀπελλῆν τὸν δόκιμον ἐν Χριστῷ ἀσπάσασθε τοὺς ἐκ τῶν Ἀριστοβούλου	Greet **Apelles, who is approved in Christ.** Greet those of the household of Aristobulus.
Rom 16:11	ἀσπάσασθε Ἡρῳδίωνα τὸν συγγενῆ μου ἀσπάσασθε τοὺς ἐκ τῶν Ναρκίσσου τοὺς ὄντας ἐν κυρίῳ	Greet **Herodion my compatriot.** Greet **those of the household of Narcissus who are in the Lord.**
Rom 16:12	ἀσπάσασθε Τρύφαιναν καὶ Τρυφῶσαν τὰς κοπιώσας ἐν κυρίῳ ἀσπάσασθε Περσίδα τὴν ἀγαπητήν ἥτις πολλὰ ἐκοπίασεν ἐν κυρίῳ	Greet **Tryphena and Tryphosa, the laborers in the Lord.** Greet **Persis, the dear friend** who has worked hard in the Lord.

Clearly the appositives here are non-restrictive since they refer to individuals well-known to the recipients. Paul's inclusion of this extra thematic information necessitates use of an article to aid the processing. The alternative would likely have been to add a topic/comment sentence to have achieved a similar two-part effect (e.g. "Greet Urbanus. He is our fellow worker in Christ."). Framed in this way, Paul's usage characterizes the referents, ostensibly for their own edification as well as to influence how their peers would view them.

Another instance from Rom 8:23 uses a right dislocation to add thematic information about a newly introduced entity:

| (9) | οὐ μόνον δέ ἀλλὰ καὶ αὐτοὶ τὴν ἀπαρχὴν τοῦ πνεύματος ἔχοντες ἡμεῖς καὶ αὐτοὶ ἐν ἑαυτοῖς στενάζομεν **υἱοθεσίαν** ἀπεκδεχόμενοι **τὴν ἀπολύτρωσιν** τοῦ σώματος ἡμῶν. | Not only this, but we ourselves also, having the first fruits of the Spirit, even we ourselves groan within ourselves while we await eagerly our **adoption, the redemption of our body.** |

The noun υἱοθεσίαν is fronted for emphasis' sake, marking it as the most important information asserted within the participial clause. If the entire noun phrase had been fronted it likely would have been misconstrued as topical rather than focal. The dislocated information describes more specifically the adoption that Paul has in mind here. Use of the dislocation construction allows Paul to introduce the concept of adoption as well as add more detail about what it entails.

The same principles apply to the use of second attributives found in Romans through Colossians; most are non-restrictive in nature, adding salient thematic information to an already identifiable concept comparable to what is observed in John (Rom 12:2 and Col 2:12). In the rest, the information in the second attributive position could easily have been included in the initial part of the noun phrase, that is, as a first attributive. Placement in the second position sets the information off from the rest of the noun phrase.

(10)	Rom 12:2	καὶ μὴ συσχηματίζεσθε τῷ αἰῶνι τούτῳ, ἀλλὰ μεταμορφοῦσθε τῇ ἀνακαινώσει τοῦ νοός, εἰς τὸ δοκιμάζειν ὑμᾶς τί **τὸ θέλημα τοῦ θεοῦ, τὸ ἀγαθὸν καὶ εὐάρεστον καὶ τέλειον.**	And do not be conformed to this age, but be transformed by the renewal of your mind, so that you may approve what is **the good and well-pleasing and perfect will of God.**
	Col 2:12	συνταφέντες αὐτῷ ἐν τῷ βαπτισμῷ, ἐν ᾧ καὶ συνηγέρθητε διὰ τῆς πίστεως τῆς ἐνεργείας **τοῦ θεοῦ τοῦ ἐγείραντος αὐτὸν ἐκ νεκρῶν·**	having been buried with him in baptism, in which also you were raised together with him through faith in the working **of God, who raised him from the dead.**
	1 Cor 7:14	ἡγίασται γὰρ **ὁ ἀνὴρ ὁ ἄπιστος** ἐν τῇ γυναικί, καὶ ἡγίασται **ἡ γυνὴ ἡ ἄπιστος** ἐν τῷ ἀδελφῷ· ἐπεὶ ἄρα τὰ τέκνα ὑμῶν ἀκάθαρτά ἐστιν, νῦν δὲ ἁγιά ἐστιν.	For **the unbelieving husband** is sanctified by his wife, and **the unbelieving wife** is sanctified by the brother, since otherwise your children are unclean, but now they are holy.
	1 Cor 12:2	οἴδατε ὅτι ὅτε ἔθνη ἦτε πρὸς **τὰ εἴδωλα τὰ ἄφωνα** ὡς ἂν ἤγεσθε ἀπαγόμενοι.	You know that when you were pagans, you were led astray to **the speechless idols**, however you were led.
	1 Cor 12:31	ζηλοῦτε δὲ **τὰ χαρίσματα τὰ μείζονα.** καὶ ἔτι καθ' ὑπερβολὴν ὁδὸν ὑμῖν δείκνυμι.	But strive for **the greater gifts.** And I will show you a still more excellent way.

1 Cor 15:4	καὶ ὅτι ἐτάφη, καὶ ὅτι ἐγήγερται **τῇ ἡμέρᾳ τῇ τρίτῃ** κατὰ τὰς γραφάς,	and that he was buried, and that he was raised up on **the third day** according to the scriptures,
Eph 1:13	ἐν ᾧ καὶ ὑμεῖς ἀκούσαντες τὸν λόγον τῆς ἀληθείας, τὸ εὐαγγέλιον τῆς σωτηρίας ὑμῶν, ἐν ᾧ καὶ πιστεύσαντες ἐσφραγίσθητε τῷ πνεύματι τῆς ἐπαγγελίας τῷ ἁγίῳ,	in whom also you, when you heard* the word of truth, the gospel of your salvation, in whom also when you believed you were sealed with **the promised Holy Spirit**,
Eph 6:13	διὰ τοῦτο ἀναλάβετε τὴν πανοπλίαν τοῦ θεοῦ, ἵνα δυνηθῆτε ἀντιστῆναι ἐν **τῇ ἡμέρᾳ τῇ πονηρᾷ** καὶ ἅπαντα κατεργασάμενοι στῆναι.	Because of this, take up the full armor of God, in order that you may be [able] to resist in **the evil day**, and having done everything, to stand.
Col 1:15	ὅς ἐστιν εἰκὼν **τοῦ θεοῦ τοῦ ἀοράτου**, πρωτότοκος πάσης κτίσεως,	who is the image of **the invisible God**, the firstborn over all creation,
Col 1:21	καὶ ὑμᾶς ποτε ὄντας ἀπηλλοτριωμένους καὶ ἐχθροὺς τῇ διανοίᾳ ἐν **τοῖς ἔργοις τοῖς πονηροῖς**,	And ⌊although you were formerly alienated⌋* and enemies in attitude, because of your **evil deeds**,

It is doubtful there was any question about which 'will of God' is intended in Rom 12:2. The unbelieving spouses are introduced in 1 Cor 7:12–13 in standard N-ADJ order, so there is no need to set off ἄπιστος unless it is for thematic reasons. Specifying that the idols were speechless in 1 Cor 12:2 is not to contrast them with those that could speak, but to highlight the fact that they are dead material rather than a living god. So although we find both simple and complex appositives in the second attributive position, both bring about the same effect of singling out the information based on its separation from the initial part of the noun phrase.

6.2.3 Summary

The fact that the Greek language adopted the article earlier than most other Indo-European languages like English has important implications. The principles of grammaticalization suggest that this longer period of development led to more innovative uses than would be found in newer adopters of the article. I noted the descriptions by Levinsohn and Read-Heimerdinger of the pragmatic (dis)use of the article with proper names. Greenberg's Stage III use of the article, as a nominalizer with non-nominal entities, is consistent with what has been observed cross-linguistically in languages. It still marks the entity as identifiable as when used with nouns, but it no longer carries the same morphological marking, identifying noun phrases. The Stage III use does not carry the same expectations of anaphora associated with Stages I or II, so caution must be exercised in claims about antecedents. This is not to say there cannot be a discourse anaphor, but merely that co-referentiality must be established on some other basis than the presence of the article. The article is only marking identifiability and signaling that what follows should be processed as a substantive, nothing more.

Second and third attributive uses of the article represent another innovation that can be credited to the high degree of the article's development in Greek. The more frequently a device is used in a language, the more likely it is to extend to less prototypical functions than those found in Stages I or II. In the sampling of data from John's gospel and Paul's epistles, these structures allow the writers to include non-restrictive information within a complex noun phrase that might otherwise have required the use of a separate clause. Although the appositives still accomplish a semantic function, the facts that they are not semantically required and that they are segmented from the initial part of the noun phrase enables them also to accomplish a pragmatic function. In most cases, this function is to activate a thematically salient, non-restrictive profile of the referent.

6.3 Conclusions

In the seminal work on grammaticalization and the development of linguistic forms, Bybee, Perkins, and Pagliuca challenge linguists to move beyond merely assigning a function to a form, noting the limitations of such an approach:

> A diachronic approach is desirable for several reasons. First, a diachronic dimension greatly increases the explanatory power of linguistic theory. Demonstrating that a given form or construction has a certain function does not constitute an explanation for the existence of the form or construction; it must also be shown how that form or construction came to have that function. (Bybee, Perkins, and Pagliuca 1994:3)

Responsible linguistic studies begin with a typologically informed understanding of the feature, that is, an understanding of how a given feature operates in other similar languages. In the case of Greek, attention would be given to pro-drop VO languages that lack an indefinite article and have a rich case-marking system. These findings would not guarantee or require that the feature in Greek would operate in exactly the same way. Rather this knowledge would provide a safeguard against claiming something that is not attested in other languages, similar or otherwise. This requires those wanting to do interdisciplinary work in linguistics and New Testament studies to develop a higher level of proficiency in the secondary discipline than has typically been observed in the past twenty years.

An intentional decision was made in this chapter to focus more on what has been said about the article outside of New Testament studies than on what has been said about it within that field. It has necessarily entailed a flyover at ten thousand feet in order to provide the intended survey of what the linguistic literature has to contribute to our understanding of the Greek article. The choice was made to consult "the usual suspects," the standard grammatical monographs, upon which most scholars rely. A natural consequence of this is the overlooking of more detailed studies (Wallace 2008; Burk 2006; Peters 2014). The objective was not to correct or challenge existing notions about the article, but to provide an overview from a discourse-functional perspective heavily grounded in cognitive linguistics. My hope is that it will help to synthesize the disparate claims about the article into a holistic understanding of its meaning and function. This study may also offer productive paths for future research.

References

Bauer, Brigitte L. M. 2007. The definite article in Indo-European: Emergence of a new grammatical category? In Elisabeth Stark, Elisabeth Leiss, and Werner Abraham, (eds.), *Nominal determination: Typology, context constraints, and historical emergence*, 103–40. Amsterdam: John Benjamins.

Blass, Friedrich, and Albert Debrunner. 1961. *A Greek grammar of the New Testament and other early Christian literature*. Translated and edited by Robert W. Funk. Cambridge: University Press.

Blass, Friedrich. 1898. *Grammar of New Testament Greek*. Translated by Henry St. John Thackeray. London: Macmillan.

Burk, Denny. 2006. *Articular infinitives in the Greek of the New Testament: On the exegetical benefit of grammatical precision*. New Testament Monographs 14. Sheffield, UK: Phoenix Press.

Burk, Denny. 2004. On the articular infinitive in Philippians 2:6. *Tyndale Bulletin* 55:253–74.

Bybee, Joan, Revere Perkins, and William Pagliuca. 1994. *The evolution of grammar: Tense, aspect, and modality in the languages of the world*. Chicago, IL: University of Chicago Press.

De Mulder, Walter, and Anne Carlier. 2011. The grammaticalization of definite articles. In Bernd Heine and Heiko Narrog (eds.), *The Oxford handbook of grammaticalization*, 522–34. Oxford: University Press.

Diessel, Holger. 1999. The morphosyntax of demonstratives in synchrony and diachrony. *Linguistic Typology* 3:1–49.

Dooley, Robert A., and Stephen H. Levinsohn. 2001. *Analyzing discourse: A manual of basic concepts*. Dallas, TX: SIL International.

Givón, Talmy. 1984. *Syntax: A functional-typological introduction*. Vol. 1. Amsterdam: John Benjamins.

Greenberg, Joseph Harold. 1978. How does a language acquire gender markers?" In Joseph Harold Greenberg (ed.), *Universals of human language: Word structure*, 47–82. Stanford, CA: Stanford University Press.

Greenberg, Joseph Harold. 1990. How does a language acquire gender markers? In Keith M. Denning and Suzanne Kemmer (eds.), *On language: Selected writings of Joseph H. Greenberg*, 241–70. Stanford, CA: University Press.

Gundel, Jeanette K., Nancy Hedberg, and Ron Zacharski. 1993. Cognitive status and the form of referring expressions in discourse. *Language* 69:274–307.

Harris, W. Hall, Elliot Ritzema, Rick Brannan, Douglas Magnum, John Dunham, Jeffrey A. Reimer, and Micah Wierenga, eds. 2012. *The Lexham English Bible*. Bellingham, WA: Logos Bible Software.

[Read-]Heimerdinger, Jenny, and Stephen H. Levinsohn. 1992. The use of the definite article before names of people in the Greek Text of Acts with particular reference to Codex Bezae. *Filología Neotestamentaria* 5:15–44.

Holmes, Michael W., ed. 2010. *The Greek New Testament: SBL edition*. Bellingham, WA: Logos Bible Software.

Huang, Yan. 2000. *Anaphora: A cross-linguistic approach*. Oxford Studies in Typology and Linguistic Theory. Oxford: University Press,.

Lambrecht, Knud. 1996. *Information structure and sentence form: Topic, focus, and the mental representations of discourse referents*. Cambridge Studies in Linguistics 71. Cambridge: University Press,.

Levinsohn, Stephen H. 2000a. *Discourse features of New Testament Greek: A coursebook on the information structure of New Testament Greek*. Second edition (revised). Dallas, TX: SIL International.

Levinsohn, Stephen H. 2009. Towards a unified linguistic description of οὗτος and ἐκεῖνος. In Stanley E. Porter and Matthew Brook O'Donnell, (eds.), *The linguist as pedagogue*, 206–19. Sheffield, UK: Phoenix Press.

Peters, Ronald D. 2014. *The Greek article*. Leiden: Brill.

Porter, Stanley E. 1995. *Idioms of the Greek New Testament*. Second edition. Biblical Languages: Greek 2. Sheffield, UK: Academic Press.

Porter, Stanley E., Matthew Brook O'Donnell, Jeffrey T. Reed, and Randall Tan. 2006. The OpenText.org syntactically analyzed Greek New Testament: Clause analysis (version 2013-04-12T20:32:29Z). Bellingham, WA: Logos Bible Software.

Prince, Ellen F. 1981. Toward a taxonomy of given-new information. In Peter Cole (ed.), *Radical pragmatics*, 223–255. New York: Academic Press.

Read-Heimerdinger, Jenny. 2002. *The Bezan text of Acts: A contribution of discourse analysis to textual criticism*. Journal for the Study of the New Testament, Supplement Series 236. Sheffield, UK: Academic Press.

Read-Heimerdinger, Jenny. 2011. The use of the article before names of place: Patterns of use in the book of Acts. In Steven E. Runge (ed.), *Discourse studies and biblical interpretation: A festschrift in honor of Stephen H. Levinsohn,* 371–412. Bellingham, WA: Logos Bible Software.

Robertson, A. T. 1923. *A grammar of the Greek New Testament in the light of historical research.* Nashville, TN: Broadman.

Runge, Steven E. 2007 A discourse-functional description of participant reference in biblical Hebrew narrative. DLitt dissertation. University of Stellenbosch. Accessed May 16, 2018. http://hdl.handle.net/10019.1/1212.

Runge, Steven E. 2010. *Discourse grammar of the Greek New Testament: A practical introduction for teaching and exegesis.* Peabody, MA: Hendrickson.

Wallace, Daniel B. 1996. *Greek grammar beyond the basics.* Second edition. Grand Rapids, MI: Zondervan.

Wallace, Daniel B. 2008. *Granville Sharp's canon and its kin: Semantics and significance.* New York: Peter Lang.

Wu, Andi, and Randall Tan, eds. 2012. *Cascadia syntax graphs of the Greek New Testament: SBL edition.* Bellingham, WA: Lexham.

7

The Function of the Article with Proper Names: The New Testament Book of Acts as a Case Study

Jenny Read-Heimerdinger

7.1 Introduction

7.1.1 Background

The fluctuation in the presence of the article with definite nouns is an issue noted in grammar books of New Testament Greek as one that is particularly intriguing.[1] Many of the rules that have been discerned for its use only work so far before they seem to be contradicted by an example that does not follow them.[2] Part of the reason for the complexity surrounding its use is that, for all that the article is often referred to as "the definite article," its

---

[1] It led one author to comment, "The development of the Greek article is one of the most interesting things in human speech" (Robertson 1934:754; he devotes a section to the topic, 1934:754–796).

[2] That the use of the article in Greek is not a straightforward matter can be seen from the discussions on the subject in the various New Testament Greek grammar books, among

presence before a noun does not necessarily denote definiteness from every point of view, just as its absence does not always signify indefiniteness.[3] To add to the confusion, even when the noun it precedes is a particular one, the same particular noun may well be found in an adjacent clause without the article. Another problem is that although the use of the article can sometimes be explained on the grounds that the referent of a noun is known, the omission of the article cannot by any means be taken as necessarily signaling that the referent is unknown. This is notably the case with the article that is found before proper nouns, a characteristic use of the article in Greek that illustrates how different its function is compared with its role in English.

The diversity in the use of the article before proper nouns by New Testament writers is made more complex by the existence of a large number of variant readings among the Greek manuscripts. Variation has tended to be dismissed by textual critics as arising from the personal style or custom of the scribe, reflecting the notion that there are no particular rules for the inclusion of the article. The absence of clear rules makes it difficult if not impossible to decide which reading is authentic at places of divergence; the common answer is to adopt an eclectic approach, whereby the non-variant text is examined to see whether the article is more often used than not with a given noun and variant readings are evaluated in the light of the results.

The approach of discourse analysis shows that where there are no explanations for linguistic variation at the level of the sentence grammar, there may well be at the level above the sentence; and pragmatic factors outside the text itself may be playing a role, too. This is the case, for example, with word order, or the choice of sentence connectives, two other issues widely affected by apparent inconsistency on the part of Greek authors as well as later copyists, which are only partially accounted for by traditional grammars. And indeed, detailed study of Greek texts on their own terms, applying the perspectives and insights of discourse analysis, does bring to light specific principles in the use of the article with proper nouns and accounts for the variation in its use.

My investigation into the use of the article in the New Testament has focused on its presence with proper nouns, which are by their nature, definite and particular, thus avoiding the uncertainty of interpretation with common nouns that are capable of being used indefinitely. The names of persons were considered in a first study carried out in collaboration with Stephen Levinsohn in 1991; ([Read-]Heimerdinger

---

which may be cited: Blass et al. 1979:§252–262 (esp. §261); Porter 1992:103–114; Turner 1963:172–184; Wallace 1996:206–290; Winer (1882)1997:131–175.

[3] What constitutes "definiteness" and how it is communicated are themselves subjects of debate. In linguistic investigation, the concept is usually seen as needing to be discussed in terms of the notions of identifiability and accessibility. For a detailed study of the topic, see Lyons 1999.

and Levinsohn 1992:15–44)[4] followed later by a consideration of the names of places in a contribution to a Festschrift for Levinsohn (Read-Heimerdinger 2011:371–402). The analysis in sections II and III below incorporates material from my earlier investigations, developing some of the examples, summarizing the findings, and modifying them on occasion.

7.1.2 Data for the study

The text selected as a sample for both studies was the New Testament book of Acts, traditionally ascribed to a certain "Luke," the author of what became the third Gospel in the New Testament canon. It is likely that the two books were initially two volumes of a single work, but whatever the connections between the two, the second volume stands as a self-contained unit insofar as the action takes place in a period of time following the end of the Gospel, and though some of the locations (Jerusalem and Judaea) and characters (notably Jesus, Peter and the apostles) appear in both books, new locations and new characters are quickly introduced in Acts as the story develops. Compared with many other New Testament books, the language of Acts is that of a native speaker of Koine Greek, who writes with a literary and sophisticated style.

The book of Acts is especially appropriate for a systematic linguistic survey of the use of the article with proper names because of its extensive narrative with a carefully developed sequence of actions, involving a wide range of participants, several of them re-appearing in more than one scene, and covering a wide geographical area where many place names occur, again often on more than one occasion. The names of both the characters and the places were examined exhaustively, taking into account the narrative setting and interaction with other characters. Consideration was also given to the meta-narrative circumstances of the author and the addressee ('speaker' and 'hearer' in discourse analysis terminology), though the absence of verifiable external information renders this aspect somewhat open to question; furthermore, the "speaker" and "hearer" are subject to change with successive copyings of the manuscript, the more so the greater the distance between the time and place of the original author and his intended audience and the date and place of the copy.

While the book of Acts was probably written in the last quarter of the first century CE, for the next two centuries the evidence for it is limited to citations and fragmentary copies on papyrus. The first complete copies, necessary for an extended study of the text, are majuscules dating from the middle of the 4th century. Among those, the one most represented in the successive editions of the Greek New Testament in use since the

---

[4] The study was adapted in Read-Heimerdinger 2002:116–144 and developed further to include common nouns in Levinsohn 2000:150–162.

early twentieth century[5] is Codex Vaticanus, B03. Dating from *circa* 350 CE, its text is attested by earlier papyri and authors from the late second century onwards; it is also widely supported by another majuscule from the same time, Codex Sinaiticus, א01. Both are taken as representatives of the Alexandrian tradition, accepted by the majority of New Testament textual critics as the "best" manuscripts available. The manuscript with the text of Acts that is most different from that of B03 is Codex Bezae, D05, dated to around 400 CE.[6] This witness is generally rejected as a witness to the original text, not least because of its frequent disagreement with the preferred text. Furthermore, though there is widespread support for its text among all the earliest translations of Acts and in citations, there is little extant evidence of support for it in Greek mss. That said, fresh archaeological discoveries over recent decades have brought to light early papyri fragments as well as new early versions that show that the readings of Acts in Codex Bezae were known well before the date of the manuscript.[7] Even so, an additional factor that has counted against the Bezan text is that many of its variant readings are difficult to make sense of or appear as simply the colorful modifications of a fanciful scribe.[8]

The difficulty of its readings and their singularity, however, are two considerations that do not impinge on the matter of the article. What is important, in contrast, is the evidence that can be retrieved from the Bezan readings for the narrator's close familiarity with the Jewish context of the events, since this is a significant pragmatic factor that serves as an indication of the perspective from which the characters and places are being viewed.[9] The text of the Vaticanus manuscript reflects, by comparison, a more distant perspective and displays less evidence of first-hand knowledge of the Jewish context of the story it tells. A further distinguishing feature of the Bezan text, which is relevant to a study of the article with names of persons in particular, is the narrator's critical appraisal of the Christian

---

[5] The current edition is Aland et al. 2013.

[6] Digital copies of Codex Vaticanus and Codex Bezae are available online as follows: http://digi.vatlib.it/view/MSS_Vat.gr.1209?sid=1f2e1a937299b864df0f51ecb18 4c2ac (accessed May 16, 2018); http://cudl.lib.cam.ac.uk/view/MS-NN-00002-00041/1 (accessed May 16, 2018).

[7] Important recent discoveries of manuscripts that attest otherwise singular readings from Codex Bezae include the Middle Egyptian version (mae or G[67]), containing Acts 1–15; the Syro-Palestinian (Aramaic) fragment (sy[pal] or sy[msK]), attesting a few verses of Acts 10; and the Greek papyrus P[127], with portions of Acts 10–16 (c. 400).

[8] Comments to this effect are found throughout the commentary on the 27th edition of the Nestle–Aland Greek New Testament, compiled by Metzger (1994).

[9] The evidence for the Jewish context is explored throughout Rius-Camps and Read-Heimerdinger 2004–2009. See also Read-Heimerdinger 2003:263–280. The general failure of textual critics to notice the Jewish context of readings of Codex Bezae in Acts has meant that the text has continued to be dismissed as a late scribal revision.

protagonists. Whereas in the Alexandrian text the characters are presented as heroes who unerringly enact the plan of God for the foundation and growth of the Church (certainly, that is how the text of Acts has all but universally been interpreted over the centuries), the narrator of the Bezan text presents a more nuanced account in which the Church's leaders make mistakes and sometimes fail to understand the divine plan correctly. It will be important to bear in mind this narratorial stance, together with the Jewish perspective, in considering variant readings concerning the article.

To be sure, the pattern of presence and absence of the article in D05 is statistically different from that found in B03, but discourse analysis shows that frequency of occurrence is an irrelevant factor in assessing the authenticity of a manuscript or even the date of its text. The differences between the two manuscripts do, however, provide useful sets of comparable data: while there is agreement concerning the article with proper names in the majority of readings, which allows the principles governing its use to be teased out, a high proportion of variant readings serve as material to refine the observations made on the basis of the common text.

There are, unfortunately, substantial portions of text missing from Acts in Codex Bezae: 8:28b–10:14a, 22:10b–20a, and also the last leaf ends at 22:29a In view of these lacunae, only names that occur up to end of Codex Bezae are included in this study but further mentions of those names that arise in portions of the text missing from D05 will be included. Where citations are given in the discussion, the variants will be identified according to the usual categories as follows: material read by only one of the manuscripts is underlined with a solid line; an arrow is placed at the corresponding place in the text of the other manuscript to indicate an absence; lexical or grammatical variation is shown by a dotted underline; words that vary in order are in italic script.

7.2 Names of persons

7.2.1 Statement of the problem

The only rule for the use of the article with names of persons that emerges from the New Testament Greek grammars, and about which there is some consensus of opinion, is that names of persons are not usually preceded by the article, in other words reference to them is anarthrous; but the article may be used (reference is arthrous) if the person has already been introduced by name before (anaphoric reference).[10] The grammars note, however, that there is a great number of unaccountable deviations from this

---

[10] Porter 1992:107 notes: "Proper names often do not appear with the article... But in some contexts a name has the article," and he includes anaphoric reference as one of those contexts. Winer, for his part, declares that "The use of the article with names of persons can hardly be reduced to any rule" ([1882]1997:140, §6).

rule. Different authors appear to adopt different practices and even two works by the same author do not necessarily conform to the same pattern, if indeed a pattern can be recognized. And then there is the complication of manuscript variation.

Several studies of the article in variant readings have been made by textual critics. For example, with regard to Peter in Acts, Elliott concludes that it is not at all clear how the article was used in the original text although there would be reason to prefer generally the arthrous reading in cases of variants because it seems to him that Luke's custom was to prefer to use the article before his name (Elliott 1972:241–256).[11] Boismard and Lamouille, looking specifically at the book of Acts, believe that the linguistic origin of the name is responsible for the variation: that the original text read the article before names of Greek origin but not before those of Semitic origin, successive scribes making their corrections according to their own linguistic background (Boismard and Lamouille 1984:110). These conclusions will be challenged to some extent by the results of the examination of the article carried out here.

7.2.2 The emergence of principles

In attempting to obtain a clearer picture, every instance of the article before the names of persons in Acts was studied exhaustively (leaving aside those arising only in the portions of text missing from D05). The movement of the characters was noted as they move in and out of the story of Acts and the interaction between the characters considered. Likewise, the opinion or the prior knowledge that hearers of the narrative could be expected to have had of the people in the story was taken into account. These factors are relevant considerations because, as discourse analysis studies acknowledge, a narrative is not told simply through the eyes of the narrator but rather the speaker constantly takes account of the point of view of the audience as well as the internal perspectives of characters within the story.

The non-variant text where both manuscripts agree on the presence or absence of the article (the "common text") was examined first to provide a base-line against which to evaluate variant readings, which in turn can be used to refine the initial deductions. The principle that emerges from this study is that the default way of referring to people by name is with the article. By "default" is meant that this is the practice a speaker would normally adopt in mentioning a person by name, unless there were special circumstances that called for the article to be omitted. Specifically, when a name is anarthrous it is because the participant is highlighted as prominent in one way or another at that point in the discourse. In other words, including the article before a name is neutral, whereas omitting the article is a

---

[11] See also Elliott 1988:250–258.

device of markedness, whose function is to draw that person to the attention of the hearer at that particular point in the narrative.[12]

It is helpful to think of a narrative as a play being acted out on a stage. As characters move on and off the stage, take center stage or wait in the wings, for example, the significance of their presence changes. At times, they are established figures on stage, whereas at others they play a particular role that on which the dramatist wishes to focus attention, which may be done with the use of a spotlight. It is clear that in some instances the choice to focus on a character at a given point is open to interpretation, and what the playwright had in mind may be viewed differently by subsequent directors, which they are at liberty to express in their staging of the play. Such freedom can frequently be seen as the cause of variation involving the presence of the article before names in Acts.

The following analysis seeks to classify the circumstances that call for spotlighting of a character and to present some of the main occurrences of variation.

7.2.2.1 First entry of participants

First entry in the book

As noted in section 7.2.1, handbooks of NT grammar generally agree that the first mention of a person by name is anarthrous, and the principle as stated above provides a reason for this to be so. When a participant is first introduced into a story, the author almost always spotlights their initial appearance as they take their place on stage, as a way of ensuring that their presence is clearly registered by the audience. The linguistic device for switching on the spotlight is to omit the article before the name of the person. Subsequently, once the participant has entered into the story, he or she can be referred to as a known factor, and the article is therefore retained.

A high level of consistency is seen in the omission of the article when a character is mentioned for the first time in the book of Acts, as there are no variant readings in this respect. Whether the name is mentioned alone (e.g. Jesus, 1:1; Matthias, 1:23; Pilate 3:13; Silas 15:22) or introduced with an expression such as τις ὀνόματι (e.g. Agabus 11:28, Timothy 16:1), or a title such as 'king' (Herod 12:1), the reference is anarthrous. The only apparent exception to this pattern is the first mention of Peter by name at 1:13. Here, the article is included and, indeed, embraces the other ten names of the list of apostles who are presented as a unified group (see §7.2.2.3.). The article

---

[12] Cf. the conclusion of the classical grammarian Basil Gildersleeve, who concluded that the article was not generally used with proper names in classical Greek: "Proper names being in their nature particular do not require the explicit article, and when the article is used with them, it retains much of its original demonstrative force" (Gildersleeve 1911:§514). See further Gildersleeve 1911:§547–561, as well as specific essays: Gildersleeve 1890:483–487; Gildersleeve 1902.

can be accounted for by the previous introduction of 'the apostles' at 1:2; its presence does, nevertheless, imply that Peter was already identified and acknowledged by Luke's addressee as the leader of the group.

The pattern of anarthrous first mention followed by arthrous, anaphoric mentions in the book of Acts is illustrated by the references to Simon Magus in Acts 8 (v. 9 anarthrous, see vv. 13, 18, 24 arthrous) or to Gallio in Acts 18 (v. 12 anarthrous, cf. vv. 14, 17 arthrous). The procedure is similar to the slight emphasis given in spoken English to the name of a person who is being referred to for the first time in a story, an emphasis that is normally absent on subsequent mentions of the name.

First entry within a speech

An important consideration to bear in mind is that portions of speech within a narrative operate as independent units, with their own speaker and audience who are distinct from the narrator and the narrator's addressee. It is not uncommon for a person to be referred to in speech who has already been established in the section of the narrative within which the speech occurs. However, when the speaker mentions that person by name for the first time the article is omitted. This is to be expected for, as far as the speaker and his or her own hearers are concerned, a true "first mention" is made. This is seen in the common text at 10:22 (the men from Caesarea speaking of Cornelius to Peter); 12:11 (Peter speaking of Herod to himself); 15:26, 27 (the Jerusalem apostles and elders speaking of Barnabas and Paul, Judas and Silas in their letter to the Gentile brethren); 19:38 (the Ephesian clerk speaking of Demetrius to the crowd).

On two occasions, the article is omitted in the Bezan text, not in direct but in indirect speech at 12:14b and 21:29. The variant reading seems to arise because the two texts are looking at the person mentioned from different points of view. At 12:14b, it is the narrator who relates that the servant girl, Rhoda, announces to the church praying in Mary's house in Jerusalem that Peter is at the door. From the point of view of Rhoda and the church, this is a first mention, which accounts for the omission of the article in D05. At the same time, from the point of view of the narrator of Acts as he speaks to his audience, this is an anaphoric reference that justifies the article in the B03 text. Similarly, at 21:29, there is ambiguity: the narrator explains that some Jewish opponents were attacking Paul because it was supposed that he had taken a Gentile into the Temple. According to the Vaticanus text, the supposition is attributed to the attackers: ὃν ἐνόμιζον ὅτι εἰς τὸ ἱερὸν εἰσήγαγεν ὁ Παῦλος, and Paul is viewed from the point of view of the narrator for whom Paul is well-established as the focal character of the story at this point. Codex Bezae presents the situation differently, attributing the supposition to Paul's companions, the "we-group," through whose eyes

Paul is seen for the first time in the present context and the name is anarthrous: ὃν ἐνομίσαμεν ὅτι εἰς τὸ ἱερὸν εἰσήγαγεν ↑ Παῦλος .

First entry from the point of view of another character

The shift in perspective just observed arises because the characters in the story of Acts not only present themselves to the hearer or reader of the story; they also interact with each other; they speak with, listen to, confront, follow one another, especially in the case of the secondary characters as they meet the Christian leaders. And when some points of meeting are referred to for the first time, this initial encounter is marked by an omission of the article before the name of the person who is the object of the meeting even if he or she is already an active participant in the scene. It is as if that person were being seen from the point of view of the other character and not of the ones telling or listening to the story. The point is illustrated by 3:3 (the lame man sees Peter and John); 13:7 (the proconsul calls Barnabas and Saul); 14:11 (the crowds in Lystra see the healing carried out by Paul). The narrator of Acts in Codex Bezae is especially sensitive to the internal point of view of the characters and the article is omitted on numerous additional occasions as a variant reading, where this more intimate perspective accounts for the highlighting of a character. See, for instance, 8:6 (the crowds were attentive to what Philip said); 13:50 (Jewish opponents persecuted Paul and Barnabas in Antioch of Pisidia); 16:14 (Lydia was attentive to what Paul said); 17:15 (Silas and Timothy receive a command from Paul); 20:9 (Eutychus listened to Paul's lecturing).

7.2.2.2 Re-entry of participants

A modified type of "first entry" is seen when, following a character's first introduction on the stage, the character leaves the stage to wait in the wings until he or she re-appears in a new scene. Thus, at the start of a new episode, the reference is sometimes anarthrous—Philip: 6:5; cf. 8:5, 12, 13, 26; Aquila and Priscilla:18:18, cf. 26. Following the initial anarthrous introduction in a new episode, subsequent mentions are arthrous unless other factors intervene (see §7.2.2.3). These anarthrous references at the beginning of a new incident can be explained by the fact that the participant has been inactive or off-stage since the last mention and is now being reintroduced as a salient participant.

When certain other characters, in contrast, re-appear in a new scene the article is maintained. In these cases, the character in question is a major participant whose presence was, as it were, always active even though they were not visible. Thus, in the first part of Acts, the name of Jesus is typically arthrous; Peter is often arthrous at the start of new scenes throughout the first five chapters; as is Paul, too, throughout the second part of the book. There are not a few variant readings in this respect (for example, the name of Peter at 1:13 is arthrous in D05, but not B03; at 5:3, it is B03 that is arthrous). It would appear that holding the presence of major characters as active over a long stretch of narrative gives rise to varying views among successive editors and copyists as to their status with regard to specific points in the developing narrative. This is not, however the same as saying that it is a matter of authorial style, as if the decision to use the article were dictated by a general, inherent personal tendency—on the contrary, the choice to use the article or not reflects how the author/editor/copyist perceives the role of the participant at a given point in a story, which in turn depends upon his or her understanding of the unfolding of the story and the prominence of the characters at the point at which they are mentioned by name.

7.2.2.3 *Participants on stage*

In the circumstances presented above, the omission of the article before the name of a participant functions as a device to draw the attention of the audience to that character. At their point of entry into the narrative or into the consciousness of the audience, characters acquire a natural prominence that causes them to stand out temporarily from any other character.

During the course of a narrative, too, once a participant is established on stage within an episode, the article may again be omitted on grounds that derive from the principle of salience, as characters need to be distinguished from other characters, or even other possible participants, on further occasions. In these instances, the anarthrous, anaphoric mentions are seemingly a way of marking the named character as salient at that point. Various circumstances can be identified that call for the absence of the article to focus the spotlight on a character after the first mention. These can be grouped according to the categories of i) selection; ii) contrast; iii) switch of focus; iv) highlighting a speech.

Selection

When more than one participant is introduced at the outset of a story and comment then made concerning only one of those initially named, the article is omitted before the second mention to indicate that that particular participant is salient at that point. The following examples show how this works.

Matthias is introduced into the account of events at 1:23 together with Joseph, both being candidates to replace Judas. The two names are anarthrous at this first mention, as would be expected. When lots are cast and the lot falls on Matthias (1:26), the name is still without the article because here 'Matthias' is the one of the pair who is selected and there is a special focus on him.

Stephen is mentioned for the first time in Acts at 6:5 at the head of the list of the seven Hellenists, without the article. Then, at 6:8, he is singled out for specific mention as he takes on a specific role. Even though the reference is anaphoric, it is anarthrous because Stephen becomes salient at this point when he becomes the focus of interest in the story of the Jerusalem church.

John is singled out from the rest of Paul's company at 13:13b as doing something different, because he alone goes back to Jerusalem.

Contrast

When there is contrast, explicit or implicit, the article is omitted. The second part of Acts from chapter 13 to the end of the book, in which Paul is the main protagonist, is characterized by many examples of such omission (see, for example, 17:6, where an angry mob look for Paul and Silas but, not finding them, seize Jason instead). There are many variants, sometimes because a person is mentioned in one text but not in the other (e.g. Judas and Silas at 15:34, 35 D05; Apollos, 19:1 B03); elsewhere, it is Codex Bezae that displays a consistent tendency to highlight contrast— to be precise, contrast between Paul and other characters (e.g. Timothy and Silas are set against Paul, 18:5 D05; the chiliarch's acquisition of Roman citizenship is contrasted with that of Paul, 22:28 D05; see also on 15:36–40 below).

Switch of focus

Once a character is established in an episode the article is usually retained, as was seen above (§§7.2.2.1 and 7.2.2.2). When, however, attention is transferred from one established participant or group of participants to another within an episode and this switch of focus needs to be emphasized, the new participants are re-introduced without the article. In this way, they re-emerge as salient. This is the case at such places as: 8.1, switch from Stephen back to Saul, already introduced at 7:58; 12:19, switch from Peter back to Herod, already named at 12:1; 12:25, switch from Herod back to Barnabas and Saul, already introduced at 11:30.

Among the manuscripts, once again there is variation on this point, for example at 12:6. Throughout Acts 12, attention moves back and forth between Herod and the threat of danger on the one hand, and Peter and his miraculous escape on the other; in the Bezan text at 12:6, the omission of the article before Herod marks his plan to have Peter accused by the people in Jerusalem as particularly salient.

Likewise at 15:35, 16:18, 25, 19:30, the article is omitted before Paul (and Barnabas or Silas) in the Alexandrian text as the story turns from a temporary focus on secondary characters to the activities of the main protagonists. D05, on the other hand, would seem to consider that they do not need to be given renewed prominence (by omitting the article) as their story is picked up; they have always been "front of stage" and the article is retained.[13]

The episode relating the separation of Barnabas from Paul illustrates the function of the omission of the article both to highlight contrast and to switch attention between characters:

(1)   **15.36–40 Codex Vaticanus, B03**   **15.36–40 Codex Bezae, D05**

[36] Μετὰ δέ τινας ἡμέρας	[36] Μετὰ δέ τινας ἡμέρας
εἶπεν πρὸς Βαρναβᾶν ↑ Παῦλος,	εἶπεν <u>ὁ</u> Παῦλος πρὸς Βαρναβᾶν,
Ἐπιστρέψαντες δὴ ἐπισκεψώμεθα	Ἐπιστρέψαντες δὴ ἐπισκεψώμεθα
τοὺς ἀδελφοὺς	τοὺς ἀδελφοὺς
↑ κατὰ πόλιν πᾶσαν ἐν <u>αἷς</u>	<u>τοὺς</u> κατὰ πᾶσαν πόλιν ἐν <u>οἷς</u>
κατηγγείλαμεν	κατηγγείλαμεν
τὸν λόγον τοῦ κυρίου, πῶς ἔχουσιν.	τὸν λόγον τοῦ κυρίου, πῶς ἔχουσιν.
[37] Βαρναβᾶς δὲ <u>ἐβούλετο</u>	[37] Βαρναβᾶς δὲ <u>ἐβουλεύετο</u>
συμπαραλαβεῖν <u>καὶ τὸν</u> Ἰωάννην	συνπαραλαβεῖν ↑ Ἰωάννην
τὸν <u>καλούμενον</u> Μᾶρκον:	τὸν <u>ἐπικαλούμενον</u> Μᾶρκον:
[38] Παῦλος δὲ <u>ἠξίου</u>	[38] Παῦλος δὲ <u>οὐκ ἐβούλετο λέγων</u>
τὸν <u>ἀποστάντα</u> ἀπ' αὐτῶν ἀπὸ	τὸν <u>ἀποστήσαντα</u> ἀπ' αὐτῶν ἀπὸ
Παμφυλίας	Παμφυλίας
καὶ μὴ συνελθόντα <u>αὐτοῖς</u> εἰς τὸ	καὶ μὴ συνελθόντα ↑ εἰς τὸ ἔργον
ἔργον	*τοῦτον* μὴ <u>εἶναι σὺν αὐτοῖς.</u>
μὴ <u>συμπαραλαμβάνειν</u> *τοῦτον.*	
[39] ἐγένετο δὲ παροξυσμὸς	[39] ἐγένετο δὲ παροξυσμὸς
ὥστε ἀποχωρισθῆναι αὐτοὺς ἀπ'	ὥστε ἀποχωρισθῆναι αὐτοὺς ἀπ'
ἀλλήλων,	ἀλλήλων,
<u>τόν</u> τε Βαρναβᾶν <u>παραλαβόντα</u>	<u>τότε</u> ↑ Βαρναβᾶν <u>παραλαβὼν</u>
τὸν Μᾶρκον	τὸν Μᾶρκον
ἐκπλεῦσαι εἰς Κύπρον.	<u>ἔπλευσεν</u> εἰς Κύπρον.
[40] Παῦλος δὲ <u>ἐπιλεξάμενος</u> Σιλᾶν	[40] Παῦλος δὲ <u>ἐπιδεξάμενος</u> Σιλᾶν
ἐξῆλθεν παραδοθεὶς τῇ χάριτι <u>τοῦ</u>	ἐξῆλθεν παραδοθεὶς τῇ χάριτι ↑
κυρίου <u>ὑπὸ</u> τῶν ἀδελφῶν,	κυρίου <u>ἀπὸ</u> τῶν ἀδελφῶν,
[41] διήρχετο δὲ τὴν Συρίαν καὶ τὴν	[41] διήρχετο δὲ τὴν Συρίαν καὶ τὴν
Κιλικίαν	Κιλικίαν
ἐπιστηρίζων τὰς ἐκκλησίας	ἐπιστηρίζων τὰς ἐκκλησίας

In the B03 text, particular attention is drawn to Paul, both by the omission of the article and also by the clause-final position, the position of natural prominence for a clausal constituent.[14] On both counts, D05 treats Paul

---

[13] When Paul is acting in unison with another participant, one article before the first named functions for the pair as a whole (see §7.2.2.3).

[14] See Runge 2010:185–189. It is not surprising that the omission of the article should often be observed to be operating in conjunction with other features, notably word

as the established main character, as he proposes to Barnabas (anarthrous, setting him up as distinct from Paul; cf. 15:35 where they are presented as a unit, especially with the single article in D05) to go and visit the cities they had previously evangelized. The independence of Barnabas in relation to Paul is then maintained as his wish (B03) or decision (D05) to take John-Mark is presented—the reference is treated as anaphoric in B03 even though the last mention was several episodes earlier (cf. 13:13), but his name is underlined by the omission of the article in the D05 text, as an indication that the choice was not necessarily the expected one.[15] Disagreement between Paul and Barnabas develops as Paul is set in contrast to Barnabas with the omission of the article as his name is mentioned verse 38. The conflict (nothing less than a παροξυσμός) is maintained with the omission of the article before Barnabas' name in verse 39, and again before Paul's in verse 40. Silas is likewise anarthrous, not because of conflict but because Paul's decision to choose him as his companion has not been anticipated, and also in contrast to John-Mark.

Clauses introducing speech

There is a noticeable tendency to omit the article before proper names in clauses that introduce speech, though this is less pronounced in the Bezan text. It arises especially when Peter or Paul either initiate a conversation or make a key speech of proclamation, encouragement or warning even though they are already established in the scene (e.g. 10:34, Peter to the household of Cornelius; 11:4, Peter to the Jerusalem brethren; 17:22 B03, Paul in the Areopagus; 19:4 B03, Paul to the disciples in Ephesus). Sometimes, the speaker is singled out from other participants as he is about to speak (1:15 B03, Peter from among the other apostles; 2:38; 4:8; 5:29 B03; 8:20), or there is a switch of focus from a minor participant back to Peter or Paul as he speaks (16:28 B03, from the jailor to Paul as he addresses the jailor for the first time). In these instances, it is not so much the speaker himself who is the focus of attention, but rather his function as the proclaimer of a key message.

7.2.2.4 Technical reasons

Some further technical factors influence the choice of the article before proper names.

---

order, as a combined means to indicate the important information of a sentence, where "important" naturally means "important for the speaker in terms of his or her communication goal" and not in any absolute sense.

[15] Barnabas' choice of John Mark is discussed in Rius-Camps and Read-Heimerdinger 2009:237–239.

Two or more names

When two or more names mentioned together are joined with καί, and the
first has the article, the second (or any subsequent) name does not take the
article if the pair or group are viewed as acting in harmony: 1:13 (Peter
and the other named apostles); 4:13 (Peter and John); 13:2 (Barnabas
and Saul); 15:22 B03 (Paul and Barnabas—both names are anarthrous
in D05). There are a further eight such instances in Codex Bezae (3:11;
13:43, 46; 15:2a, b; 16:19, 29; 17:15), where the Alexandrian text reads
the article before both names, apparently reflecting the importance that
Paul acquired as a character distinct from his co-workers. Codex Bezae
does not view him with the same degree of approval and often purpose-
fully points out his weaknesses.

Stereotyped phrases

In stereotyped phrases that include a reference to a named person, the reference is anarthrous whether the person has already been mentioned in the
story or not. This is notably so for the repeated occurrences of τὸ βαπτίσμα
Ἰωάννου, 'the baptism of John' at 1:22; 18:25; 19:3; and τὸ ὄνομα Ἰησοῦ,
'the name of Jesus' at 2:38; 3:6; 4:10; 16:18.

Dependent genitive

A final issue concerns a name in the genitive, dependent on an articular
phrase. The article is retained before the person's name, without variant
readings in the manuscripts studied, whenever the reference to the person
is anaphoric (e.g. 12:7, 14; 20:37; 21:11). When the article is omitted, the
reference is either a set phrase like 'the name of Jesus' or a first mention.
In other words, the presence or absence of the article with such dependent genitives is not determined by the syntax. The principle is clearly
illustrated in Acts 10 where, at verse 17, (διερωτήσαντες) τὴν οἰκίαν τοῦ
Σίμωνος, 'the house of Simon', is an anaphoric reference (cf. 9:43, D05
lac.) and as such Simon is prefaced by the article; however, at verse 32, we
see ἐν οἰκίᾳ Σίμωνος, quoting the earlier conversation of 10:3–6, where
it is a first mention in direct speech, and the name Simon is therefore
anarthrous.

It is worth noting that grammatical case does not, in general, affect
the use of the article before names of persons, despite apparent statistical evidence to the contrary. For example, a numerical count shows that
a high proportion of names in the nominative case are anarthrous—that is
not because of the case but because the subject of a sentence is frequently
salient.

7.2.3 Conclusion on the use of the article with names of persons

In summary, it may be observed that first mentions of a person by name are anarthrous with practically no variation within or between the manuscripts. Secondly, reference to named persons is anarthrous when attention is being drawn to their presence or to their actions at that particular point in the text. This factor, described here as salience, is determined by several aspects, all of which are characterized by a fair amount of variation both within and between the manuscripts. There are, finally, technical reasons for anarthrous reference to named persons that tend to apply with a high degree of consistency. In the absence of any of these three factors, the article is used to refer to persons by name.

The identification of the main principle of saliency tallies with the result of a study regarding ordinary nouns in Classical Greek. There, too, salience has been recognized as the overall factor that lies behind the omission of the article before a noun where it would normally be expected. Thus, in a recent study of the use of the article in Plato, David Sansone concludes that the "definite article tends to be more at home with topic than with focus" (Sansone 1993:199). This will be a feature of the use of the article to take into account in considering names of places in the next section.

7.3 Names of places

7.3.1 Statement of the problem

Like names of persons, place names also fall into the category of nouns that have a sole, identifiable referent. To use the classification proposed by Stanley Porter, place names are identifiable as "particular" (Porter 1992:313). In fact, they are even more particular than names of persons since there is rarely more than one referent designated by any given geographical name, unlike the many people called "Mary," "Peter" or "Jesus," for example, even though in a given context there may well be only one such person. The aim of this present study is to see if the pattern that has been established with respect to the use of the article with names of persons also applies to the place names. The book of Acts is again a most useful source of data, because both the narrative and the speeches within it abound in references to geographical locations of many kinds, whether associated with the land or the sea: countries, regions, cities, mountains, islands, and seas.

Consideration of the article with geographical names in the standard grammars suggests that, as with names of persons, there are no real rules. Blass–Debrunner–Rehkopf, for example, present a list of observations, noting the "frequent," "many" or "occasional" occurrences of the presence or the absence of the article with certain names or categories but without explanation; Robertson speaks of "obscurity and uncertainty" (Blass et al.

1979:§261; Robertson 1934:1397). Other works make no distinction between proper names of people and proper names of places, any "clear and consistent principles" being rated in any case as undetectable.[16] Gildersleeve identifies the general "rule" that the article is present with geographical names, while noting that exceptions occur chiefly in enumerations, with conjoined nouns functioning as a unity and the predicate (Gildersleeve 1911:§568, §603, §666). It is telling that, commenting on Gildersleeve's analysis of the spectrum of Classical works, Robertson notes that usage of article with place names "greatly varies among Greek writers" (1934:759). Winer ([1882]1997:139–140), for his part, gives the impression that apart from a regular tendency for the first mention of a name to be anarthrous, the presence or absence of the article depends on the nature of the place (e.g. country versus cities) or on the grammatical context (e.g. after prepositions, or in oblique cases) or on the author.

The situation in the grammar books is thus not a little confused, despite some extensive and detailed analysis and a genuine search for general principles. It lends itself to the conclusion that the choice to use the article or not is "as much a question of style as of grammar" (Sansone 1993:204).[17] Taking into account the additional variation found in the different manuscripts, only occasionally if ever mentioned in the New Testament grammar books, it would be an easy step to assume that scribal custom should also figure in the list of factors determining the use of the article.[18]

In view of the principles that were able to be identified with respect to personal names using the tools of discourse analysis, there is reason, however, to have some optimism about recognizing the linguistic factors influencing a speaker's choice to use the article with geographical names. In order to reach a full and complete explanation, a range of texts and authors would need to be examined in detail, elucidating patterns and testing the principles that evolve in a variety of situations. This study of geographical names in the book of Acts is presented as one small part of that examination, in the hope that it can contribute to a wider and more complete study of the question that will achieve the all-important goal of "explanatory adequacy" (Wallace 1996:246).[19]

7.3.2 Emergence of principles

The following analysis tends to confirm that salience is the key factor affecting the use of the article. With all of the different types of places, the default

---

[16] E.g. Wallace 1996:245–247.

[17] Referring to the work of Gildersleeve.

[18] Sansone does draw attention to the existence of variant readings concerning the presence of the article in the text of Plato and the need to take account of it in establishing patterns of use (1993:202).

[19] Wallace, citing Chomsky.

usage is to include the article with geographical names, and omission of the article is a way of marking the place as having particular significance. Unlike names of persons, however, the first mention of the name of a place is not marked in this way, except for cities which generally are anarthrous at their point of introduction into the narrative.

7.3.2.1 Countries

Among the places mentioned in Acts, only a few can be classified as countries because of the changing nature of their boundaries and identity as they were absorbed by foreign powers, notably the Roman Empire by the time of the events recorded in Acts. Areas that had been made into Roman provinces are dealt with under the next heading of "Regions."[20]

Egypt is the most frequently mentioned country, principally in the speech of Stephen in Acts 7. The name first occurs before that speech, at the head of the list of countries (regions) cited as being represented in Jerusalem at Pentecost (2:9), and thereafter is mentioned eleven times (+ 1 B03; + 1 D05) by Stephen. On all save two occasions the name is anarthrous, even when it occurs twice in successive sentences (e.g. 7:10a b, 34a b).

At 7:11, the article is used where Egypt is mentioned in conjunction with Canaan, as famine came ἐφ' ὅλης τῆς Αἰγύπτου καὶ Χανάαν. The name of Egypt has just occurred in the previous sentence in a salient reference to Moses being appointed the governor of the country; when the country is mentioned again in 7:11 it is a true anaphoric reference with no need to highlight its salience. The article is then found at 7:36 B03 with some support:[21] ἐν τῇ Αἰγύπτῳ, where Egypt is mentioned as a place in conjunction with the Red Sea and the desert where miracles were performed. The similarity of the majuscules Γ and T could have led to confusion with ἐν γῇ Αἰγύπτῳ of the other manuscripts, but even if the article is secondary from a linguistic point of view that does not make it an "error" or even a scribal preference. On the contrary, the arthrous reference could be the default form, altered by the fixed nature of the phrase ἐν γῇ...(cf. comments on Midia, below).

When the article is omitted the country is always salient for one reason or another. For example, at 7:12, Jacob is said to have heard at the time of the famine that there was corn in Egypt, where the country is seen as being of particular importance from his point of view. At 7:15, Egypt occurs in a

---

[20] Israel is not included in this study because whenever it is mentioned in Acts, the name refers to Israel as a people or ethnic identity rather than a geographic location. It may be noted, however, that while the majority of references to Israel are anarthrous, all of them arise in a fixed expression such as 'the people/house/ sons of Israel'. On the two occasions when the article is present (4:8 D05 et al.; 5:31), the mention occurs in a phrase that is not stereotypical.

[21] The reading of the article is supported by C04 36 453 *pc*. Other manuscripts read ἐν γῇ Αἰγύπτῳ (Αἰγύπτου D05 et al.).

sentence full of weighty significance: καὶ κατέβη Ἰακὼβ εἰς Αἴγυπτον,[22] a statement that is central to Stephen's argument in his speech. The omission of the article before Egypt tallies with the anarthrous, though anaphoric, mention of Jacob and combines with the asyndetic introduction to the sentence to highlight the statement in a powerful way. The omission of the article in other references to Egypt can be justified similarly, as a device used to draw attention to the name for one reason or another.

Other Mesopotamian countries mentioned by Stephen: as indicated in the paragraph above, Canaan is mentioned anarthrously once (7:11), where it is associated with Egypt. Midian is named without the article (7:29), in the phrase ἐν γῇ Μαδιάμ, which is typically anarthrous.[23] Finally, the name of Babylon occurs (7:43) in an adapted quotation from Amos, where the reference is highlighted as the destination corresponding to Israel's punishment: μετοικιῶ ὑμᾶς ἐπέκεινα Βαβυλῶνος.[24]

Greece is named as a country only at 20:2, where Paul is said to go there (ἦλθεν εἰς τὴν Ἑλλάδα, 20:2). Although the reference is not strictly anaphoric, it corresponds to the decision earlier attributed to Paul at 19:21 to go to 'Achaia' (see §7.3.2.2), and so the information is not especially salient. Anaphora, however, is probably not the factor that accounts for the retention of the article with Ἑλλάς. Comparison with 'Italy', the one other country mentioned in Acts, shows that the article is present at both isolated references: at 18:2, Aquila is said to have recently come (to Corinth) from Italy, which is of only indirect relevance to the narrative and plays no further role; at 27:6, the centurion found a boat for Paul to travel with as it was going to Italy, the country that had long been presented as his final destination, hitherto referred to by the capital of Rome.

In sum, as far as countries are concerned, it can be deduced that the use of the article is the default way of referring to them. Omission of the article occurs either in a fixed expression (ἐν γῇ...) or, more usually, as a means to highlight the country, but this is not a device used for the first occurrences of the name, unlike the pattern observed with names of persons.

7.3.2.2 Regions

For ease of classification, the names of regions are discussed according to the section of the Acts narrative with which they are particularly associated.

Judaea is of crucial significance for the first part of the book of Acts since the action is centered there for the first five chapters. All the references are arthrous irrespective of the criterion of first mention, except for

---

[22] B03 alone omits the mention of Egypt in this sentence.

[23] Cf. Luke. 2:4 D05: Ἀνέβη δὲ καὶ Ἰωσὴφ ἀπὸ τῆς Γαλιλαίας ἐκ πόλεως Ναζαρὲθ εἰς γῆν Ἰούδα (εἰς τὴν Ἰουδαίαν, B03).

[24] At 7:43, D05 reads ἐπὶ τὰ μέρη Βαβυλῶνος, a chorographic genitive, which Gildersleeve observes to be usually anarthrous (1900:2; 1911:§552).

a variant anarthrous reading at 10:37 D05. Here, Peter is seen, exceptionally, to be addressing an audience of Gentiles to whom he mentions Judaea as the region where Jesus had been active among the Jewish people. The absence of the article in the Bezan text seems to reflect Peter's awareness of the viewpoint of his audience, for whom Judaea is not their country in the same sense that it is the country of the Jews, and he will go on in the next sentence to contrast it with Galilee (arthrous). The sensitivity of the writer of Acts, especially the Bezan narrator, to the viewpoints of different characters was already noted with reference to the names of persons in section 7.2.

One other variant reading involving the article with Judaea is found at 8:1, where D05 has an anarthrous reference: πάντες δὲ διεσπάρησαν κατὰ τὰς χώρας τῆς (om. D05) Ἰουδαίας καὶ Σαμαρείας. Since the one other reference to the two regions is arthrous with one article serving the two names (see 1:8), and since there is no obvious cause for the narrator to highlight the names at 8:1, the D05 reading could be interpreted as an example of what Gildersleeve calls the "chorographic genitive."[25] The perspective of discourse analysis, however, prompts the consideration that the narrator has a reason for highlighting the reference to Judaea and Samaria at this point, at least in Codex Bezae. The text goes on to specify that πάντες does not include the apostles, for they were not dispersed (πλὴν τῶν ἀποστόλων), and at that point an additional clause is read by D05: οἳ ἔμειναν ἐν Ἰερουσαλήμ. This comment carries a great deal of weight in the Bezan text, where the narrator uses the dual spelling of the city of Jerusalem to evaluate the spiritual progress of the characters, reserving the Hebrew-derived spelling to refer to the seat of Judaism as opposed to the geographical city. Thus the disciples of Hierosoluma (ἐν Ἰεροσολύμα, 8:1b) were driven out of Judaea and Samaria by the persecution, but the apostles remained in Jerusalem (ἐν Ἰερουσαλήμ, 8:1c), under the protection of the Jewish authorities as will emerge in due course.[26] On this reading, the contrast between the apostles, who had been commanded by Jesus precisely to go to all of Judea and Samaria (ἐν πάσῃ τῇ Ἰουδαίᾳ καὶ Σαμαρείᾳ, 1:8) and the disciples who in fact do go there is stark, and may be the explanation for the omission of the article before the regions on this occasion in the Bezan text.

At 2:9, Judaea is mentioned in a list of nine regions and countries from where people were present at Pentecost: οἱ κατοικοῦντες τὴν Μεσοποταμίαν Ἰουδαίαν τε (om. D05) καὶ Καππαδοκίαν Πόντον καὶ τὴν Ἀσίαν Φρυγίαν τε (om. D05) καὶ Παμφυλίαν, Αἴγυπτον τε (om. B03) καὶ τὰ μέρη τῆς Λιβύης τῆς κατὰ Κυρήνην. The article is found before Mesopotamia, before Asia and before Libya. The reason for its presence with certain names and not others may depend on the particular way the countries are grouped. The first three, which include Judaea, may be considered to form an initial grouping (especially with the linking τε), for which a single article suffices (as

---

[25] See previous note.

[26] See Rius-Camps and Read-Heimerdinger 2006:117–120.

discussed in §7.2.2.3). Mesopotamia is arthrous on its single other appearance (7:2). Asia itself will be considered separately below, but meanwhile it may be observed that both Phrygia and Pamphilia could be being viewed as belonging to the larger land mass of Asia. As for Libya, the article in the phrase τὰ μέρη... is not surprising given that the area is specifically qualified as τῆς κατὰ Κυρήνην. There remains Pontus as the only name without an article that is not accounted for by any of the explanations presented so far, and in this sense it is, indeed, something of an anomaly.

Samaria and Galilee are always arthrous, sometimes by virtue of their being linked to one or two other regions of which the first named bears the article (but note the D05 variant at 8:1, on which see above in this section; and 15:3, where many manuscripts including D05 repeat the article before Samaria–διήρχοντο τήν τε Φοινίκην καὶ τὴν Σαμάρειαν, thus treating the two regions as distinct).

The places beyond the ancient territory of Israel take on a greater importance after Acts 8 once the Church moves out beyond the boundaries of Judaea and Samaria, and especially once the believers begin to proclaim the gospel to the Gentiles from Acts 10 onwards. Most locations are associated with the travels of Paul, though they are often already mentioned before he becomes an active participant in the narrative.

Asia is mentioned nine times (+ 1 B03; + 2 D05; + 1 B03 [D05 lac.]), first at 6:9 after appearing in the list of 2:9 on which see above in this section. The name is usually arthrous, even when the country is referred to for the first time in the context. The article is also retained when the region is set in contrast to Jerusalem at 19:1 D05:

(2)   **19:1 B03**   **19:1 D05**

↑ Ἐγένετο δὲ ἐν τῷ τὸν Ἀπολλῶ   ↑ Θέλοντος δὲ τοῦ Παύλου
                                                        κατὰ τὴν ἰδίαν βουλὴν
                                                        πορεύεσθαι εἰς Ἱεροσόλυμα
εἶναι ἐν Κορίνθῳ ↑ Παῦλον ↑   εἶπεν αὐτῷ τὸ πνεῦμα
                                                        ὑποστρέφειν εἰς τὴν Ἀσίαν
διελθόντα ↑ τὰ ἀνωτερικὰ μέρη   διελθὼν δὲ τὰ ἀνωτερικὰ μέρη
ἐλθεῖν εἰς Ἔφεσον   ἔρχεται εἰς Ἔφεσον

Although the mention of Asia in the D05 reading is particularly salient—indeed, critical information in terms of the Bezan narrator's portrayal of Paul as someone whose own plans are not endorsed by the Holy Spirit—Paul had already indicated when he was last in Asia that he would return (18:21). So Asia represents the direction both expected and intended for Paul and, as will be seen with reference to Syria and Macedonia at 20:3 (see ex. [3]), this factor apparently plays a part in the retention of the article before names of places.

The three anarthrous references to Asia stand out as exceptional, though none is a firm reading. At 6:9, it is a question of people who began to argue with Stephen, people who were from Cilicia and from Asia (D05 omits this mention of Asia). Neither region has the article. It could be that the narrator is highlighting Cilicia as being of special importance, for this is the province from which Paul originated, and his later role in the story concerning Stephen (see 7:58; 8:1) suggests he would have been among those Jews from Cilicia disputing with Stephen. Asia, too, will later emerge as the place from which the fiercest Jewish opponents of Paul as a Jesus-believer came (τὴν Ἀσίαν, 21:27); pointing out their presence here anticipates the part they will continue to play in opposing the attitudes of Jewish Jesus-believers to the Temple. For the unexpected absence of the article before Cilicia and Asia at 6:9 to have such a highlighting function, it may be supposed that the addressee of the narrative would have had some prior knowledge of this aspect of the conflict between believers and non-believers.[27]

At 19:26, 27 the references to Asia made by Demetrius in his address to the Ephesian craftsmen could be seen as salient according to the articulation of the narrative. At 19:26, he speaks of the harm caused by Paul not only in Ephesus but also in the whole of Asia, where an adverbial καί in D05 underlines the spread of the damage: οὐ μόνον Ἐφέσου ἀλλὰ καὶ σχεδὸν πάσης (τῆς B03) Ἀσίας. When Demetrius then goes on to praise the goddess Artemis who is worshipped throughout Asia and the inhabited world, B03 (alone) omits the article before both places ἦν ὅλη ἡ (om. B03) Ἀσία καὶ ἡ (om. B03) οἰκουμένη σέβεται. The first omission could have arisen through homoioteleuton (ΟΛΗΗΑCΙΑ) and the second then could be a means to balance the two phrases. Alternatively, both omissions of ἡ by B03 in this sentence could be a way of highlighting the broad extent of the worship of the goddess of Ephesus.

Cilicia is always arthrous after the mention at 6:9 analyzed above, except for one occurrence of the name at 23:34 (D05 lac.). Here, the mention of the province provides important and new information about the origin of Paul to the governor Felix, from whose perspective Cilicia is named. This would seem to be the factor that accounts for the omission of the article.

Phoenicia is introduced into the narrative of Acts at 11:19 as the first-named in a group of places (Phoenicia, Cyprus and Antioch) outside Jewish territory that the Jesus-believers ventured to. As such, the name is in no way anticipated and is of particular significance for the account of the spread of the gospel. (Note the preposition ἕως which, in itself, highlights the places named). At 21:2, Phoenicia is again anarthrous, being the destination of the ship Paul and his companions were fortunate enough to find. In that sense,

---

[27] This point is of particular relevance for the addressee of the Bezan text for whom there is strong evidence of a Jewish, non-Christian, origin. See Rius-Camps and Read-Heimerdinger 2004:40, 2006:3–4, 2007:3–4, and 2009:3–4 for the possibility that he was Theophilus the High Priest of 37–41 CE.

the place is not an expected or anticipated destination, but is implicitly singled out from among other potential landing places along the Syrian coast.

The one remaining reference to Phoenicia at 15:3 is arthrous—in this
instance, the region is named together with Samaria as places Paul and Barnabas
travelled through on their way from Antioch to Jerusalem. Insofar as these
regions lie on the path of the itinerary between the two cities, that they are cited
as places where the travellers met with other believers occasions no surprise.

The next three regions mentioned are Pamphylia, Pisidia, Lycaonia, beginning with Pamphylia. This region was discussed previously with reference to
the list of 2:9, where it was suggested that the absence of the article could be due
to its being considered as a part of the larger area of Asia. It is then mentioned
again in 13:13 as the area of the mainland at which Paul and his companions
arrived on leaving Cyprus, with particular reference to the town of Perga, εἰς
Πέργην τῆς Παμφυλίας. Here, it is Perga that is in focus, Pamphylia being the
region that serves to identify it. In that respect, the reference is similar to that of
27:5, where it is a question of crossing the 'open sea off Cilicia and Pamphylia'
(τὸ πέλαγος τὸ κατὰ τὴν Κιλικίαν καὶ Παμφυλίαν).

At the one remaining occurrence of Pamphylia (14:24), the article is
present in B03 but not in D05. The region is mentioned in the course of
the description of the return journey of Paul and Barnabas from Pisidia to
Syrian Antioch (14:23–26), where they retrace the steps of their outward
journey. The narrator has the travelers go through the region of Pisidia and
on to Pamphylia, where they stop in the town of Perga. B03 has the article
for both regions, unlike D05 which only has the article for Pisidia:

(3) **14:24–25 B03**   **14:24–25 D05**

²⁴ k̲a̲ὶ̲ διελθόντες τὴν Πισιδίαν   ²⁴ διελθόντες δ̲ὲ̲ τὴν Πισιδίαν
ἦλθο̲ν̲ εἰς τ̲ὴ̲ν̲ Παμφυλίαν,   ἦλθα̲ν̲ εἰς ↑ Παμφυλίαν,
²⁵ καὶ λαλήσαντες ἐν Πέργῃ τὸν   ²⁵ καὶ λαλήσαντες ἐν Πέργῃ τὸν
λόγον κατέβησαν εἰς Ἀττάλειαν   λόγον κατέβησαν εἰς Ἀττάλειαν
κἀκεῖθεν ἀπέπλευσαν εἰς   κἀκεῖθεν ἀπέπλευσαν εἰς
Ἀντιόχειαν...   Ἀντιόχειαν...

That Pisidia should be arthrous can be explained by the geographical
situation, for the last town the pair stopped in, Antioch, belonged to the
province of Pisidia (cf. 13:14).²⁸ In other words, after finishing their busi-
ness in the church there, they travelled through the province not as a new
place but as one in which they were already present. Arriving in Pamphylia,
on the other hand, is a new stage where a significant stop is made in Perga
to 'speak the word' for the first time in the town (cf. 13:13). B03 links the

---

²⁸ At 13:14, most manuscripts read with D05, παρεγένοντο εἰς Ἀντιόχειαν
τ̲ῆ̲ς̲ Πισιδίας, where the article serves to define which Antioch is meant; other
manuscripts including B03 read παρεγένοντο εἰς Ἀντιόχειαν τ̲ὴ̲ν̲ Πισιδίαν.

account of the return journey to the previous narrative with καί and has the article before Pamphylia, in keeping with the fact that the region was an inevitable stage in their journey as Paul and Barnabas headed towards the seaport. D05, on the other hand, marks the development at 14:24 with the connective δέ and presents Pamphylia anarthrously. If absence of the article is to be taken as a marker of salience, as the analysis of this section so far has been suggesting, it causes the province to be highlighted, seemingly marking thus the action of speaking in its capital, Perga.

Lycaonia is also mentioned in the context of the travels of Paul and Barnabas in the same area, as they moved on to cities in the province on leaving Iconium after their initial visit there (14:6). It is the only reference to the region and the name is arthrous without variant.

The first of the five references to the province of Syria belongs to the address of the letter from the Jerusalem leaders to the churches of Antioch, Cilicia and Syria (15:23), where the names of both regions are arthrous, being covered by the one article at the head of the list: οἱ πρεσβύτεροι ἀδελφοὶ τοῖς κατὰ τὴν Ἀντιόχειαν καὶ Συρίαν καὶ Κιλικίαν ἀδελφοῖς. The defining function of the place names accounts for the article. When the names are repeated by the narrator as he reports that the letter was delivered to the named regions (15:41), the names are again arthrous, the intention being fulfilled: διήρχετο δὲ τὴν Συρίαν καὶ (τὴν D05) Κιλικίαν.

Syria as the intended destination likewise accounts for the article before the name at 18:18 and 20:3 B03. In both cases, it is a matter of Paul returning by sea, from Corinth and Greece respectively, to the place of his mission's origin: ἐξέπλει/ἀνάγεσθαι εἰς τὴν Συρίαν, Syria being the general area that was essentially his familiar base. Verse 20:3 presents, however, a telling variant reading, for D05's reference to Syria is anarthrous in the midst of considerable divergence between its text and that of B03:

(4) **20:3–4a B03**   **20:3–4a D05**

³ ποιήσας τε μῆνας τρεῖς   ³ ποιήσας δὲ μῆνας τρεῖς
↑ γενομένης ἐπιβουλῆς αὐτῷ   καὶ γενηθείσης αὐτῷ ἐπιβουλῆς
ὑπὸ τῶν Ἰουδαίων   ὑπὸ τῶν Ἰουδαίων
μέλλοντι ἀνάγεσθαι εἰς τὴν Συρίαν ἠθέλησεν ἀναχθῆναι εἰς ↑ Συρίαν
ἐγένετο γνώμης τοῦ   εἶπεν δὲ τὸ πνεῦμα αὐτῷ
ὑποστρέφειν   ὑποστρέφειν
διὰ ↑ Μακεδονίας.   διὰ τῆς Μακεδονίας.
⁴ συνείπετο δὲ αὐτῷ   ⁴ ↑ Μέλλοντος οὖν ἐξιέναι αὐτοῦ
↑   μέχρι τῆς Ἀσίας,
Σώπατρος, κτλ.   Σώπατρος, κτλ.

There is here an instance where the variation in the use of the article reflects a difference in the narrative purpose. According to the articulation of the familiar B03 text, there is nothing surprising or exceptional about Paul's intention to go to Syria, as was commented above; it is Macedonia that is unexpected, a change of itinerary forced on him by the plot. In D05, on the other hand, his decision to go to Syria was only prompted by the plot of the Jews—nothing more is said about the plot or why it caused Paul to turn back to Syria when, to all intents and purposes, he was already on his way to Rome.[29] The mention of Syria is, in consequence, very much contrary to expectation, although to recognize this requires an appreciation of the wider narrative beyond this local variation. The unexpected nature of the destination of Syria at this point in the Bezan text could account for the absence of the article. In this text, it is the Spirit who tells Paul to go back through Macedonia, as a place he had already been directed to (cf. 16:6–10) and which would put him back on the route to Rome.

The extensive account of the sea-voyage from Greece to Syria finally reaches its conclusion at 21:3b (D05 lac.). The article at this mention could be expected since this is the destination that has been in view throughout the journey. The explanation for its absence is not obvious, though within the perspective of the Bezan version of the narrative, a comparison could be being made with Cyprus (21:3a) which, the narrator makes a point of noting, was not visited, the implication being that it ought to have been.[30] This example of the principles directing the use of the article with place names illustrates the importance of taking account of the message that the narrator wishes to communicate, which is not always possible to do with certainty in the absence of firm knowledge about the circumstances of the writing and the identity of the intended addressee.

Macedonia is a place of key importance for Paul's travels, as was seen above in the D05 reading of 20:3. It represents an obligatory stage on the itinerary between the home province of Syria and the divinely appointed final destination of Rome. It is introduced into the narrative at the point when Paul was first called to take the step of moving away from his familiar territory to proclaim the gospel there: in 16:9–12 it is mentioned three times, the first anarthrously as an unexpected destination that had not figured in Paul's plan hitherto, and thereafter arthrously.

Macedonia becomes topical again when Paul, in Ephesus, planned to revisit places where he was intending to take up the collection from the Gentiles in order to deliver it to Jerusalem. Thus, at 19:21, Macedonia is named along with Achaia, the latter having been mentioned several times in Acts 18 as the province in which the city of Corinth, the center of action, was situated (18:2 D05, 12, 27)—all three references to Achaia are arthrous

---

[29] The Bezan presentation of Paul's struggle to resist the divine plan for him to go to Rome until he had taken the collection of the Gentiles to the Temple in Jerusalem is explored in detail in Rius-Camps and Read-Heimerdinger 2009, see esp. Excursus 3, 168–170.

[30] See Rius-Camps and Read-Heimerdinger 2009:149–150.

by virtue of their association with the prior mention of Corinth. D05 reads the article before both Macedonia and Achaia at 19:21, so treating them as distinct, but in B03 one article groups them together. This accounts for the anarthrous reference to Macedonia in 19:22 B03, when it is singled out as the country to which Paul sent Timothy and Erastus ahead of him. In contrast, D05 retains the article, simply picking up the reference to Macedonia from the previous sentence, as the first place Paul planned to travel to.

In the event, Paul's departure is delayed by trouble in Ephesus, and attention is focused strongly on his activity there in countering the opposition as well as in talking with the disciples. Then, when he finally did get away, there is a marked switch of focus from Ephesus to Macedonia so that even though it had been anticipated as the next stopping place, it is introduced anarthrously as a new area of activity (20:1). The painful nature of Paul's separation from the Ephesian community is highlighted in the Bezan text of this verse:

(5)   **20:1 B03**   **20:1 D05**

Μετὰ δὲ τὸ παύσασθαι τὸν   Μετὰ δὲ τὸ παύσασθαι τὸν
θόρυβον   θόρυβον
<u>μεταπεμψάμενος</u> <u>ὁ</u> Παῦλος τοὺς   <u>προσκαλησάμενος</u> ↑ Παῦλος τοὺς
μαθητὰς   μαθητὰς
καὶ ↑ <u>παρακαλέσας</u>,   καὶ <u>πολλὰ</u> <u>παρακελεύσας</u>,
<u>ἀσπασάμενος</u> ἐξῆλθεν <u>πορεύεσθαι</u>   <u>ἀποσπασάμενος</u> ἐξῆλθεν ↑
εἰς <u>τὴν</u> Μακεδονίαν.   εἰς ↑ Μακεδονίαν.

Paul's involvement in Ephesus is underlined as attention switches from the riot in the city back to Paul (anarthrous Παῦλος), and his close ties with the disciples are brought into focus with the lexical choice of προσκαλησάμενος...παρακελεύσας...ἀποσπασάμενος, the inclusion of πολλά and finally the absence of the infinitive πορεύεσθαι. The insistence on the separation seems to be what justifies the omission of the article before the new destination, Macedonia. This analysis is intimately linked to a recognition of the accentuated interest in the difficulties posed by the Ephesians to Paul's plan for the Gentile collection, as expressed by the Bezan narrator throughout these episodes of Acts.

The mention of Macedonia at 20:3 and the variant reading involving the use of the article are discussed in relation to Syria, just before example (4).

Mysia, Bythinia, and Thessaly are regions that Paul and Silas either passed through or attempted to go to towards the beginning of the second phase of Paul's mission Following the intervention of the Holy Spirit to stop them from speaking the word in Asia (arthrous,16:6), they arrived at the border of Mysia (arthrous, 16:7a) to the north west of Asia from where they wanted to go east into Bithynia (arthrous, 16:7b B03 et al.; anarthrous 16:7b D05) but being prevented they headed south through Mysia (arthrous, 16:8a) to Troas (16:8b). The consistently arthrous references confirm what has been seen so far, that when regions are not particularly salient, especially if they lie on the route of an itinerary, the article is retained. The variant reading with regard to Bithynia illustrates this. It would be a possible, expected step to go from Mysia to neighboring Bithynia. Indeed, B03 says that Paul and Silas attempted to go there: ἐπείραζον εἰς τὴν Βιθυνίαν πορευθῆναι. The Bezan text presents the direction as a wish rather than an actual attempt: ἤθελαν εἰς ↑ Βιθυνίαν πορευθῆναι. Given the sustained reference in the Bezan text to Paul's tactics of avoiding Rome until he had accomplished plans of his own, and given the three successive measures of divine intervention in the episode of 16:5–10 to keep him moving towards Rome, Paul's desire to turn east instead of west at the border of Mysia is a significant narratorial comment on his resistance to God's leading.

In the Bezan text, an additional intervention is recorded to prevent Paul from speaking the word to a region that would take him away from Rome. As he headed towards Athens to escape from the threats to his life in Berea, it is reported that he sailed past Thessaly (παρῆλθεν τὴν Θεσσαλίαν, 17:15 D05), since he was not permitted to evangelize there. The name is arthrous, Thessaly being a region he would necessarily pass and one that remains in the background of the narrative.

To sum up the pattern that can be detected regarding the use of the article with regions, it may be noted that the default use is the arthrous name, just as it is with names of countries. The name is anarthrous when the place is being highlighted as particularly salient. However, it is important to note that recognizing the reason for an author's drawing attention to the place depends on understanding the author's purpose and message more generally.

7.3.2.3 Islands

Several islands are mentioned in the course of Paul's final journey to Jerusalem. Cos and Rhodes (21:1), are arthrous in B03, as is Crete during Paul's sea voyage to Rome (27:7, 12, 21 [D05 lac.]). In D05, however, Cos and Rhodes are anarthrous which could mean that the names are viewed as cities rather than islands, since cities are typically anarthrous at the first mention (see §7.3.2.5) and there is no apparent reason in the narrative for highlighting the islands. This possibility is supported by the references to the islands of Chios and Samos (20:15), which are also names of cities doubling for names of islands, and anarthrous in Acts without variant. It can thus be concluded that islands are generally referred to with the article, even at the first or an isolated mention, but that where its name is shared with the name of the city found on the island this may cause the article to be omitted.

Cyprus stands out for the amount of variation concerning the use of the article, both in the firm text and among the two manuscripts B03 and D05. Its introduction into the narrative at 11:19 has been mentioned above with reference to Phoenicia, where the name is anarthrous, apparently because of its narrative importance. The island readily acquires symbolic significance at 13:4, as the first place across the sea to which the gospel was taken by Barnabas and Paul, and as such the omission of the article is a means to draw attention to this information. The next mention of Cyprus at 15:39 alludes back to this event, when Barnabas chooses to return there after his separation from Paul (see ex. [1]).

The use of the article at the other two references to Cyprus in Acts demonstrates the highlighting purpose of its omission, even though the symbolic significance of the island is still relevant with the arthrous name. The narrator's comment on Cyprus at 21:3 (D05 lac.) has been noted in the last section in connection with Syria, which is negatively highlighted (anarthrous) as Paul's goal in preference over and against (arthrous) Cyprus. Finally, as Paul eventually sets off to Rome his ship sails under the protection of the lee of Cyprus, reflecting the protection of the Roman guard on his mission to the Gentiles.[31]

7.3.2.4 Mountains

The only mountain mentioned in Acts is Sinai (7:30, 38), prefixed each time with the arthrous noun ὄρος.

7.3.2.5 Cities

When a city is mentioned for the first time it is almost always anarthrous, and at subsequent mentions within the same episode the article is then frequently present, for example, Damascus in 9:2 (D05 lac.). See also 9:3 (D05 lac.), Paphos 13:6, compare 13:13: Perga 13:13, compare 13:14; Athens 17:15, compare 17:16 and 18:1, and Miletus 20:15, compare 20:27. From this it may be concluded that the article is present by default and that its omission reflects the salience of a town when it is mentioned for the first time. In that respect, the pattern of the article with the names of cities is similar to that noted with the names of persons. There are, however, several exceptions where the first mention (in the book or in an episode) is arthrous. And there are many more references that are anarthrous although anaphoric. On top of all that, there are numerous variant readings.[32] In order to justify each reading, it would be necessary to ascertain the intention of the narrator at each point and to examine how that corresponds to the articulation of the narrative in the distinct texts of the manuscripts.

---

[31] This point is elaborated upon in Rius-Camps and Read-Heimerdinger 2004:384.
[32] The full list of cities can be found in the appendix to Read-Heimerdinger 2011.

That represents a separate study in itself, such is the importance that the narrator assigns to certain geographical locations. Some analysis, however, is possible here and serves to shed light on the question.

In the case of isolated arthrous references (Amphipolis 17:1; Assos 20:13) it is difficult to justify the presence of the article without comparison to references in other literature. Where place names are introduced arthrously and occur later anarthrously, the contextual situation may help to account for the presence of the article on the first occasion. For example, Rome is first mentioned (18:2) where the narrator presents Aquila and his wife as having recently left Italy because of the emperor's edict for all Jews to leave Rome. In this context, Rome is anticipated by the prior mention of Italy of which it is the capital. It may also be presumed that the addressee of Acts, being a contemporary of these events, would have already been familiar with them and the mention of Rome would be expected. The next reference to Rome is made by Paul in direct speech as he told the Ephesians that he knew that after his visit to Jerusalem he had to go to Rome: Μετὰ τὸ γενέσθαι με ἐκεῖ δεῖ με καὶ Ῥώμην ἰδεῖν, which is the first time he had made any mention of Rome to anyone. At the third and final mention of Rome when Paul eventually arrives there (οὕτως εἰς τὴν Ῥώμην ἤλθαμεν, 28:14 D05 lac.), B03 reads the article as may be expected since it is his long-anticipated destination; manuscripts that omit the article[33] highlight, just as does the position of the name before the verb, the importance of the city in the context of Paul finally reaching his goal.

The place name that occurs most frequently in Acts is Jerusalem (47 times in D05; 41 times in B03), with its dual spelling used to designate either the geographical location (Ἱεροσόλυμα) or the seat of Judaism (Ἱερουσαλήμ), as explained in section 7.3.2.2.[34] Both forms are always anarthrous with one exception (5:28), where the Hebrew-derived spelling is found without variant as the president of the Sanhedrin accuses the apostles of having contravened their orders not to teach about Jesus in the Temple (see 4:18), and thereby to have "filled Jerusalem" with their teaching: πεπληρώκατε τὴν Ἱερουσαλὴμ τῆς διδαχῆς ὑμῶν. In this situation, the reference is to the immediate and specific environment of the holy city in which the Sanhedrin meeting is taking place.

---

[33] For the full list of witnesses, see Rius-Camps and Read-Heimerdinger 2009:400.

[34] At the majority of references to Jerusalem in the text of Acts extant in Codex Bezae (up to 22.29a), the same spelling is found without variant. There are four places of variant reading and six additional mentions of the city in D05, as follows: Ἱερουσαλήμ: 2:42 D05; 8:1b D05, 14 D05; 11:2 B03; 15:2a D05, 4 D05; 20:22 B03; Ἱεροσόλυμα: 8:14 B03; 11:2 D05; 15:4 B03; 18:21 D05; 19:1 D05; 20:22 D05, 23 D05. After 22:29b, there are a further 13 references to the city by name in the extant manuscripts, always anarthrous as in the earlier parts of the book. For a detailed study of the two spellings for Jerusalem in Acts, see Read-Heimerdinger 2002:311–344.

Comparison with the words of Gamaliel as he addresses the Sanhedrin in similar circumstances is instructive, as he speaks of everyone living in Jerusalem (πᾶσιν τοῖς κατοικοῦσιν Ἰερουσαλήμ) having heard about the apostles' healing activity, but there it is the people who are in focus rather than the city. On one other occasion, Jerusalem is mentioned in a similar context to that of 5:28, where the chiliarch was informed that "all of Jerusalem is in confusion" (21:31, ὅλη συγχύννεται Ἰερουσαλήμ) but this reference is indirect, made anonymously via the narrator.

7.3.3 Conclusions on names of places

It has been contended by present-day scholars who are native Greek speakers that Koine Greek is closer to Modern Greek than is often supposed, that the development of the language was such that once Koine usage had been established it then changed relatively little.[35] That being so, it is of interest to know the practice in Modern Greek with regard to the article with geographical names. Discussion with a contemporary speaker reveals that Greek today always has the article with names of places (towns, islands, countries and so on), unless the sentence wants to give some kind of emphasis.[36] The following were given as examples: "Here is [arthrous] Athens," but "[arthrous] Patra is nice, but it is not like [anarthrous] Athens." This picture tends to suggest that the presence of the article with names of places could have been the expected usage even in New Testament Greek, and that anarthrous names were not the rule, which is in line with the findings of the present study.

It is, on the other hand, in contrast with Gildersleeve's observations concerning Classical Greek. On particular categories of places, he observes that Asia is always arthrous though other names of countries vary; postpositive, partitive and chorographic genitives are generally articular; towns or cities are generally anarthrous though the more notable regularly take the article. He suggests that names that are substantivized adjectives (frequently ending in -ια) are more likely to be arthrous.[37]

At the heart of the difference between the present findings and the observations of grammarians such as Gildersleeve is the factor of frequency. What a discourse analysis approach demonstrates is that frequency as such is not of relevance for ascertaining default usage. Because the principal

---

[35] See notably Caragounis 2006.

[36] Personal communication with Andreas Andreopoulos, Senior Lecturer in Orthodox Christianity, University of Winchester, UK. He reports that omission of the article is sometimes perceived by present-day Greeks as a sign of laziness in oral discourse. So, although in the question "Do you live in Athens" the city is often anarthrous, it would be considered more "correct" to use the article. Caragounis (2006) makes no specific mention of geographical names in his extensive investigation.

[37] This claim is also made by Blass–Debrunner–Rehkopf but is dismissed by Hemer as "misconceived" (see Hemer 1989:243).

effect of marked usage is emphasis, it may well happen that in a given text place names are particularly highlighted because they have a rhetorical function. Thus, where place names in a narrative such as Acts are used as indicators of the inner development of characters, which the geographical journeys are seen as mirroring, the article before the names is liable to be more often omitted than in a text where the places are mentioned for the purpose of simply transmitting factual information.

7.4 General conclusions

This study has been focused on the use of the article with names of people and names of places, which by their very nature provide workable sets of comparable data because they both reflect the function of the article to designate entities that are "uniquely identifiable" (Levinsohn 2000:133). In examining the patterns of usage in a narrative text, it has been found that in both sets, the principle factor affecting the choice to use the article or not is salience. The default usage is to include the article with names of people and names of places; when it is omitted, it is because the speaker wishes to mark out a participant or a place as particularly significant at that point.

Within this context, the role of the named person or place in what is being related is of crucial importance. This is true, on the one hand, of the function of the character or location within the unfolding story; on the other, it also true of their function in connection with the purpose of the speaker and the message to be communicated. In other words, marking a name as salient is not a matter of absolute or objective reality but of the perspective and intention of the speaker. To a meaningful extent, the speaker plays a part in the choice to use the article or not, and in that sense the article with proper names can be likened to verbal aspect, whereby the choice of one "tense" in preference to another depends on how the speaker views the situation or wants to present it to the audience.

What is more, in order to communicate effectively, the speaker must also take into account the prior knowledge and understanding of the hearer. Thus, pragmatic factors play a key part in the choice to use or omit the article before proper names. Far from being a simple grammatical component in the language, the article serves to articulate the story on a deeper level and to give coherence as well as cohesion to the discourse, with a much broader scope than the immediate sentence in which the name is found. Grammatical context is, indeed, rarely relevant, though some few exceptions were noted in relation to names of people.

The patterns elucidated in this exploration of the article in a Koine Greek narrative are not "rules" in the sense traditionally associated with languages, where there is one correct form and others that are incorrect. Rather they are principles, which a speaker can make use of in order to express the relative saliency of a participant or location in the story at a given point. They are not rules that have to be followed in order to conform to grammatical accuracy, but they are a device that reflects the flexibility of the language to adapt to situational aspects of the discourse as well as the nature of the discourse itself.

Given this inherent flexibility in the use of the article with proper names, variant readings in successive renderings of a narrative are a valuable source of information that provides data for comparison and for furthering the analysis. The examination presented here demonstrates the importance of reading variants in their context, of both the immediate passage and the wider discourse. This means that assessing them cannot be done effectively on a piecemeal basis but must take account of the perspective and purpose of the overall text. The findings suggest that the numerous variant readings among the early New Testament manuscripts of Acts that affect the article with proper names should be ascribed not to scribal habit but to the changing narratorial intentions, which may vary from one copying to another, and to the different audiences for whom the copies were intended. The article with proper names is part of the story-teller's collection of tools that serve to enhance the articulation of the story and to adapt it to the people listening to it.

References

Aland, Barbara, Kurt Aland, Eberhard Nestle, Erwin Nestle, and Institut für Neutestamentliche Textforschung, eds. 2013. *Novum Testamentum Graece.* Twenty-eighth edition. Stuttgart: Deutsche Bibelgesellschaft.

Blass, Friedrich W., and Albert Debrunner. 1979. *Grammatik des neutestamentlichen Griechisch.* Fifteenth edition. Edited by Friedrich Rehkopf. Göttingen: Vandenhoeck & Ruprecht.

Boismard, M.-É., and A. Lamouille. 1984. *Le texte occidental des Actes des Apôtres: Reconstitution et rehabilitation 1: Introduction et textes.* Paris: Éditions Recherche sur les Civilisations.

Caragounis, Chrys C. 2006. *The development of Greek and the New Testament: Morphology, syntax, phonology, and textual transmission.* Grand Rapids, MI: Baker Academic.

Elliott, J. Keith. 1972. Κηφᾶς: Σίμων Πέτρος: ὁ Πέτρος: An examination of New Testament usage. *Novum Testamentum* 14:241–256.

Elliott, J. Keith. 1988. The text of Acts in the light of two recent studies. *New Testament Studies* 34:250–258.

Gildersleeve, Basil L. 1890. On the article with proper names. *American Journal of Philology* 11:483–87.

Gildersleeve, Basil L. 1902. Problems in Greek syntax: II: The article. *American Journal of Philology* 23: 121–141.

Gildersleeve, Basil L. 1900. *Syntax of Classical Greek from Homer to Demosthenes 1: The syntax of the simple sentence, embracing the doctrine of the moods and tenses.* New York: American Book Company.

Gildersleeve, Basil L. 1911. *Syntax of Classical Greek from Homer to Demosthenes 2: The syntax of the simple sentence continued, embracing the doctrine of the article.* New York: American Book Company.

[Read-]Heimerdinger, Jenny, and Stephen H. Levinsohn. 1992. The use of the definite article before names of people in the Greek text of Acts with particular reference to Codex Bezae. *Filología Neotestamentaria* 5:15–44.

Hemer, Colin J. 1989. *The book of Acts in the setting of Hellenistic history.* Edited by Conrad H. Gempf. Wissenschaftliche Untersuchungen zum Neuen Testament 49. Tübingen: J. C. B. Mohr.

Levinsohn, Stephen H. 2000. *Discourse features of New Testament Greek.* Second edition. Dallas, TX: Summer Institute of Linguistics.

Lyons, Christopher. 1999. *Definiteness.* Cambridge Textbooks in Linguistics. Cambridge: University Press.

Metzger, Bruce M. 1994. *A textual commentary on the Greek New Testament.* Second edition. Stuttgart: Deutsche Bibelgesellschaft.

Porter, Stanley E. 1992. *Idioms of New Testament Greek.* Second edition. Vol. 2 of Biblical Languages: Greek. Sheffield, UK: JSOT Press.

Read-Heimerdinger, Jenny. 2002. *The Bezan text of Acts: A contribution of discourse analysis to textual criticism.* Journal for the Study of the New Testament: Supplement Series 236. Sheffield, UK: Academic Press.

Read-Heimerdinger, Jenny. 2003. The apostles in the Bezan text of Acts. In Tobias Nicklas and Michael Tilly (eds.), *Apostelgeschichte als Kirchengeschichte: Text, texttraditionen und antike auslegungen,* 263–280. Beihefte zur Zeitschrift für die neutestamentliche Wissenschaft 120. Berlin: Walter de Gruyter.

Read-Heimerdinger, Jenny. 2011. The use of the article before names of places: Patterns of use in the book of Acts. In Steven E. Runge (ed.), *Discourse studies and biblical interpretation: A festschrift in honor of Stephen H. Levinsohn,* 371–402. Bellingham, WA: Lexham Press.

Rius-Camps, Josep, and Jenny Read-Heimerdinger. 2004. *The Message of Acts in Codex Bezae 1: A comparison with the Alexandrian tradition: Acts 1:1–5:42.* Library of New Testament Studies 257. Edinburgh, UK: T. & T. Clark.

Rius-Camps, Josep, and Jenny Read-Heimerdinger. 2006. *The Message of Acts in Codex Bezae 2: A comparison with the Alexandrian tradition: Acts 6:1–12:25.* Library of New Testament Studies 302. Edinburgh, UK: T. & T. Clark.

Rius-Camps, Josep, and Jenny Read-Heimerdinger. 2007. *The Message of Acts in Codex Bezae 3: A comparison with the Alexandrian tradition: Acts 13:1–18:23.* Library of New Testament Studies 365. Edinburgh, UK: T. & T. Clark.

Rius-Camps, Josep, and Jenny Read-Heimerdinger. 2009. *The Message of Acts in Codex Bezae 4: A comparison with the Alexandrian tradition: Acts 18:1–28:31*. Library of New Testament Studies 415. Edinburgh, UK: T. & T. Clark.

Robertson, Archibald T. 1934. *A grammar of the Greek New Testament in the light of historical research*. Fourth edition. Nashville, TN: Broadman.

Runge, Steven E. 2010. *Discourse grammar of the Greek New Testament: A practical introduction for teaching and exegesis*. Peabody, MA: Hendrickson.

Sansone, David. 1993. Towards a new doctrine of the article: Some observations on the definite article in Plato. *Classical Philology* 88:191–205.

Turner, Nigel. 1963. *A grammar of New Testament Greek 3: Syntax*. Edinburgh, UK: T. & T. Clark.

Wallace, Daniel B. 1996. *Greek grammar beyond the basics*. Grand Rapids, MI: Zondervan.

Winer, George B. (1882) 1997. *A treatise on the grammar of New Testament Greek*. Translated by W. F. Moulton. Reprint. Eugene, OR: Wipf & Stock.

Index

SIL International®
Publications in Translation and Textlinguistics Series
ISSN 1550-588X

9. **Paul's anthropological terms in the light of discourse analysis,** by Sunny Chen, 2019, 286 pp., ISBN 978-1-55671-421-4.

8. **Studies in the Psalms: Literary-structural analysis with application to translation,** by Ernst R. Wendland, 2017, 538 pp., ISBN 978-1-55671-401-6.

7. **Prophetic rhetoric: Case studies in text analysis and translation.** Second edition, by Ernst R. Wendland, 2014, 719 pp., ISBN: 978-1-55671-345-3.

6. **Orality and the Scriptures: Composition, translation, and transmission,** by Ernst R. Wendland, 2013, 405 pp., ISBN 978-1-55671-298-2.

5. **Lovely, lively lyrics: Selected studies in Biblical Hebrew verse,** by Ernst R. Wendland, 2013, 461 pp., ISBN 978-1-55671-327-9.

4. **LiFE-style translating: A workbook for Bible translators.** Second edition, by Ernst R. Wendland, 2011, 509 pp., ISBN 978-155671-243-2.

3. **The development of textlinguistics in the writings of Robert Longacre,** by Shin Ja Hwang, 2010, 423 pp., ISBN 978-1-55671-246-3.

2. **Artistic and rhetorical patterns in Quechua legendary texts,** by Ågot Bergli, 2010, 304 pp., ISBN 978-1-55671-244-9.

1. **Translating the literature of Scripture: A literary-rhetorical approach to Bible translation,** by Ernst R. Wendland, 2004, 509 pp., ISBN 978-1-55671-152-7.

SIL International Publications
7500 W. Camp Wisdom Road
Dallas, TX 75236-5629 USA

General inquiry: publications_intl@sil.org
Pending order inquiry: sales@sil.org